*Elementary School
Librarian's Almanac:
A Complete Media Program
for Every Month of the School Year*

Elementary School Librarian's Almanac

A Complete Media Program for Every Month of the School Year

Hilda K. Weisburg
Ruth Toor

The Center for Applied Research in Education, Inc.
West Nyack, New York 10994

Library of Congress Cataloging in Publication Data

Weisburg, Hilda K
    Elementary school librarian's almanac.

    Includes bibliographies and index.
    1. School libraries--Activity program. I. Toor,
Ruth   joint author. II. Title.
Z675.S3W44   027.82'22   78-31808
ISBN 0-87628-299-0

Printed in the United States of America

To our understanding families
for their support and encouragement—

Marvin
Rona and Jeffrey

Jay
Mark and Cary

ABOUT THE AUTHORS

Hilda K. Weisburg has been working in libraries since she was 18 years old, with time off for marriage and two children. She earned her M.L.S. from Columbia University as a specialist in Children's and Young Adult Services and is continuing with further graduate education. She is presently the library media specialist at the Harry S. Truman School in Sayreville, New Jersey. She has also been a high school librarian and has held positions in public libraries as Children's Department Head and Director of Young Adult Services.

Ruth Toor has been a library media specialist at Southern Boulevard School in Chatham Township, New Jersey, since 1972. Before that, she had experience teaching in all grades from kindergarten through eighth. After graduating from the University of Delaware, getting married, and raising two sons, she returned to school and earned her M.L.S. from Rutgers University. She is continuing with further graduate education and has had several articles published in various professional journals.

About the Elementary School Librarian's Almanac . . .

The *Elementary School Librarian's Almanac* is a practical tool for both the experienced library media specialist and the recent library school graduate. It provides a unique store of useful tips, techniques, and activities for planning and implementing a year-round media program, and solutions to many everyday problems that confront the library media specialist in his or her work. You will find that the *Almanac* is also a valuable aid in administering your media center and in working with your faculty to develop and teach library skills and multimedia units. As two practicing library media specialists with a combined total of over 20 years' experience, we have developed, refined, and successfully incorporated these multiple aspects of librarianship into our own programs.

From the opening of the media center in September to its closing in June, the *Elementary School Librarian's Almanac* is filled with hundreds of new ideas and tips of the trade. Each of the ten chapters focuses on one month of the school year; each one provides:

- birthdates of famous authors and illustrators
- bulletin board ideas with accompanying student activities
- library art activities
- annotated storytelling suggestions
- library skills teaching units with suggestions for joint classroom/media center projects
- library skills learning centers and games that are ideal for small groups and individualized instruction
- how-to descriptions of areas of professional responsibility not encompassed by library service courses
- detailed guides to projects and tasks performed by volunteers or clerks
- discussions of problems in librarianship that offer several alternatives rather than absolute answers

Here are a few of the highlights you'll find in the *Almanac*: directions on using an overhead projector to create impressive bulletin board displays even if you have little artistic talent; numerous ideas for stimulating student reading through book talks, contests, and even television; a gold mine of easy-to-implement tips designed to make your job simpler; and a sensible, nuts-and-bolts approach to handling audio-visual hardware. The *Almanac* also offers guidelines for carrying out such basic responsibilities as providing orientations for students and teachers, running a book fair, and taking an end-of-year inventory. These guidelines describe typical

problems and give suggestions on how to anticipate and solve them almost immediately. With the *Elementary School Librarian's Almanac* in hand, even a first-year
library media specialist can function with the confidence of an "old pro."

To use the *Almanac* to best advantage, feel free to adapt and enlarge upon our
ideas and suggestions and to experiment with your own. Each media center and
each library media specialist is unique. We want this book to be a stimulus to your
creativity, not a recapitulation of our own experiences. Although the chapters are
divided according to the months of the year, your program must flow throughout
the year and not be constricted by the divisions of the calendar. A teaching unit or
library art project begun in one month may carry through to the next. Every idea
included here cannot possibly be utilized by one media specialist in one year.
However, by judiciously sampling the ideas offered in the *Almanac*, you can add
to your program over the years, creating one that is original, effective, and respon-
sive to the changing needs of your faculty and students.

Hilda K. Weisburg
Ruth Toor

Table of Contents

March

April

May

June

Elementary School
Librarian's Almanac:
A Complete Media Program
for Every Month of the School Year

September

Happy Birthday To . . .

3   **Aliki** (1929)—author and illustrator
        Easy-to-read fiction and nonfiction including *Keep Your Mouth Closed, Dear* and *My Five Senses*

4   **Syd Hoff** (1912)—author and illustrator
        Cartoon illustrations in easy-to-read stories such as *Grizzwold, Julius*, and *Oliver*

        Joan Aiken (1924)—author
        Historical suspense fiction for upper grades such as *Wolves of Willoughby Chase*

7   **C. B. Colby** (1904)—author
        Brief descriptions of military and governmental subjects accompanied by black-and-white photographs; works include *Fighting Gear of World War II* and *The F.B.I.*

9   **Aileen Fisher** (1906)—author
        Nature poetry and general nonfiction including *Cricket in a Thicket* and *Human Rights Day*

        Phyllis Whitney (1903)—author
        Light mysteries for intermediate and upper grades including *The Vanishing Scarecrow*

11   **Alfred Slote** (1926)—author
        Sports fiction such as *My Father, the Coach* and *Tony and Me*

13   **Roald Dahl** (1916)—author
        Modern fairy tales in which virtue is handsomely rewarded and evil is severely punished such as *Charlie and the Chocolate Factory* and *James and the Giant Peach*

        Else Minarik (1920)—author
        Easy-to-read fiction, notably the Little Bear series

15 **Robert McCloskey** (1914)—author and illustrator
Picture books such as *Make Way for Ducklings* and *Lentil*; the Homer Price series

16 **H. A. Rey** (1898)—author and illustrator
Creator of the popular picture books about Curious George

19 **Arthur Rackham** (1867)—illustrator
Richly detailed illustrations of fairy tales such as *Grimm's Fairy Tales, Aesop's Fables,* and *Cinderella*

Rachel Field (1894)—author
Historical fiction for upper grades, such as *Calico Bush* and *Hitty: Her First Hundred Years*

21 **H. G. Wells** (1866)—author
Science fiction classics including *War of the Worlds* and *The Invisible Man*

24 **L. Leslie Brooke** (1862)—author and illustrator
Wrote and illustrated *Johnny Crow's Garden*; noted primarily as an illustrator of vividly colored animal characters

Jane Curry (1924)—author
Science fantasy for intermediate and upper grades, including *Mindy's Mysterious Miniature* and *Parsley, Sage, Rosemary, and Time*

27 **Bernard Waber** (1924)—author and illustrator
Picture books including the Lyle the Crocodile series and *Ira Sleeps Over*

28 **Kate Douglas Wiggin** (1856)—author
Remembered for *Rebecca of Sunnybrook Farm*

30 **Alvin Tresselt** (1916)—author
Picture books about nature, such as *Hide and Seek Fog* and *Wake Up, City!*

AMAZE Yourself

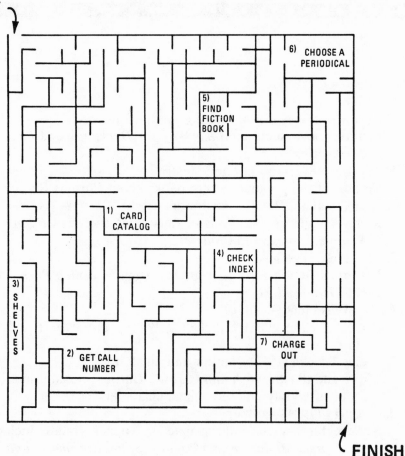

START

6) CHOOSE A PERIODICAL

5) FIND FICTION BOOK

1) CARD CATALOG

4) CHECK INDEX

3) SHELVES

2) GET CALL NUMBER

7) CHARGE OUT

FINISH

Know your
  Media Center:

1. Enter all boxes
   in Numerical Order

2. Do NOT Retrace
   your steps.

TAKE ONE,
HAVE FUN

Bulletin Boards

AMAZE YOURSELF

As an eye-catcher for the opening of the media center, a puzzle bulletin board is highly effective. It can serve to remind students of basic library terminology. If you feel intimidated by the idea of constructing the Amaze Yourself bulletin board shown in the illustration, you might do a hidden word puzzle or a crossword instead. A maze takes more time, especially when reproducing it, but the response is worth the effort.

> *Note:* All of the bulletin boards in the *Almanac* are mounted on standard-size (22″ × 28″) posterboard. However, they are easily adaptable to existing bulletin boards covered with construction paper or butcher paper.

MATERIALS:

—1 sheet of 22″ × 28″ light-colored posterboard
—wide-tip felt marker
—narrow-tip felt marker of another color
—a 10″ × 13″ manila envelope
—ditto master
—1 sheet of graph paper
—rubber cement
—1 sheet of acetate
—overhead projector
—pencil
—scissors

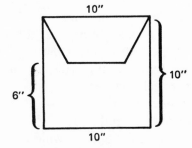

PREPARATION:

1. Design a maze or use the one shown. Use graph paper to keep your lines straight.
2. Trace the maze onto the acetate sheet.
3. Use an overhead projector to enlarge the acetate transparency. Trace the maze onto the posterboard with a pencil.

> *Note:* Directions on how to use the overhead projector are given in the October Library Enrichment Activity.

4. Use the wide-tip marker to outline the maze.
5. Use the narrow-tip marker to label the boxes within the maze.
6. Use the wide-tip marker to copy the title "Amaze Yourself."
7. Copy the directions using the narrow-tip marker.
8. Cut the manila envelope down to 10″ × 10″.
9. Cut the front of the envelope so that it measures 6″ × 10″. (See above.)
10. Use the narrow-tip marker to write "Have fun, take one" on the manila envelope.
11. Use the rubber cement to glue the manila envelope to the posterboard.

12. Prepare the ditto master. Take the graph paper with the maze on it and place a sheet of carbon paper between the maze and the ditto master. Retrace the maze.

13. Run off the ditto master and put the copies in the manila envelope.

ILLUSTRIOUS ILLUSTRATORS

Here is another bulletin-board game for launching the school year. As you can see from the illustration, this one focuses on famous illustrators. Several of the illustrators named in the clues were born this month, as was the venerable Arthur Rackham, the "Mystery Answer." This game is more complex than the one in the previous bulletin board because students will need to use the card catalog to find the answers. The students will come to you to see if their responses are correct, so have an answer sheet at the circulation desk or announce that you will post the answers at the end of the month. A complete answer sheet is provided at the end of the construction directions.

MATERIALS:

—1 sheet of 22″ × 28″ light green or blue posterboard
—pink construction paper
—yellow construction paper, at least 16″ wide
—brown construction paper
—black felt markers, wide tip and fine tip
—brown felt marker
—rubber cement
—ditto master and paper
—1 manila envelope, 9″ wide
—scissors

PREPARATION:

1. Cut a piece of pink construction paper into a 2″ × 4″ bullet shape. This piece will form the eraser.

2. Cut a piece of yellow construction paper into a 15½″ × 2″ rectangle. This piece will form the main part of the pencil. The last 2″ of the pencil should be cut with rippled edges. This will form the metal cap that holds the eraser. The other end of the pencil should have a jagged edge. The point of the pencil will begin here.

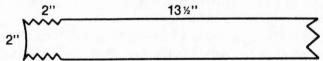

3. Paste the pencil body over the pink eraser so that 2½″ of the eraser shows.

4. Use the fine-tip felt marker to complete the circle representing the top of the eraser.

ILLUSTRIOUS ILLUSTRATORS

Directions: 1. Fill in the blanks with the illustrators of the books listed below. (Sometimes they are the authors, too.)
2. Use the CARD CATALOG for help.
MYSTERY ANSWER: The first letters of the illustrators' names will spell out the name of a famous illustrator born this month.

1. Keep Your Mouth Closed, Dear
2. Lentil (Whole Name)
3. Allumette (Whole Name)
4. Julius (Last Name Only)
5. The Fool of the World and the Flying Ship (Whole Name)
6. Thirteen (Whole Name)
7. Spectacles (Last Name Only)
8. Lucille (Whole Name)
9. And I Mean It, Stanley (First and Last Name)
10. Albert's Toothache (Whole Name)
11. Curious George (First 2 Initials & Last Name)
12. Little Tim and the Brave Sea Captain (Last Name Only)
13. Where the Wild Things Are (Whole Name)

MYSTERY ILLUSTRATOR~ OOOOOOO OOOOOOO

5. Use the brown felt marker to make curved lines on the rippled section to simulate the metal cap of the pencil.

6. Cut a piece of brown construction paper in a shape resembling the one shown here. This will form the sharpened end of the pencil.

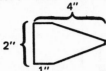

7. Paste the pencil body over the 1″ long section of the brown construction paper so that only the triangular part shows.

8. Use the fine-tip marker to color the pencil point. The point should take up ½″ of the brown construction paper.

9. Use the wide-tip marker to print "Illustrious Illustrators" on the pencil body in large letters.

10. Outline the body of the pencil with the fine-tip marker.

11. Attach the pencil to the posterboard. The body of the pencil should be 1″ from the top of the posterboard; the end of the eraser should be 3½″ from the left edge.

12. Use the fine-tip marker to print the directions.

13. Use the fine-tip marker to make a wavy line around the directions. The line should begin at the pencil point.

14. Use the fine-tip marker to print the clues.

15. Use the wide-tip marker to print "Mystery Illustrator" in large letters near the bottom of the posterboard.

16. Prepare a ditto master with the same directions and clues as those on the bulletin board. The clues may be typed, but use a pen for drawing the blanks and circles in the right-hand column. If you try typing these, you will not be able to tell how many letters are in each answer. Run off copies of the ditto master.

17. Cut down the manila envelope to about 5″ high so that students can remove the directions easily.

18. Insert the directions in the envelope and attach the envelope onto the bulletin board or onto a nearby wall.

ANSWER KEY:

1.	*Keep Your Mouth Closed, Dear*	Aliki
2.	*Lentil* (whole name)	Robert McCloskey
3.	*Allumette* (whole name)	Tomi Ungerer
4.	*Julius* (last name only)	Hoff
5.	*The Fool of the World and the Flying Ship* (whole name)	Uri Shulevitz
6.	*Thirteen* (whole name)	Remy Charlip
7.	*Spectacles* (last name only)	Raskin
8.	*Lucille* (whole name)	Arnold Lobel
9.	*And I Mean It, Stanley* (first and last name)	Crosby Bonsall
10.	*Albert's Toothache* (whole name)	Kay Chorao
11.	*Curious George* (first 2 initials & last name)	H. A. Rey
12.	*Little Tim and the Brave Sea Captain* (last name only)	Ardizzone
13.	*Where the Wild Things Are* (whole name)	Maurice Sendak

MYSTERY ANSWER: ARTHUR RACKHAM

Library Art Activity

THIS SUMMER I READ WHILE . . .

Encourage creative flights of fancy, and the media center will soon be decorated with student work. A simple poster asking for artwork is all it takes. (See the illustration.) Instead of asking for mundane "How I Spent My Summer" drawings, the poster asks students to imagine themselves reading while engaged in an activity that would normally preclude books. This serves a dual purpose; it draws attention to reading as an activity, and it requires original thinking.

Have on hand a supply of drawing paper or construction paper to distribute to

the students. If there is time for students to make the drawing while in the media center, provide them with crayons as well. When the drawings are turned in, be sure that each student's name and classroom are included.

You can expect this art activity to have a slow start. Once some completed drawings are posted, however, you may have trouble keeping up with the students' ideas. Some of the better ideas could be displayed in the hall outside the media center.

UNMARKED MAP OF THE MEDIA CENTER

This is a good way to familiarize fourth, fifth, and sixth grade students with the library at the beginning of the school year.

MATERIALS:

—stencil
—mimeograph paper, enough sheets to run off a copy for each student
—pencils, enough for a large class

PROCEDURE:

1. Before the orientation session, draw a map of your media center on a stencil. Include book shelves, the card catalog, the circulation desk, tables and chairs, study carrels, the magazine rack, and other important items. As shown in the sample map, nothing should be labeled.
2. Run off enough copies for all of your students.
3. During the orientation, hand a copy of the unmarked map and a pencil to each child.
4. Make sure that everyone has the map turned the correct way by calling attention to the entrance of the media center and the circulation desk.
5. Tell the students that they should explore the media center with map in hand. They should mark the map to show where fiction books are kept, where nonfiction and biography are shelved, and where the card catalog, the circulation desk, and other landmarks are located.
6. The older students can be more specific and mark where on the shelves certain call numbers are located. (For example: Fiction A-Bu, Nonfiction 540-599.)
7. Tell the students that the maps will be guides for their use throughout the year and that they should keep the completed maps in their notebooks where they can refer to them until they are completely familiar with the location of everything.
8. Allow sufficient time for the students to fill in the labels on their maps. This will depend on the size and complexity of your media center.
9. At the end of the period, collect the pencils so that you will have them for the next class.

Library Enrichment Activity

HAPPY BIRTHDAY GREETINGS

Call attention to authors and illustrators, reminding children of old favorites or introducing them to new ones. Have a year-round Happy Birthday display on a

Unmarked Map of the Media Center

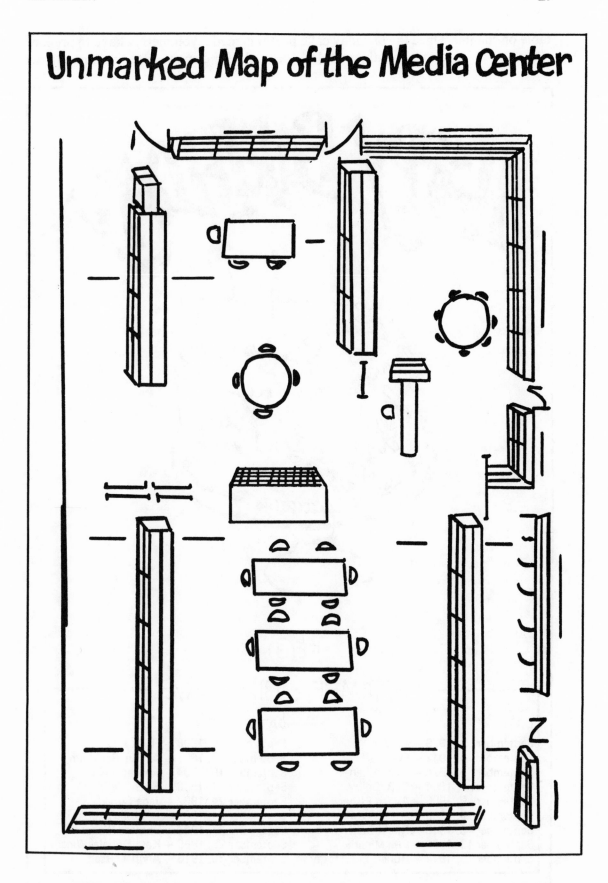

table or counter. Once the birthday cake poster is made, you merely have to prepare a new 9″ × 4″ card each month and select the books for display. (See the illustration.)

HAPPY BIRTHDAY

to

SEPTEMBER BIRTHDAYS

DATES	DATES
September 3, 1929 — Aliki	September 16, 1898 — H. A. Rey
September 4, 1912 — Syd Hoff	September 19, 1867 — Arthur Rackham
September 4, 1924 — Joan Aiken	September 19, 1894 — Rachel Field
September 7, 1904 — C. B. Colby	September 21, 1866 — H. G. Wells
September 9, 1906 — Aileen Fisher	September 24, 1932 — Jane Curry
September 9, 1903 — Phyllis Whitney	September 24, 1862 — L. Leslie Brooks
September 13, 1916 — Roald Dahl	September 27, 1924 — Bernard Waber
September 13, 1920 — Else Minarik	September 28, 1856 — Kate Douglas Wiggin
September 15, 1914 — Robert McCloskey	September 30, 1916 — Alvin Tresselt

Students enjoy discovering that someone famous was born on or near their birthdays. As each month's birthdays are posted and the new books are displayed, the Happy Birthday area will draw fresh attention.

MATERIALS:

—1 sheet of 11″ × 14″ colored posterboard
—cardboard easel back (available in several sizes from library supply houses)
—felt markers
—1 large sheet of white construction paper (or 2 sheets of 9″ × 12″ paper)
—tracing paper
—pencil
—glue stick
—rubber cement
—crayons or pastels (optional)
—scissors

PREPARATION:

1. Make the birthday cake:
    a. Find a good picture in a cookbook.
    b. Trace the cake. You can draw the candles later.
    c. Use the glue stick to attach the tracing onto white construction paper. Cut away the excess paper.
    d. Use pastels or crayons if you wish to color the cake.

Note: An alternative to tracing a fancy cake is to make a very simple cake like the one shown in the small illustration.

2. Cut the remaining construction paper into a 4″ × 9″ strip.
3. Type or print the September birthdays on the 4″ × 9″ strip.
4. Position the birthday list on the posterboard.
5. Position the cake drawing on the posterboard. If you drew the simple cake, place it near the top; if you have a more elaborate drawing, center it.
6. Lightly outline the words Happy Birthday; try to make happy-looking letters. If you made the simple cake, write Happy on the second tier and Birthday on the bottom tier.
7. Use the felt marker to darken the letters. If you prefer, you might cut the letters out of construction paper and paste them onto the posterboard.
8. Use rubber cement to paste the cake and the birthday list onto the posterboard.
9. Place the poster on the easel back and set it up on a counter top, window sill, or table top.

Note: Throughout the *Almanac*, directions for making posters usually refer to easel backs. Although an easel back is convenient for placing a poster anywhere in the media center, you may prefer to simply attach the poster to a wall.

10. Select books by the authors and illustrators born during the month and arrange them around the poster.
11. Do not remove all of the appropriate titles from the shelves. You will need these to replace the books that students borrow from the display. Also, some students will be motivated to use the card catalog to locate additional titles by themselves.

Note: If a student complains that no author or illustrator was born on his or her birthday, guide the student to *Famous First Facts*, 3rd ed. by Joseph N. Kane (Wilson, 1964) or *The Book of Days* edited by Robert Chambers (reprint of 1862 edition by Gale Research Co., 1967). These books will help the child discover other important occurrences on his or her birthday.

STUDENT ORIENTATION

September is the month for organizing your schedule for the school year. One of your first priorities should be student orientation to the media center. During the first days of school, the library media specialist needs to seek out the teachers and schedule classes for orientation.

In arranging the schedule, bear in mind that students in grades one to three need a general orientation as soon as possible. The upper grades are more familiar with the media center, and if time is a consideration, they need not be scheduled for orientation. However, teachers should be advised that any new students should be sent to the media center to receive individual or small group tours.

Kindergarten classes are normally scheduled for the end of the month, since it takes several weeks until the children have settled down enough to cope with any new excitement. During the kindergartners' first visits, you should cover the location of books they will like, how to charge out and return books, and how long books may be borrowed. You might conclude the sessions with a short story.

Orientation for Grades 1–3

When conducting these half-hour introductions to the media center, remember three simple rules:

- be prepared
- be friendly
- be brief

If your media center is carpeted, the floor is a great place to begin! Otherwise, group the tables in as informal a manner as possible. Display selections that illustrate the types of materials found in the various sections of the media center. Throughout the orientation, your underlying message to the students is: The media center is a super spot. It offers help with classroom assignments, and it has all kinds of resources to make free time more interesting.

The basic steps for sending out this message are:

1. *Greetings* — Welcome the group. Ask some general questions about what the children did during the summer. If the children are first graders, ask if they remember your name. With mock seriousness, you might applaud their eagerness to get back to school.

2. *Tour* — Depending on the size of the class and of the media center, you may decide to "tour" by pointing out sections while the group remains seated. To avoid a lecture with grades two and three, you could choose a student and send him or her to a given area. Ask the class if the student is in the right place. Then choose another student to go to the next section.

- *Fiction*—Review the meaning of the word *fiction*. Point out the special sections where students in the group will find books that they can enjoy.
- *Nonfiction*—Ask the class what kinds of books can be found in the nonfiction area. Use questions to get the students to realize that whenever factual material is needed, they will find it in the nonfiction section. Sometimes this information is needed for class, sometimes a student is independently interested in a particular subject. Sports and hobby books are often chosen for the latter reason.
- *Biography and Collective Biography*—Ask the class the meaning of the word *biography*. If you wish, you can ask about autobiography too. Explain what is meant by collective biography. Point to several preselected examples of biographical works. Your selection should include famous historical figures (George Washington, Abraham Lincoln) and well-known sports figures (Tom Seaver, Julius "Dr. J." Erving).
- *Reference*—Indicate the encyclopedias and highlight the ones that are easy to read. The subject encyclopedias in such areas as science and sports should also be shown.
- *Special Sections*—Point out periodicals, pamphlets, picture files, and any other special areas in the media center. Any restrictions on borrowing these materials should be explained.
- *Charge Out Desk*—Review the procedures for borrowing, renewing, and reserving materials. If fines are charged, explain the rules and rates. Discuss what is meant by *overdue*. Point out how and where to return material. Emphasize that books are *not* to be returned to the shelf once they have been charged out.
- *Rules for the Media Center*—Now is the time to briefly remind students about acceptable noise levels in the media center, passes (if they are required), behavior in the halls, and proper handling of the books. It sounds dreary, but if done with a light touch, your demonstration of flagrant examples of improper behavior, such as calling across the room to a friend or leaning back on a chair, will help maintain the friendly mood.

3. *Windup* — Ask if there are any questions. Of course, you have been answering questions all along, but there may be some more. To forestall the questions designed to make this trip last forever, tell the group that as soon as questions are over, they may look for books to take out. When the students charge out their books, it would be nice to have bookmarks or library maps to give them. Bookmarks can be purchased commercially or made by students. (See the June Library Art Activity for directions on making bookmarks. See this month's Library Art Activity for making media center maps.)

Orientation for Grades 4–6

Since students at this level are familiar with the media center, the orientation given to the lower grades would be redundant. Although they have also had experience with the equipment, a review of media center hardware will be of more interest to them and will possibly save you time. Too much equipment out for repair can play havoc with your program and scheduling.

Schedule each class for a 45 minute session. If a shorter period is required, make smaller groups and use less equipment.

PREPARATION:

1. Set up the pieces of equipment that are used by most students. These would include a filmstrip projector, cassette player, 8 mm. loop projector, and headphones. Each type of equipment should be placed in a different area.
2. Each equipment area should be identified with a number. (For example: Station 1, Station 2.)
3. Place the appropriate software next to the equipment.
4. Make a list of key directions for each piece of equipment on standard-size paper. (See illustration.) Use felt markers to make bold letters.

CASSETTE RECORDER
(with built-in microphone)

PLUG IN RECORDER

To Play
1. Push eject button to open
2. Insert cassette
3. Plug in headphones or jack box
4. Set volume
5. Push play button
6. Adjust volume
7. REW means Rewind
8. FF means Fast Forward
9. Push STOP after step 7 or 8
10. Push eject to remove cassette

To Record
1. Push eject to open
2. Insert cassette
3. Set volume
4. Push RECORD and PLAY at the same time
5. Count silently 2 seconds
6. Begin recording
7. Push STOP when through
8. Push eject to open

5. Tape the directions next to the appropriate equipment.
6. Place sheets of lined paper next to the directions. Head each sheet with the name of the equipment. As the students check out on the machines, they will sign their names on the sheets.

PROCEDURE:

1. Divide the class into groups of four or less. If the teacher is with the class, the teacher can select the groups. If there are more groups than types of equipment, use additional pieces of equipment.
2. Explain to the students what is expected of them. Then assign the groups to different pieces of equipment. Each student is to go through the steps for correctly operating the machine while the other members of the group supervise. After checking out on the equipment, the student signs the sheet, and another member of the group goes through the same operation. When all of the students in all of the groups have checked out on the equipment at one station, the groups advance to another station. The students who began at the highest numbered station go to Station 1.
3. Circulate freely among the groups to spot problems and to provide assistance.
4. Compare the check-out sheets with the class list. Send the names of students who did not check out to the classroom teacher. These students can be scheduled at another time.
5. If there is time remaining, the students may borrow books or work with the equipment.

NEW TEACHER ORIENTATION

New teachers must be made aware of the scope of services provided by the media center as soon as possible. In addition, it is frequently the responsibility of the library media specialist to see that new teachers are checked out on the equipment.

Try to schedule all of the new teachers at one time. Usually there are not many additions to the faculty, so the number is quite manageable. The best time for this orientation is before the school is open to students.

Explain the system for faculty charge out and describe services such as the organization and delivery of a multi-media unit for classroom use. (See the December chapter for an example of a multi-media unit.) Be sure the teachers understand that requests for a service are not a bother. Teachers who have little experience with a media center seem almost fearful of "imposing." They usually recover from this initial apprehension with a vengeance, but this means that you have succeeded in becoming an integral part of their teaching.

You should then check out the teachers on all of the basic equipment. A teacher is checked out only after he or she has operated the equipment under your close observation. Teachers must *demonstrate* competency even on a record player. Do not assume anything. Do not accept a verbal review; there must be a demonstration. Keep a record of teachers and the equipment on which they are checked out.

Because several machines are covered at one session, you should quickly review the key points of operating a piece of equipment the first time a teacher borrows the software for it.

Caution teachers about the procedure they should follow in case of equipment malfunction. The rules are simple: Turn the machine off and send a message to the media center. This will bring temporary equipment replacement and, when possible, the aid of the library media specialist. Tell the teachers not to attempt to repair the damage. It is simpler to discover what has gone wrong if attempted repairs do not complicate matters.

Storytelling Suggestions

SHORT AND SURE-FIRE HITS

The stories you will be reading to your classes in September will differ somewhat from those you read later in the school year. To introduce the story hour, you will want to choose books that are guaranteed to be successful so that the children will look forward to this event all year.

Why is it important to read stories to children? It is an effective way to acquaint them with good literature. You can introduce material that is beyond their reading level, yet not beyond their interest level. Reading stories to children makes them aware that listening is an activity. Listening skills are essential and need to be encouraged. Your early selections should be fairly short. As the listening skills of the group develop during the year, you can begin reading longer tales.

It is a good idea to keep a record of what you have read to each class. You might also want to note the children's reactions to particular stories. If you have a lot of classes, the record will save you from reading the same story several times to the same class. Although there is nothing wrong with repeating a story, there are so many good ones to choose from that you need not repeat any unless you have a specific reason for doing so.

Here are some stories with which you might begin the school year:

Aliki   *Keep Your Mouth Closed, Dear*
Dial Press, 1966

Charles the crocodile swallows everything in sight, causing his parents to try all kinds of solutions to his problem. (kindergarten and first grade)

Asch, Frank   *Monkey Face*
Parents, 1977

Monkey shows a picture he has painted of his mother to his friends, who all suggest changes that should be made. (kindergarten)

Brown, Myra Berry   *Benjy's Blanket*
Watts, 1962

Benjy is very attached to his blanket, but he soon finds someone who needs it more. (kindergarten and first grade)

Chorao, Kay   *Molly's Moe*
Seabury, 1976

Molly is always losing things, but on a shopping trip with Mother, she resolves that she will watch everything very carefully. (second and third grade)

Delton, Judy   *Two Good Friends*
illus. by Giulio Maestro
Crown, 1974

Neat duck and sloppy bear prove that two characters with different personalities can complement each other and be good friends. (first grade)

Groves, Paul   *Mr. Egbert Nosh*
                                    illus. by Hilary Hayton and Graham McCallum
                                    Childrens, 1972

Egbert Nosh's house gets lonely and begins to follow him wherever he goes. (first and second grade)

Hoban, Russell   *Bedtime for Frances*
                                    illus. by Garth Williams
                                    Harper & Row, 1960

Frances keeps postponing her bedtime until she discovers that it is her job to go to sleep. (first to third grade)

Johnston, Johanna   *That's Right, Edie*
                                    illus. by Paul Galdone
                                    Putnam's, 1966

Edie loves to scribble and doesn't want to take the time to write properly until she almost loses her birthday bike. (first grade)

Kellogg, Steven   *Much Bigger Than Martin*
                                    Dial Press, 1976

Henry dreams of being a giant who towers over his brother Martin. (kindergarten and first grade)

Kraus, Robert   *Whose Mouse Are You?*
                                    illus. by Jose Aruego
                                    Macmillan, 1970

A little mouse belongs to no one, but soon he restores his family—complete with little brother. (kindergarten and first grade)

Maestro, Giulio   *The Remarkable Plant in Apartment 4*
                                    Bradbury, 1973

Michael buys a plant that changes his whole apartment house as it becomes monstrous overnight. (first and second grade)

McGovern, Ann   *Too Much Noise*
                                    illus. by Simms Taback
                                    Houghton Mifflin, 1967

Peter's house is too noisy, but after filling it with animals, he discovers the true joy of quiet. (kindergarten to third grade)

Peet, Bill   *The Wump World*
                                    Houghton Mifflin, 1970

The tranquillity of the Wump world is destroyed by the landing of the Pollutians. An ecological tale. (second to fourth grade)

Viorst, Judith   *Alexander and the Terrible, Horrible, No Good,*
                                    Very Bad Day
                                    illus. by Ray Cruz
                                    Atheneum, 1973

Everything that could possibly go wrong happens to Alexander in one day. (second grade)

Williams, Barbara   *Albert's Toothache*
                                      illus. by Kay Chorao
                                      Dutton, 1974

No one but grandma believes that a turtle can have a toothache. But he does!
(first to third grade)

Teaching Unit

BOOK SPINES

Get your library skills program off to a quick start with a book spine unit designed for a classroom learning center or media center learning activity.

The nonfiction "book spines" (which are made of posterboard) can be placed in the fifth or sixth grade, the fiction spines in the third or fourth grade. At these levels, the book spines serve to reinforce existing library skills. After two months the unit can be routed to the lower grade levels, where it can be used in conjunction with a basic library skills unit.

> *Note:* Library skills are learned in many ways and through much reinforcement. The first three Teaching Units cover specific library skills for the intermediate grades. The January Teaching Unit is an intense, six-session unit that brings together all of the basic library skills. Other Teaching Units give the lower grades an introduction to encyclopedia use and expose the upper grades to a periodical index and other specialized reference tools. You can easily adapt all of these teaching units to students at any grade level who seem to need a particular skill.

OBJECTIVES:

At the conclusion of this unit, students should be able to:

1. Explain how nonfiction and fiction books are arranged.
2. Arrange a series of call numbers in correct shelf sequence.

Nonfiction Book Spines

MATERIALS:

—50 strips of 1" × 6½" posterboard in 4 different colors
—4 pieces of 6" × 9" posterboard in the same 4 colors
—1 sheet of 8½" × 11" colored construction paper (or another 6" × 9" piece of posterboard)
—felt marker
—1 manila envelope, large enough to hold all of the materials

PREPARATION:

1. Go to the nonfiction shelves in your media center and prepare a list of 50 call numbers, preferably in sequence. A suitable sequence might look like the one shown.

620	620.09	621	621	621	621.32	621.381	
LAR	BRA	BOU	EPS	FIN	RUS	KLE	
621.382	621.384	621.386	621.386	621.386	621.388	621.388	
NAT	GOU	EVA	KNI	SCH	HAE	WIL	
621.389	621.389	621.4	621.4	621.48	621.702	621.8	
MUR	OLN	WEI	ZIM	COL	WIL	ZAF	
621.9	621.9	621.9	621.909	621.97	621.97	622	
MEY	YAT	ZIM	EPS	EDS	EPS	BUE	
623	623.4	623.4	623.409	623.7	623.82	623.82	
GRA	BER	COL	NIC	COO	BUR	COO	
623.82	623.82	623.82	623.88	623.89	624	624	
GIL	HAN	SNY	GIB	CHA	CAR	CUL	
624	624	624	625.1	625.2	625.2	625.7	625.7
PEE	SUL	VEG	HAR	KES	OPP	PAR	PAR

2. To help the teacher keep track of the level of difficulty, use one color poster-board for all spines with a three-digit Dewey decimal number, a second color for spines with one number after the decimal point, a third color for spines with two numbers after the decimal point, and a fourth color for spines with three or more numbers after the decimal point.

3. Use a felt marker to print each call number on the appropriate part of a book spine.

4. Use the 6″ × 9″ pieces of posterboard to prepare answer cards that are color-coded. For example, if blue posterboard was used for spines with three-digit call numbers, use blue for the answer card.

5. Print the following directions for using the book spines on either the construction paper (if the unit is to be mounted on a bulletin board) or the extra 6″ × 9″ posterboard piece (if it is to be kept as a learning packet).

DIRECTIONS FOR USING THE BOOK SPINES:

1. The teacher assigns the students one color or several colors of book spines, depending on their abilities and knowledge of library skills.

2. The students are to arrange the spines in correct numerical sequence. (The teacher should remind the students that nonfiction is arranged in numerical order.)

3. After arranging the spines, the students are to check their responses with the appropriate answer card.

4. The teacher may then direct students to choose one spine in a given color, to take the spine to the media center, and to check the shelves there. The students are to find the name of the author and the title of the book with that call number.

5. All of the materials should be put back in the manila envelope for delivery and storage.

Fiction Book Spines

MATERIALS:

—25 strips of 1" × 6½" colored posterboard
—2 pieces of 6" × 9" colored posterboard
—1 sheet of 8½" × 11" colored construction paper (or another 6" × 9" piece of posterboard)
—felt marker
—1 manila envelope, large enough to hold all of the materials

PREPARATION:

1. Go to the fiction shelves in your media center and prepare a list of 25 authors and titles. Choose several that require alphabetizing by the second or third letter. The list might look like this:

Alcott, Louisa M.	*Little Women*
Asimov, Isaac	*Fantastic Voyage*
Babbitt, Natalie	*Goody Hall*
Bulla, Clyde	*White Bird*
Cameron, Eleanor	*The Court of the Stone Children*
Carlson, Natalie Savage	*The Empty Schoolhouse*
Cleary, Beverly	*Ramona the Pest*
Dahl, Roald	*James and the Giant Peach*
Dickens, Monica	*The House at World's End*
Edwards, Julie	*Mandy*
Haywood, Carolyn	*Eddie and Gardenia*
Henry, Marguerite	*Brighty of Grand Canyon*
Key, Alexander	*The Golden Enemy*
Lawson, Robert	*Ben and Me*
Lenski, Lois	*Judy's Journey*
Lindgren, Astrid	*Pippi Longstocking*
Mendoza, George	*GWOT!*
Sachs, Marilyn	*Laura's Luck*
Stevenson, Robert L.	*Black Arrow*
Stolz, Mary	*Noonday Friends*
Sutcliff, Rosemary	*Witch's Brat*
Thurber, James	*The 13 Clocks*
Tolkien, J. R. R.	*The Hobbit*
Watson, Sally	*Magic at Wychwood*
White, E. B.	*Charlotte's Web*

2. Use a felt marker to label the spines. Be sure to include the author, title, and call number. Authors' names should be written first name first.
3. Use a 6" × 9" piece of posterboard to prepare the alphabetized answer card.
4. Print the directions for using the book spines on construction paper or 6" × 9" posterboard.
5. Use a 6" × 9" piece of posterboard to prepare a question card with three or four questions. Answer can be written upside down on the card, or the students can check with the teacher. Here are a few sample questions:

   • Who wrote *Mandy*?
   • What is the title of the book by George Mendoza?
   • Who is the author of the book that has $\boxed{\begin{array}{c} \text{FIC} \\ \text{THU} \end{array}}$ as a call number?

DIRECTIONS FOR USING THE BOOK SPINES:

1. Students are to arrange the spines in correct alphabetical sequence. (Your directions to the students should remind them that fiction is arranged in alphabetical order.)
2. After arranging the spines, students are to check their responses with the answer card.
3. Students who successfully alphabetize the spines are to answer the question card.
4. All of the materials should be put back in the manila envelope for delivery and storage.

Professional Responsibilities

DISTRIBUTING HARDWARE

Placing equipment in classrooms presents two separate problems. The first concerns interpersonal relationships and the equitable distribution of a limited amount of equipment. The second problem is maintaining a record of where a given piece of equipment is located.

Storing all of the equipment and circulating it as needed would require a large support staff as well as more storage space than most schools have. The areas used for storage over the summer are usually used for other purposes during the school year. Therefore, equipment should be assigned to the classroom teachers for use during the school year. When there is not enough equipment to go around (a frequent occurrence), it becomes necessary for teachers to share. Sharing procedures can be worked out based on physical locations. Each section or wing, for example, could be assigned an overhead projector, a record player, a tape recorder, and a filmstrip projector. Rely on your awareness of how well the teachers in a given area interact in deciding whether to assign all of the equipment to one teacher for use by the entire section, or whether to dole it out piece by piece to all of the teachers and then make clear how it is to be shared. After each section has one of each type of equipment, additional pieces can be assigned. For example, there may be only one overhead projector per section, but three record players.

Be sure that the media center keeps at least one and preferably two of each type of equipment. These reserves are needed for students in the media center, for classroom teachers when the assigned equipment is being used by another teacher in the section, and as temporary replacements in cases of equipment malfunction.

After the equipment is distributed, keeping track of where it is at a given time can be difficult. Equipment never stays put. Teachers borrow from one another and make exchanges when a machine breaks down and is sent out for repairs. One of the best methods of keeping track of equipment is an equipment control board. (See illustration on next page.) Once the board is set up, the library media specialist can tell at a glance the location of each piece of equipment. The equipment is color-coded by type to double-check that it has been distributed fairly.

In the sample equipment control board, grades one and two are shown sharing equipment, as are grades three and four, grades five and six, the kindergarten and the specialists. The equipment control board can be a bulletin board that is set up

Equipment Control Board

Media Center	1 + 2	3 + 4	5 + 6	K + Spec.
	1	6	11	K-1
	3	8	13	ART
	5	10	15	Music
	2	7	12	P.E.
	4	9	14	RE-PAIR

in the equipment storage area or back room, or a large sheet of posterboard that is fastened to a wall. To construct an equipment control board, you will need the following materials and directions.

MATERIALS:

—bulletin board or 1 large sheet of posterboard
—1″ squares of posterboard, enough for each piece of equipment
—pushpins or map tacks in assorted colors, 1 color for each type of equipment and 1 pin for each piece
—3″ squares of white construction paper, 1 for each classroom plus 1 to be labeled "Repairs"
—5″ × 3″ pieces of construction paper, 1 for each group of classrooms
—felt markers
—yarn (if you are using a bulletin board)
—stapler

PREPARATION:

1. Use yarn or a felt marker to divide the control board into sections. (Yarn is stapled onto the bulletin board.)
2. Label the 5″ × 3″ cards representing groups of classrooms and staple them to the top of the control board.
3. Label the 3″ squares representing room numbers and staple them in the proper locations. Do not forget the repair label.
4. Label the 1″ square pieces of posterboard to correspond to the numbers on the equipment. For example, if there are ten overhead projectors and they are marked OP/1 through OP/10, make ten squares and number them OP/1 through OP/10.
5. For each type of equipment, use only one color of push pins or map tacks to attach the squares to the control board. You might have squares for overhead projectors attached with blue pins, and squares for record players attached with white pins.

PROCEDURE:

1. All of the squares in the left column represent equipment in the media center.
2. As equipment is assigned, move the square with the equipment number to the appropriate classroom box.
3. When equipment is returned, return the appropriate square to the left column.
4. When equipment is sent out for repair, the square with the equipment number is placed in the repair box. When repairs are completed, the square is returned to the column labeled media center.

Volunteers

RECRUITING AND SETTING UP A SCHEDULE

A strong support staff is required to assist a library media specialist in carrying out a successful program. Staff members put cards back into books that have been returned (this is known as "slipping" the books), file cards for books that have been charged out, and replace books on the shelves properly. They mend old books and process new ones. They type catalog cards, book cards, and bibliographies. They care for magazines, work on the vertical file, and take inventory at the end of the year. Some of them help with bulletin boards. When a paid support staff is limited or nonexistent, it becomes necessary to recruit volunteers who are senior citizens, parents of school children, or other interested community members. A good group of volunteers is an important ingredient of a successful media center.

> *Note:* In each chapter of the *Almanac,* you will find a section discussing the tasks performed by volunteers. Although the general instructions are applicable to all media centers, you may want to change some of the specific procedures to conform with your own practices. Therefore, the Volunteers sections sometimes seem to be addressed to the volunteers and sometimes to you. After you have explained any of your procedures that are different from those described here, feel free to share these sections with your volunteers.

When recruiting volunteers it is extremely important that you:

- make the volunteers feel that they are performing a useful service
- have tasks ready for them at all times
- make use of any special talents they have (such as typing or artistic ability)

The volunteers are a pipeline to the community. To a great extent, the way they view your media center is the way the community will also look at it. But don't let this scare you, because they are generally enthusiastic and willing; besides being extremely helpful, they are the public relations people who spread the message that the media center is the hub around which the entire school revolves.

A library chairperson, generally chosen by the school P.T.A., has the job of recruiting volunteers for the year. You can also help. If you speak at kindergarten or new parent orientations, put in a plug for volunteers. This is often a good way to interest mothers who are anxious to meet people or to learn more about the school.

The schedule for the year, set up by the library chairperson, should be based on your specific needs. It seems to work out well when two or more people are scheduled for each morning and afternoon. This way, if one person can't come at the last minute, the time period will still be covered. The volunteers should receive a copy of the library schedule that includes names and telephone numbers, so that they will know whom to contact if they cannot come. It is a good idea to schedule each new person at the same time as an experienced volunteer, but this will not always be possible.

VOLUNTEER ORIENTATION

The beginning of the school year is usually too hectic for a formal orientation for media center volunteers. If it is convenient, you might schedule a meeting during the last hour of school midway through September. Serve coffee and danish to keep the mood informal. The library chairperson will contact the volunteers to inform them of the meeting. Do not be concerned if several cannot attend. This is just a simple get-together.

Introduce yourself and briefly explain how important their services are to the media center. Calm those who are worried because they don't know anything about libraries, media centers, or whatever else you call them by pointing to the experienced volunteers who were once equally agitated. Schedules can be distributed at this time. Stress the importance of volunteers coming at the scheduled time and arranging for substitutes if they cannot. Be sure to thank the group, both for coming and for volunteering.

When your new volunteers report for duty, you should try to spend some time with each one discussing tasks and touring the media center. It may be helpful to have the volunteer read the appropriate section in this book as a general overview before attempting a new task; you can then mention any specific procedures that might differ in your media center. If you can devote the time to training your new volunteers, they will learn the correct procedures and save you a lot of future problems.

CHARGE OUT AND RETURN

The term *charge out* refers to the procedures for borrowing library materials. There are a number of ways in which this may be done. One way is to have a person at the circulation desk at all times to help children charge out their books. A student writes his name on the space provided on the book card and enters his classroom number or class code. The person at the desk stamps the due date on the appropriate section of the book pocket and on the book card. The book card is then filed in the circulation desk drawer.

If you cannot spare a person to be at the circulation desk continuously, the children can charge out their books by themselves. In this instance, a student signs his or her name, the day's date and the classroom number or class code, and then files the book card alphabetically by the last name of the author in a card sorter placed on top of the circulation desk. (Even first graders learn to do this very quickly and are proud to be able to arrange their cards alphabetically.) The student then takes a prestamped date due card from a box on the desk and places it in the book pocket; the book is now charged out. When a number of cards have accumulated in the card sorter, a volunteer can file them in the circulation desk drawer after checking to make sure that they have been charged out correctly.

Book cards can be filed in the circulation drawer in several ways. The most popular way is by the date they are due. Cards with the same due date are filed alphabetically by the author's last name. They can also be separated into fiction, nonfiction, and biography and then arranged in the same order as they would be on the shelves. Another way to file book cards is alphabetically by author, regardless of the date the book is due. With this method, you always know the whereabouts of a particular book, but it can cause a lot of problems when you are looking for overdue books (See the Volunteers section in the January chapter.) A third method is filing the cards behind the classroom teacher's name. This system works well if students borrow books only when they come with their class, but any open scheduling interferes with it.

Teachers and parents may borrow material for an extended period of time. You may want to have a separate file for parents and another one that shows the books borrowed under each teacher's name. Parents and teachers would not take prestamped date due cards or have the date due section of a book pocket or book card stamped. They would either write their names on a date due slip, or, if there were none, write their last names on a slip of paper and place it in the book pocket for identification upon the return of the material.

Magazines can be charged out in a manner similar to books. In some media centers, they are only allowed to circulate overnight. One idea for spotting magazine cards quickly is to use a different color (such as blue) for magazine cards.

When books are returned, they must be "slipped." This means putting the book card back in the returned material. Everyone who uses the media center should know the one place where all materials must be returned.

If you have filed the book cards by due date, check to see when the book is due by looking at the book pocket slip or the date due card. Then look for the book card under that date. Be sure that the author's last name, the title of the book, and the accession or copy number (see the January chapter) on the book card and the book pocket agree. This will avoid mix-ups if there is more than one copy of a book. If the book was checked out by a teacher or parent, which you can tell by the name written on the book pocket slip or on the slip of paper placed in the pocket, look in the file for parents or for the teacher's name. If, after searching, you cannot find the correct book card, put it aside where you keep "snags" (books for which the correct card cannot be found). (See the March chapter.)

When all of the materials have the proper cards in them, they should be placed on a cart for "shelving"—returning material to its proper location for future circulation. (See the October chapter.)

CIRCULATION STATISTICS

Daily Circulation Statistics

It is important for the library media specialist to have a record of how many items are borrowed each day and of how many students use the media center. These statistics are used to determine which areas of the collection need strengthening, and they are included in reports to the school administration. Statistical records help you compare the degree of activity in the media center from month to month and from year to year. Although numbers by themselves are not the only measure of accomplishment, they can be used as an indication of how things are proceeding. Therefore, it is necessary to make a count of all circulated materials.

This may be done at the time the cards are filed into the circulation drawer, or the previous day's circulation may be noted each morning. There should be a pad on the desk with the date on it and space to enter statistics. Daily circulation pads may be made to your design by the high school graphic arts class or purchased from library supply houses.

Statistics can be recorded for the total number of books circulated, or a separate count can be kept for fiction, nonfiction, biography, magazines, and other materials. You may want to keep the count for teachers and parents separate, though you may find it easier to include them with the other statistics. When introducing a new service such as paperbacks, circulation of media software, or a vertical file, you may want to temporarily maintain a separate record of these items in order to gauge interest and degree of success.

Permanent Circulation Record

The daily slips should be transferred to a permanent circulation record. Although many media centers do not maintain a permanent record, it is standard practice in public libraries and it has several long-range advantages. Again, it is true that numbers do not tell the entire story, but statistics can be helpful if you are called upon to justify the need for a library media specialist. In a more positive vein, a permanent record enables you to compare the statistics for several years and to determine circulation patterns.

Although it is difficult to record, you should also be aware of in-house circulation. This refers to materials that are used only in the media center such as encyclopedias, reference books, and books that have been placed on reserve for a specific class to use while doing a report. Although these materials will not appear on your circulation record, they are an important element of media center use.

Only one volunteer should be responsible for maintaining the permanent record. Select a conscientious volunteer for the task. Care is necessary in transferring data from the daily circulation pad to the permanent circulation book. Although this book can be purchased from the same library supply houses as the pad, the two do not always correlate. Once the figures have been entered, the daily counts may be thrown out.

If there is no convenient place to enter faculty statistics separately, divide the boxes with a slash and use the top for student figures and the bottom for the staff. It is helpful to do weekly totals first and to then do the monthly totals.

Open End

SUMMER RESPONSIBILITIES?

Almost all library media specialists are on ten-month contracts from the beginning of September through the end of June. But what happens to your media center during July and August? Do you just lock up in June and return after Labor Day to begin again?

If that is the case, your return is greeted by mountains of mail—advertisements, catalogs, magazines, and other assorted materials. You open the door refreshed from your summer vacation and eager to begin again, and you are inundated. Your good intentions may be slightly shattered by the necessity of going through everything that has piled up over the summer just when your schedule is the heaviest. It is truly amazing how much can pile up over a period of ten or eleven weeks!

In many cases, your budget for the next year is due within a few weeks of your return. Some school districts will allow books and audio-visual materials to be ordered only once a year, and that time may also be in September. To be faced with all of these tasks at once can cause even the most experienced library media specialist to dream of being back on the beach relaxing!

If you dread having to catch up on the summer, you have only two alternatives. One is to gather up everything and place it in large cartons until you eventually get around to it. Obviously, this is not a good practice because there may be some important materials waiting for you and some of them may have a time limit on them. The other alternative is to visit your school regularly during the summer, pick up your mail, and go through it at your leisure.

This approach can also cause problems. First of all, you are not getting paid to work in the summer, and regular visits to your school may set a precedent that is better left unestablished. This approach also presupposes that you are at home most of the summer and have the time to give to this task. Many library media specialists spend their summers traveling or taking summer courses or otherwise making use of their free time.

Unless it is possible to get your administration and school board to recognize that the library media specialist's work is not just a ten month job, that certain tasks need to be performed during the summer, and that one additional week or a series of days throughout the summer should be budgeted and paid for, your method of coping with summer responsibilities will depend on your personality and needs.

If you feel that it is worth the unpaid work to have all of your summer mail and paper work up-to-date so that you can open your media center in September with a clear desk and an easy mind, then you will make one decision. If, on the other hand, you know that you will be able to work better in September after having a complete rest and change from doing any type of library work, then the other approach will be best for you.

October

Happy Birthday To . . .

3   **Natalie Savage Carlson** (1906)—author
Fiction for intermediate grades, including the Orpheline series and *Ann Aurelia and Dorothy*
Molly Cone (1918)—author
Fiction and nonfiction for intermediate grades, including *A Promise Is a Promise* and *Purim*

4   **Julia Cunningham** (1916)—author
Poignant fiction including *Onion Journey* and *Burnish Me Bright*
Robert Lawson (1892)—author and illustrator
His own stories include *Ben and Me* and *Mr. Revere and I*
Munro Leaf (1904)—author and illustrator
Fiction and nonfiction including *The Story of Ferdinand* and *Manners Can Be Fun*
Donald J. Sobol (1924)—author
Author of the Encyclopedia Brown mystery series for intermediate grades

5   **Louise Fitzhugh** (1928)—author
Creator of Harriet the Spy

7   **Alice Dalgliesh** (1893)—author
Fiction and nonfiction about American history, such as *The Courage of Sarah Noble* and *The Fourth of July Story*

10   **James Marshall** (1942)—author and illustrator
Animal picture books whose characters include those famous hippopotamuses George and Martha

Get going on programs and then make way for ghosts, goblins, and things that go bump in the night.

===

13   **Arna Bontemps** (1902)—author
      Accounts of the contributions of black Americans to this country, including *Frederick Douglass* and *Famous Negro Athletes*

14   **Lois Lenski** (1893)—author and illustrator
      Picture books including *Cowboy Small*, and intermediate fiction set in regional locations, such as *Strawberry Girl* and *Judy's Journey*

16   **Edward Ardizzone** (1900)—author and illustrator
      Creator of the Little Tim picture books

      Noah Webster (1758)—lexicographer
      Compiler of *Webster's Dictionary*, considered the finest English dictionary of its time

20   **Wylly Folk St. John** (1908)—author
      Mysteries including *Secret of the Seven Crows* and *Mystery of the Gingerbread House*

23   **Marjorie Flack** (1897)—author and illustrator
      Picture books including the Angus series and *The Story About Ping*

24   **Phyllis Fenner** (1899)—compiler
      Collections of short stories including *Ghosts, Ghosts, Ghosts* and *Feasts and Frolics*

      Bruno Munari (1907)—author and illustrator
      Picture books including *Bruno Munari's Zoo* and *ABC*

Bulletin Boards

USE THE DICTIONARY

Children love to play with long words. Encourage or stimulate this interest with a dictionary bulletin board. (See illustration.) This bulletin board will provide a good introduction to ''Looking Up Unusual Words in the Dictionary,'' this month's Library Enrichment Activity.

MATERIALS:

—1 sheet of 22″ × 28″ colored posterboard
—4 balloons
—ball of lightweight yarn or string
—cellophane tape
—rubber cement
—stapler
—9″ × 12″ sheets of construction paper in various colors
—fine-tip felt marker
—1 sheet of white construction paper
—medium-tip felt marker
—scissors
—3″ × 5″ white card
—crayons or colored felt markers (optional)
—list of 14 words from the dictionary or the following list:

> absterge (ab sterj′) verb—to wipe off
> bombastic (bom bas′tik) adj.—inflated
> carcharodon (kär kar′ ə don) noun—large man-eating tropical shark
> dhow (dou) noun—ship with triangular sails
> eulogium (yü lō′ jē əm) noun—praise
> googol (gü′ gol) noun—the number one followed by one hundred zeros
> imbricate (im′brə kāt) verb—to overlap (as tiles or shingles)
> klompen (klom′pən) noun—wooden shoes worn by the Dutch
> natator (nā ta′ ter) noun—a swimmer
> plenitudinous (plen′ ə tu′ də nəs) adj.—stout
> somnambulate (som nam′byə lāt) verb—to walk in your sleep
> troglodyte (trog′lə dīt) noun—cave man
> vicinal (vis′ə nəl) adj.—neighboring, near
> waggery (wag′ər ē) noun—joking, clowning

Source: *World Book Dictionary* (Field Enterprises, 1970)

PREPARATION:

1. Write four of the words from your list on the four balloons (one word on each balloon) with the fine-tip felt marker.
2. Blow up the balloons, knot them, and attach long strings of yarn to them.
3. Cut out the letters for the word *inflate* from different colored construction paper. The letters should be 4″ high.
4. Choose any word from your list. Write the word in capital letters with a felt marker on a sheet of colored construction paper. Below the word in smaller letters, write the pronunciation, the part of speech, and the meaning. Draw a balloon shape around what you have written and cut out the balloon.

5. Repeat step 4 with each word on the list. Use different colors of construction paper.
6. Staple a long piece of yarn to each balloon cutout. The yarn can be trimmed later.
7. Draw or trace the cartoon figure holding the dictionary on white construction paper and cut it out. You may color the figure with crayons if you wish.
8. Print or type the source of the pronunciations and definitions on the 3″ × 5″ card.
9. To assemble the bulletin board:
   a. Position and paste the cartoon figure on the posterboard. Do not paste down the raised arm.
   b. Roll pieces of cellophane tape and attach the pieces to the backs of the inflated balloons. Attach the balloons to the top of the posterboard.
   c. Catch the four pieces of yarn behind the cartoon figure's upraised arm and staple the yarn to the posterboard. Cover the staples with the figure's hand.
   d. Use a felt marker to print "Your Vocabulary" and "Use the Dictionary" on the posterboard.
   e. Position the letters for the word *inflate* and paste them onto the posterboard.
   f. Staple the construction paper balloons to the sides of the posterboard.
   g. Trim excess yarn.
   h. Attach the 3″ × 5″ card to the bottom of the posterboard.

UNFINISHED HAUNTED HOUSE

Begin October with a spooky bulletin board. It is quite simple to construct, and the students will add most of the finishing touches. (See this month's Library Art Activity for directions on how to finish the house.) By Halloween you will have a completed eerie bulletin board—and a successful library art project. (See illustration on facing page.)

MATERIALS:

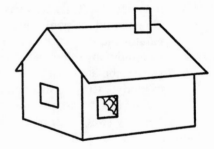

—1 sheet of 22″ × 28″ orange posterboard
—yellow construction paper
—black felt marker
—rubber cement
—clear self-stick vinyl (optional)
—pencil
—scissors

PREPARATION:

1. Use a pencil to draw a horizon line across the posterboard.
2. Cut the yellow construction paper to make a circle. This will be the moon.
3. Use a pencil to lightly draw a haunted house on the posterboard. Copy the one in the sample bulletin board or use your own ideas. If you find it difficult, you might draw a simple house like the one shown above. Draw only one or two windows. A spider web will help you make the house look haunted.
4. Cut away the inside of the moon so that it outlines the house.

5. Paste the moon to the posterboard.
6. Use a felt marker to darken the lines of the house and the horizon.
7. Add eerie details such as a grave, spooky tree, ghost, or bat. Do not add too much. Leave something for the children to do.
8. You might cover the posterboard with clear self-stick vinyl. If you do, you will be able to wipe off the students' additions and reuse the bulletin board in the future.

Library Art Activity

COMPLETE THE HAUNTED HOUSE

Get the students into the Halloween spirit early. As soon as your Unfinished Haunted House bulletin board goes up, start this art activity to get the house finished.

MATERIALS:

—white construction paper
—scissors
—black felt marker
—1 sheet of 11″ × 14″ orange posterboard
—rubber cement
—washable felt markers or transparency markers

PREPARATION:

1. Cut 3″ high ghost shapes out of the white construction paper. Keep them simple.
2. Draw two large black eyes on each ghost.
3. Prepare a poster explaining the art activity on the orange posterboard. See the sample poster (on facing page) for directions to the students.

PROCEDURE:

1. When students return books in the suggested subject areas, give them one ghost for each book. The ghosts are proof that they have read the books. They can then make additions to the bulletin board during their free time.
2. Collect the ghosts as the students return them and paste them onto the windows as additional decorations.
3. Give the students washable felt markers to draw additions to the haunted house.

Library Enrichment Activity

LOOKING UP UNUSUAL WORDS IN THE DICTIONARY

This activity is an extension of this month's Use the Dictionary bulletin board. Students in all grades beginning with second can participate.

Mention to each of your classes that you are highlighting Noah Webster and the dictionary this month. Suggest that they may want to participate by finding some

1. Read a mystery, horror story, or a ghost story.

2. When you return the book ask for a ghost.

3. For every ghost you receive, you may add one item to the HAUNTED HOUSE.

Add windows, doors, bats, witches, or whatever you wish.

unusual words in one of the dictionaries available in the media center, writing them down, and having the cards posted for others to see. This may be done during a class period or when the children come in during their free time.

MATERIALS:

—several dictionaries at different grade levels
—pack of 3″ × 5″ index cards
—pens
—tape

PROCEDURE:

1. Give each student some 3″ × 5″ cards and a pen.
2. The students may check any dictionary to find words that interest them.
3. Each word is written on the center of the card, and the pronunciation is written in parentheses next to it. At the bottom of the card, the name of the dictionary in which the word was found is noted. The card is then turned upside down, and the meaning of the word is written on the back.
4. The cards (and the pens) are returned to you to post around the room. If there is time, it is a good idea to do this right away so that the students can see where you place their cards.
5. Stick a piece of tape to the top of each card and attach it to the bulletin board. Leave the bottom free so that the card can be turned over and the definition can be read easily. Place each card low enough so that the children can read it.
6. The cards can be posted near the bulletin board, near the area where the dictionaries are kept, or all around your media center, depending on the amount of space you have.

The children will enjoy looking for unusual words and will learn the meanings of several new ones during the time that this activity takes place.

STORYTELLING TIPS FOR KINDERGARTEN

Kindergarten children love to hear stories. The expedition to the media center is frequently the high spot of their week. At first the attention spans of the children will be limited. Your object is to build their attention spans until they can listen to longer stories and be able to recall the sequence of events in them.

Have an oversupply of stories ready for the first visit. If you are well prepared, you can respond to the mood of the class. The books you select should be short, colorful, and preferably large so that the pictures can be easily seen.

A good selection for this visit might include:

Rosie's Walk by Pat Hutchins (Macmillan, 1968)
Titch by Pat Hutchins (Macmillan, 1971)
Herman the Helper by Robert Kraus (Windmill, 1974)
Goodnight Moon by Margaret Wise Brown (Harper & Row, 1947)
Caps for Sale by Esphyr Slobodkina (Addison-Wesley, 1947)

Although this selection has no unifying theme, all of the books get a strong response from students. While listening to *Rosie's Walk*, students can be asked several times if they think the fox will catch Rosie. The class can "help" do the part of the monkeys in *Caps for Sale*. *Titch* and *Herman the Helper* can be used to elicit the students' feelings about themselves. *Goodnight Moon* is excellent for achieving a special quiet feeling. The children's bedtime routines can be discussed.

Before you start to read, reassure the children that all of them will see the pictures. Demonstrate how you will move the book while you read. Suggest that they save their questions until the end of the story. Be prepared for nonsequiturs such as "My aunt's birthday is tomorrow"! Do not squelch these "questions," but turn back to a discussion of the story; otherwise, each student in the class will tell you of every birthday in the family—including pets—and you will lose the atmosphere that you worked to create.

If you handle these kindergarten visits with warmth and interest, the students will develop happy attitudes toward books, libraries, and reading that may well last into adulthood.

OVERHEAD PROJECTOR TECHNIQUES

The overhead projector is one of the most helpful tools in the modern classroom. Teachers can use acetate sheets to prepare information at home, saving class time that would be spent putting the information on a chalkboard. Overlays can be used to clarify and expand on concepts. Students preparing oral reports can use transparencies to add interest. These are only a few examples of ways to utilize the overhead projector. Unfortunately, in many schools only a few teachers really use the overhead. Others feel that the blackboard has always worked well enough, so why bother.

But there are other uses for this versatile piece of equipment. Once students begin to use it to produce high quality illustrations, teachers also become interested. You can use the following overhead projector techniques to teach a class that comes to the media center to learn about report writing or to be shown the resources applicable to a particular unit. You can also demonstrate these techniques to individual students and let others acquire the necessary interest and skills from watching the overhead projector in operation. Its simple operation and excellent results are tremendous incentives to students. As a result, second graders who begin by making pictures of animals often follow up with simple reports.

The Overhead Projector as a Shadow Box

If your collection of permanent transparencies includes maps, pictures of famous people, or drawings of animals, students can copy them easily by placing them on the overhead projector. Cover the transparency with a sheet of white drawing paper, or even construction paper, and turn on the light. The underlying transparency will show through in clear detail. Students can use a pencil to trace the outline. Later they can color the drawing. While the students are tracing, tell them that they can find out what still needs to be drawn by turning off the light. Also caution them to turn off the light whenever the paper begins to feel uncomfortably warm. Remind the students that if they leave the machine for any reason, no matter for how short a time, they should turn off the light, run the fan, and allow the bulb enough time to cool. Be sure that they do not look at the light source when there is no paper covering the transparency.

Opaque material such as covers of booklets, pages from a pamphlet, or pictures from a magazine can be traced in the same fashion, although construction paper cannot be used for this. If the material to be copied is printed on two sides, the print from the underside will show through; however, students are amazingly good at discounting these annoyances when tracing. Care should be taken to insure that magazines are handled carefully during this operation. Restrict the use of this technique with magazines to adults or to the more responsible students.

Others wishing to copy from magazines or from books need to add one step to achieve the same results. They should trace the picture onto acetate, put the acetate on the overhead projector, cover it with paper, and retrace the picture onto the paper.

The Overhead Projector as an Enlarger

When making a poster or copying a drawing that is too small, use the overhead projector to magnify the illustration. Trace the picture onto acetate and place the acetate on the overhead. Lightly tape the construction paper, posterboard or other type of paper to a wall or a door at a convenient height for drawing. Turn on the overhead projector and focus it; then move it until the focused image is the correct size and is projected at the desired location. Trace the picture onto the paper. To see what still has to be drawn, turn off the overhead projector.

It is also possible to use this technique to transfer a drawing from a filmstrip to a poster. Insert the filmstrip into an individual viewer, choosing the model with the largest screen. Put a sheet of acetate over the screen and trace the illustration in the frame. Then transfer the acetate to the overhead projector and project the image onto posterboard.

Students can easily learn these methods and use them to copy almost anything. The only difficulty is when the original illustration is too small or detailed to be traced with even fine-tip felt markers. As they achieve results that look realistic, students become very enthusiastic; this, in turn, motivates them to further efforts. You, too, will be pleased to create impressive bulletin boards using the enlarging techniques, and your success will encourage teachers to use the overhead projector. Then you will have only one problem—not enough projectors and felt markers to keep up with the demand!

Note: Everyone who uses the overhead projector—or any other type of copying equipment—should be aware of the changes in the copyright law that became effective on January 1, 1978. The law does place restrictions on the type and amount of copying that may be done for teaching and research purposes. You should not only take care not to violate this law but also be able to explain its ramifications to your faculty and administration. A short bibliography of up-to-date information on the copyright law is given below. For specific local questions, a good source of advice would be your regional or district public library. When in doubt, you would be wise to write to the publisher asking permission to duplicate specific materials.

Sources of information:

U.S. Government Printing Office
Washington, D.C. 20559
(request material prepared by Copyright Office, Library of Congress)

Copyright and Educational Media: A Guide to Fair Use and Permissions Pro-
   cedures
(prepared by Association for Educational Communications and Technology and
   Association of Media Producers)
AECT Publication Sales Department
1126 16th Street, N.W.
Washington, D.C. 20036

A.L.A. Librarian's Copyright Kit: What You Must Know
(eleven pamphlets on implementing the new copyright law)
American Library Association
50 East Huron Street
Chicago, Illinois 60611

Explaining the New Copyright Law
Association of American Publishers
1707 L Street, N.W.
Washington, D.C. 20036

Storytelling Suggestions

HALLOWEEN TALES

Since this is the month of Halloween, here is a list of ghostly tales. Children in
grades three and up seem to enjoy the spookier stories. In choosing books for the
lower grades, avoid stories that might cause nightmares.

Balian, Lorna   *Humbug Witch*
                                 Abingdon, 1965

This very spooky but ineffectual witch at last gives up, unmasks, and goes to
bed. (kindergarten to second grade)

Barton, Byron   *Hester*
                                 Greenwillow, 1975

When Hester the alligator goes trick or treating, she finds a strange group
celebrating in an unusual looking house. (first grade)

Boggs, Ralph S. and   "The Tinker and the Ghost"
   Mary Gould Davis   in *Feasts and Frolics*
                                 ed. by Phyllis Fenner
                                 Knopf, 1949

Esteban remains unconcerned as parts of a body come down the chimney.
(third grade and up)

Bright, Robert   *Georgie's Halloween*
                                 Doubleday, 1958

Georgie the ghost gets left behind on Halloween, but later joins the fun.
(kindergarten to second grade)

Harper, Wilhelmina (compiler) *Ghosts and Goblins*
                                 Dutton, 1965

Thirty-four stories and poems for this eerie season. Starred selections are especially good for younger children. (all grades)

Jacobs, Joseph (compiler)   "Teeny Tiny"
                                 in *English Folk and Fairy Tales*
                                 Putnam's, no copyright date

A variation on the famous Golden Arm tale. In this case, the subject is a teeny, tiny bone. (third grade and up)

Leach, Maria   *The Thing at the Foot of the Bed and Other Scary Tales*
                                 World, 1959

A gold mine of stories for a Halloween story hour. (third grade and up)

Mendoza, George   *The Crack in the Wall and Other Terribly Weird Tales*
                                 Dial Press, 1968

Four shivery tales. The title story is about a crack in a wall that spreads until the house is consumed. (third grade and up)

Mendoza, George   *GWOT! Horribly Funny Hairticklers*
                                 Harper & Row, 1967

Three stories from American folklore; each is very scary but without a true climax. (third grade and up)

Riley, James Whitcomb   "Little Orphant Annie"
                                 in *The Illustrated Treasury of Poetry for Children*
                                 ed. by David Ross
                                 Grosset & Dunlap, 1970

As this classic Halloween poem warns, "the Goblins will get you, if you don't watch out!" (second grade and up)

Serraillier, Ian   *Suppose You Met a Witch*
                                 illus. by Ed Emberley
                                 Little, Brown, 1973

Intense illustrations heighten the impact of this happily ending poem by Serraillier. (second grade and up)

Teaching Unit

A TRIP AROUND THE MEDIA CENTER USING THE DEWEY DECIMAL SYSTEM

This unit, in which children become acquainted with the Dewey Decimal Classification System, can be easily adapted to your own schedule. The material takes approximately 17 sessions to cover; however, the unit can be stretched over a longer period by interspersing occasional stories and by periodically reviewing what has been learned, or it can be shortened by covering a block of 100 three-digit numbers at each session. During each session, the children are taught about one area of nonfiction and are able to choose from a group of books that you have preselected from that area. Allow 15 to 20 minutes for this part of the lesson. During the rest of the period, allow the children to select additional books from the section that was covered. The unit is designed for about the third grade level.

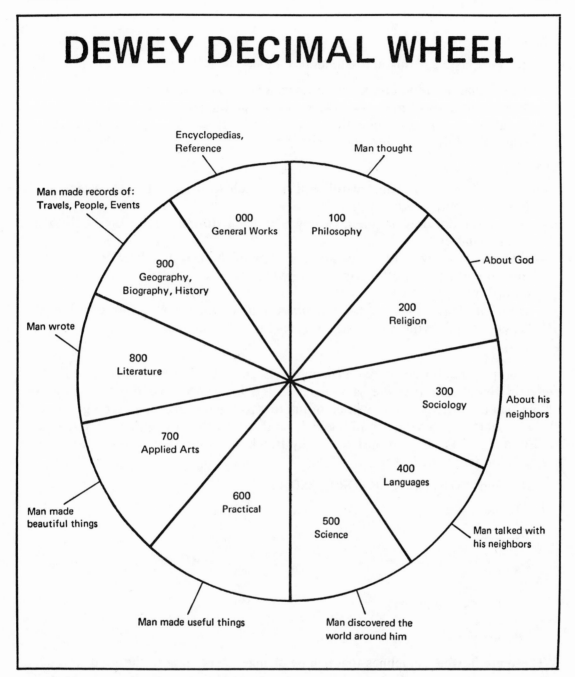

DEWEY DECIMAL WHEEL

Encyclopedias, Reference

Man thought

Man made records of: Travels, People, Events

About God

000 General Works

100 Philosophy

900 Geography, Biography, History

200 Religion

Man wrote

800 Literature

300 Sociology

About his neighbors

700 Applied Arts

400 Languages

Man made beautiful things

600 Practical

500 Science

Man talked with his neighbors

Man made useful things

Man discovered the world around him

One excellent way of familiarizing children with the Dewey Decimal System is to introduce them to the Dewey Blocks©. The Dewey Blocks are copyrighted by Modern Learning Products, a subsidiary of Fordham Equipment Company, Inc., 3308 Edson Avenue, Bronx, New York 10469. They are a set of 12 large, paper-covered blocks, ten of which represent the ten major Dewey divisions. There are separate blocks for 398 and for biography. The number is given on one surface, and five popular categories within that number are depicted on the other five surfaces. If you put the blocks in a prominent place in your media center, the children will become used to referring to them when they are interested in certain subjects. They will in no way supplant the card catalog for subject access; they are just another tool for making the classification system more meaningful to young children.

OBJECTIVES:

At the conclusion of this unit, students should:

1. Be familiar with the nonfiction arrangement of the media center.
2. Have read books from every section of the nonfiction shelves.
3. Be able to identify popular Dewey numbers such as 796—sports, 398.2—folk tales, and 568—dinosaurs.

MATERIALS:

—sheet of 8½″ × 11″ white cardboard on which to draw a Dewey wheel (see illustration on preceding page)
—felt markers for drawing the Dewey wheel (use a different color for each block of one hundred)
—ditto master on which to draw another copy of the Dewey wheel
—enough paper to run off a copy of the wheel for each student
—set of Dewey Blocks
—*Abridged Dewey Decimal Classification and Relative Index*, 10th ed. (Forest Press, 1971) for your use in selecting categories of books

PREPARATION:

The preparation for each lesson is similar. Decide how large an area you wish to cover in your lesson (see the sample schedule). Jot down some of the categories within that area that you feel will be of interest to the students, and then go to the shelves and choose a sampling of books from that area that are within the students' ability range. Take the appropriate Dewey Block and your Dewey wheel, and you are ready to teach the lesson.

SUGGESTED SCHEDULE FOR LESSONS:

1. Biography
2. 000's
3. 100's
4. 200's
5. 300–349
6. 350–398
7. 398.2 to end of 300's
8. 400's
9. 500–549
10. 550–589
11. 590 to end of 500's
12. 600–629.4
13. 630 to end of 600's
14. 700's
15. 800's
16. 900–929
17. 930 to end of 900's

These are flexible guidelines that can be changed according to the needs of your students and the availability of particular categories of books in your media center. For example, there are usually not too many books in the 400's in an elementary school media center, so one lesson could cover that section more than adequately. However, if you have a very large number of books in any one area with which you want to acquaint your students, you can certainly spend extra time on that area. You might even consider splitting up the suggested categories into smaller sections.

Introducing the Unit:

Explain to the children that they will be taking a trip around the media center using the Dewey Decimal System. Let them know that by the time this unit is finished, they will know where to find books on all different kinds of subjects.

Discuss some terms first. Ask the students if they know what nonfiction means, and make sure they are aware that all books in this category contain factual information. Explain that Melvil Dewey invented a system of classifying books that will help them find any book they want, and that if they become familiar with the Dewey Decimal System in your media center, they will be able to use it in other media centers as well as public libraries that follow the same system. Mention that nonfiction books are arranged on the shelves by numbers and are therefore unlike fiction books, which are arranged alphabetically by the author's last name.

Sample Lesson:

In many media centers, biographies are labeled with a *B* and shelved according to the last name of the person that they are about. Since this is an exception to the general rule for nonfiction, this is a good place to begin or end your unit.

Before the class arrives, go to the biography section and pull out 20 to 25 biographies that you feel are appropriate to the reading and interest levels of that class. Take your Dewey wheel and the Dewey Block that covers biography, and you are ready to begin.

When the children are seated, ask if anyone knows what a biography is. Explain the term and mention autobiography as well. Some of the children will probably suggest that when they grow up and become famous, someone will write biographies about them. You can add that they might even write their own autobiographies. Sometimes the children will mix up the terms biography and bibliography. Be sure to straighten this out before going further.

Show the students the Dewey wheel and let them find where biography is located on it. Since biography is the one exception to the Dewey System, explain that in some libraries biographies are filed separately and that you will therefore discuss them first as a special unit. Then point out how biographies are filed on the shelves; if there are five biographies about George Washington and all of them are written

by different people, they will all be found together under $\boxed{\begin{array}{c} \text{B} \\ \text{WASHINGTON} \end{array}}$. Show

the Dewey Block to the students and point out that in some libraries they might find biographies filed under 92.

Pull out the books you have chosen. Tell the children that you have selected some of the biographies available in your media center that they might want to read and enjoy. Display each one separately, showing the spine label (this reinforces the lesson of how biographies are shelved), the cover, and a few pages of the book. If a student wants to charge out the book, give it to the student right away. Keep doing this until you have gone through all of the books. The children will generally vie for the privilege of taking them out. If there are any that no one wants, just set them aside without comment.

When all the books have been shown and discussed, review the rules for shelving biographies. Then take the whole class over to the section where biographies are shelved. Point out the beginning and the end of the biography section so that the students will know this for the future. Each child should take out *at least one* book from the section that you discussed during the session; in this way he will become familiar with books on a variety of subjects during the course of the unit. Let the children spend the remainder of the period browsing among the biography shelves.

> *Note:* If you file the 920's (collective biography) with the biography section, you might want to introduce these books now. Otherwise, wait until you teach the 900's. See the Open End section of this chapter for a discussion about shelving collective biography.

Continuing the Unit:

Follow the same procedure discussed in the sample lesson for every lesson. Each time you cover a nonfiction section, select a variety of books from that section that are at the appropriate reading and interest level and allow the children to choose from them. Look through your Dewey Decimal Classification book in advance to find categories that you might want to mention. During the lesson on 590 to 600, for example, you might pay special attention to 590—general zoology; 591—how animals live, their habits and behavior; 594—mollusks and shells; 595.7—insects; 597—fishes and amphibians; 598.1—reptiles; 598.2—birds; and 599—mammals.

At the end of the unit, give the students copies of the Dewey wheel to keep in their notebooks as a reminder of their trip around the media center using the Dewey Decimal System.

Professional Responsibilities

HOW TO COMPILE A BIBLIOGRAPHY

There are many instances when you will be called upon to make up a bibliography or will feel the need to compile one for yourself.

Sometimes teachers assign certain categories for their students' book reports such as mysteries, adventure stories, science fiction, and animal stories. When you know that you will be inundated by 30 students all clamoring at once to find out on which shelf you keep the fantasy books for sixth graders (even though they have had library instruction, students don't always realize that books aren't kept neatly in one spot for their use), it is good for your peace of mind to be able to pull out a bibliography that you have prepared for just this occasion.

When a teacher introduces a new unit to the curriculum, a bibliography of the media center's holdings in that subject area would be gratefully received. Holidays are another occasion for preparing a bibliography.

Obviously, preparing a bibliography is time-consuming, but the time involved is usually well worth spending, because you will probably be able to use the bibliography more than once. Also, a bibliography is a good way to give professional guidance to a number of children at the same time, rather than making each child wait until you can help him or her individually.

There are several steps to take in compiling a bibliography. Suppose you are doing one on animal stories for the fifth grade. You could begin by checking your card catalog under various subject headings such as ANIMALS—FICTION, BEARS—FICTION, CATS—FICTION, DOGS—FICTION, and HORSES—FICTION. You can easily spot most of the books that you will not include by checking the number of pages listed on the cards. When you come to a title with which you are not familiar, go to the shelf and examine the book so that you can determine whether or not to use it.

You will want to include some titles that are somewhat below fifth grade reading ability and some that are above it. It is important not to put the exact grade level on the bibliography, because someday you may want to use it for an advanced fourth grade or a slow sixth grade reading class. You might want to make a note on your copy about what reading levels are covered.

After checking your card catalog, you could check some professional bibliographies that you might have in your media center. Some examples are:

Adventuring with Books, new edition.
prepared by Patricia Cianciolo and the Committee on the Elementary School Booklist of the National Council of Teachers of English. Citation, 1977

The Best in Children's Books
edited by Zena Sutherland
University of Chicago Press, 1973

The Elementary School Library Collection: A Guide to Books and Other Media,
10th ed.
edited by Phyllis Van Orden
Bro-Dart, 1976

You could use these sources to look up subject headings similar to those you checked in your card catalog. See if they have included any books that you have in your media center but didn't find in your subject search.

When you have compiled a list of sufficient length and arranged it in alphabetical order by author (as the books would appear on the shelves), have it typed on a stencil and have sufficient copies run off so that you will have a good supply on hand. This type of bibliography doesn't have to be annotated; the children can find annotations in the card catalog, and you will save a lot of time by not including them. You might want to keep all of your bibliographies in one place, such as a file cabinet, so that they will be easy to find and distribute.

Keep one copy of each bibliography in a folder in your desk and date it. Every few years, the bibliographies will need updating and retyping in order to take into account the new titles you have received. This task can be simplified if, whenever you check through new books, you jot down any titles that are appropriate to the bibliographies you have compiled. The titles should be added to the master copies that you keep in your desk. When it is time for a revision, your updated copy will be all ready for retyping.

RECLASSIFICATION OF COMMERCIAL CATALOG CARDS

Most library media specialists purchase books with commercial catalog cards or with complete processing. Either way enables you to avoid cataloging and classifying them yourself. The cost for the service is more than offset by the professional time saved. Convenient as commercial services are, however, they do not entirely relieve you of cataloging responsibilities.

The cataloging itself rarely requires alteration, although some choices for the main entry overstep the bounds of even simplified rules. Problems do occur with classification numbers. The assigning of these numbers is not an exact science, and it is a truism that no two catalogers will ever agree completely. However, sometimes you must emphatically disagree. If a simple counting book is placed in 510, it might never be used, for the young students for whom it is intended choose their books from the picture book or beginning reader section. In order to take your users into consideration, you must change the number. (See the discussion on shelving easy books in the Open End section of the January chapter.)

Notations for books going into the reference or professional collection must be added to the commercial catalog cards. This can be done by marking the designation on the shelf list card as you examine the new book. Your volunteers can make the additions to the remaining cards and to the book card, pocket, and spine label.

You must make sure that your commercially processed book is not a second copy with a completely different classification number. For example, it is possible to have a picture book that is written in rhyme come through once with cards assigning it an *E* classification and then to have the same book come through later with a set of cards placing it in 811. You must resolve this disparity and determine how the books will be classified. But first you must discover that the disparity exists. All titles that are not newly published should be checked against the card catalog by a responsible volunteer.

It will be necessary to make changes on catalog cards occasionally, but you must also learn to accept classifications that would not be your first choice. Otherwise, you will defeat the purpose for which you originally purchased commercially produced cards.

Volunteers

PROCESSING NEW BOOKS

Processing refers to all of the procedures involved from the time a book is taken out of the shipping carton until it is placed on the shelf ready to be charged out.

You, the library media specialist, will probably check in shipments of new books, place printed catalog cards inside them, and affix the call number labels and any other special markings to the spines.

Then the volunteers will take over and perform the following tasks:

1. Check through each book quickly to determine if there are any flaws such as upside-down pages, faulty binding, or errors in illustrations.
2. If the book is in good condition, stamp it with the school name and address according to the practice in your media center.
3. Paste in the book pocket. If it has been commercially printed, only a few drops of paste are necessary to attach it to the page; too much paste will soak through the paper and ruin some of the pages. If the pockets are typed in your media center, consider using the self-sticking kind. This saves time and paste, for the pockets can be quickly run through a moistener and attached to the page.
4. If the book is for reference use only, do not paste in the pocket. Generally a sticker noting that the book is for reference use and does not circulate is placed in the front and back of the book.

5. The accession or copy number is placed in the book, on the book pocket and card, and on the shelf list card. (See the January Volunteers section.)

6. If the book does not have a dust jacket, a small amount of white paste should be put over the spine label where it adheres to the book spine. The paste will be clear when it dries and will make the spine label last much longer. An alternative method is to write on transfer tape with an electric stylus and to cover the call number with plastic spray.

7. If the book has a dust jacket, it should be covered with an adjustable vinyl book jacket. Measure the size of the book with a ruler, find the appropriate size jacket, slip the dust jacket inside, and attach both jackets to the book (front and back, top and bottom) with four strips of vinyl tape.

After all of these operations have been performed, the book is ready for you to check again. Remove the catalog cards for filing, taking out the ones you don't need and saving them for scrap paper and other uses (see Index); separate the shelf list card, noting the price paid for the book, the purchase date, and from whom it was purchased; and then look over the book before putting it out to circulate.

SHELVING

Shelving—returning material to its proper location for future circulation—can be a relatively simple process. After the books have been slipped, place them on a cart arranged according to fiction, nonfiction, biography, and paperbacks.

1. Fiction books are put in alphabetical order by the author's last name.
2. Nonfiction books are arranged by numbers, including decimal points. Books with the same number are arranged alphabetically by the author's last name.
3. Biographies are arranged alphabetically by the last name of the person they are written about. Books written about the same person are arranged alphabetically by the author's last name.
4. Paperbacks can be filed in many different ways; they should be arranged according to the instructions of the library media specialist.
5. It is a good idea to check to be sure that the material has been properly slipped before shelving it. Mistakes can occur during the slipping procedure, and this is an excellent time to find them. (An explanation of slipping is given in the September Volunteers section.)

Because the books have been placed in exact order on the cart, they will be much easier to replace on the shelves in their correct spots.

Open End

SHELVING COLLECTIVE BIOGRAPHY

Where do you put collective biography? Should you shelve the books strictly according to numerical sequence, or should collective biography follow immediately after biography?

If you shelve numerically, collective biography comes after the geography of arctic regions and before ancient history; it is nowhere near biography. As a result of this separation, students and teachers frequently forget that collective biography exists. The library media specialist must therefore seek out occasions to bring it to the attention of students. This can be accomplished when the students are doing reference work. A more emphatic way of focusing on collective biography is to suggest to teachers that it be either a required book report topic or an alternative to a biography or short story book report.

If you shelve collective biography after biography in order to keep similar types of books together, there is a large numerical gap in the shelves. Students looking for 920 go to the shelves and find nothing. They may be aware that collective biography is shelved after biography, but they may not realize that the number for collective biography is 920. Too often, only the term is stressed and the number is forgotten. If you shelve this way, make sure that you call attention to the Dewey decimal number. A sign reading "920—Collective Biography" is more helpful than one that just reads "Collective Biography." To reduce fruitless searching by students, you can order a book block (a cardboard block shaped like a library book) from any library supply company. Write on the block, "920 books are shelved after biographies," and place it on the shelf where 920 would begin.

You must choose the method that seems best to you. No matter which approach you select, there will be some problems. The best solution is frequently determined by the physical structure of your media center; that is, wherever you have the most suitable shelf space.

November

Happy Birthday To . . .

1   **Helen Fuller Orton** (1872)—author
     Mysteries for intermediate grades, including *A Treasure in the Little Trunk*

12   **Dahlov Ipcar** (1917)—author and illustrator
     Picture books such as *Bug City* and *Hard Scrabble Harvest*
     Marjorie Weinman Sharmat (1928)—author
     Easy-to-read books such as *Nate the Great* and intermediate fiction such
     as *Getting Something on Maggie Marmelstein*

13   **Nathaniel Benchley** (1915)—author
     Easy-to-read books including *Small Wolf* and *Sam the Minuteman*
     Robert Louis Stevenson (1850)—author
     Adventure stories and poems including *Treasure Island, Kidnapped,* and
     A Child's Garden of Verses

14   **Astrid Lindgren** (1907)—author
     Creator of Pippi Longstocking and picture books such as *The Tomten*
     William Steig (1907)—author and illustrator
     Picture books such as *Sylvester and the Magic Pebble* and intermediate
     fiction such as *Dominic*

15   **Manus Pinkwater** (1941)—author and illustrator
     Offbeat fiction including *Blue Moose* and *Lizard Music*

16   **Jean Fritz** (1915)—author
     Historical fiction such as *Brady* and intermediate biographies such as *And
     Then What Happened, Paul Revere?*

A bulletin board, a book fair, and book talks
set the tone for Children's Book Week.

18   **Miroslav Sasek** (1916)—author and illustrator
Picture books with splashy illustrations of locations around the world, such as *This is Greece* and *This is New York*

21   **Leo Politi** (1908)—author and illustrator
Picture books on Mexico and California such as *Rosa* and *Song of the Swallows*

24   **C. Collodi** (1806)—author
Author of *Adventures of Pinocchio*

26   **Doris Gates** (1901)—author
Realistic fiction, notably *Blue Willow*, the story of an Okie family
Charles Schulz (1922)—cartoonist
Creator of Charlie Brown and the Peanuts family

28   **Tomi Ungerer** (1931)—author and illustrator
Humorously macabre picture books such as *The Three Robbers* and *The Beast of Monsieur Racine*

29   **Louisa May Alcott** (1832)—author
Author of *Little Women*
Madeleine L'Engle (1918)—author
Science fiction and fantasy for upper grades, including *A Wrinkle in Time*

30   **Samuel Clemens (Mark Twain)** (1835)—author and journalist
Creator of Tom Sawyer and Huckleberry Finn
Margot Zemach (1931)—illustrator
Picture books including *The Judge* and *Duffy and the Devil*

MARK TWAIN'S AMERICA

FACTS ABOUT MARK TWAIN 1835 ~ 1910

1. He was born and died in years when Halley's Comet appeared.

2. His real name was Samuel Langhorne Clemens.

3. He was a riverboat pilot on the Mississippi River.

4. Mark Twain means 2 fathoms of 12 feet ~ a safe depth for a river boat.

5. He was a great teller of ghost stories. His best tale was "The Golden Arm."

6. He grew up in Missouri along the Mississippi River.

Bulletin Boards

MARK TWAIN'S AMERICA

Mark Twain is not one of the most popular authors of the elementary school set. However, some of his books, notably *The Adventures of Tom Sawyer,* are not beyond the ability of the better upper grade readers. Since Twain is one of America's great writers, introduce his work by presenting him as a historical figure. Make a bulletin board map of "Mark Twain's America." (See illustration on next page.)

Teachers can adapt this idea by having students find four or five facts about the lives of authors with whom the students are more familiar.

MATERIALS:

—1 sheet of 22″ × 28″ yellow posterboard
—1 acetate sheet
—blue fine-tip felt marker
—black fine-tip felt marker
—1 sheet of 8″ × 18″ light blue construction paper
—blue wide-tip felt marker
—rubber cement
—overhead projector

PREPARATION:

1. Locate a map of the United States in the 1840's—the years when Mark Twain was growing up. One source is *The American Heritage Pictorial Atlas of United States History* (American Heritage Publishing Co., 1966).
2. Trace the map on the acetate sheet and transfer it to the posterboard using an overhead projector.
3. Outline the major rivers of the Midwest with the blue fine-tip marker. This highlights the way the rivers form state boundaries. It also shows how many rivers flow into the Mississippi.
4. Complete the outlines of the states with the black felt marker.
5. Use the blue fine-tip marker to print "Facts About Mark Twain" on the construction paper.
6. Use the blue wide-tip marker to make a wavy line around the construction paper.
7. Paste the construction paper to the posterboard.
8. Use the wide-tip marker to letter "Mark Twain's America" across the posterboard.

IT'S CHILDREN'S BOOK WEEK

Efforts of library media specialists notwithstanding, some children read nothing more substantial than T-shirts. Now you can construct a T-shirt bulletin board and use it to send any kind of message you wish. (See illustration.)

MATERIALS:

—1 sheet of 22″ × 28″ dark-colored posterboard
—2 sheets of 9″ × 14″ white construction paper
—crayons, pastels, or colored felt markers
—1 strip of 4″ × 18″ construction paper, in a light shade complementary to the posterboard
—several sheets of light-colored construction paper. (If you do the corresponding Library Art Activity, more construction paper is necessary.)
—rubber cement
—scissors

PREPARATION:

1. Draw or copy from the sample the two cartoon figures. Use the white construction paper.
2. Use crayons, pastels, or felt markers to color in the figures.
3. Use two different colors of construction paper to make T-shirts for the two figures. The T-shirts should be 3½″ long and 4″ wide. For best results, fold a piece of scrap paper in half, draw half a shirt, cut it out, and unfold. The paper can then be used as a pattern for the construction paper shirts.
4. Use a felt marker to write the slogans on the T-shirts.
5. Paste the T-shirts on the figures.
6. Use a felt marker to letter "It's Children's Book Week" on the 4″ × 18″ strip of construction paper.
7. Paste the figures onto the posterboard.
8. Paste the banner onto the posterboard so that the figures are holding it.
9. Cut out additional T-shirts from construction paper and letter slogans on them.
10. Glue the T-shirts onto the posterboard. If you are doing the corresponding Library Art Activity, do not make too many shirts. Instead, post the first efforts of the students.

Library Art Activity

WRITE A T-SHIRT SLOGAN

To expand on the Children's Book Week bulletin board and to encourage the students to "think books," decorate the media center with T-shirts whose slogans have been invented by the students. A poster encouraging students to "write a T-shirt slogan" is shown on the following page.

MATERIALS:

—sheets of construction paper in assorted light colors
—fine-tip felt markers
—1 T-shirt cut out of scrap paper to use as a pattern
—1 light-colored sheet of 11″ × 14″ posterboard
—2 manila envelopes, 6″ × 2½″
—rubber cement
—scissors

IT'S CHILDREN'S BOOK WEEK

CELEBRATE!

write a slogan
for a T-shirt
See your shirt
on display

**BLANK
T-SHIRTS**

**BLANK
T-SHIRTS**

PREPARATION:

1. Have a volunteer use the pattern to cut from 50 to 75 T-shirts from the construction paper. This is sufficient to begin the activity and more than enough to use up the patience of even a very kindly volunteer.
2. Outline a huge T-shirt on the posterboard.
3. Letter the directions in freehand. A casual look is what you wish to achieve.
4. Print ''Blank T-shirts'' on each of the manila envelopes.
5. Paste the envelopes onto the poster.
6. Put blank shirts into the envelopes.
7. Completed T-shirts can be pasted on a bulletin board or window or hung on a yarn ''clothesline.''

Library Enrichment Activity

BOOK TALKS FOR CHILDREN'S BOOK WEEK

One way to make Children's Book Week a special event in your media center is to give book talks to your third through sixth grade classes that week. In addition, you might read a special story to the kindergarten and first and second grades to commemorate the event.

> *Note:* Children's Book Week is *usually* the third week of November, but it is best to check with the Children's Book Council, 67 Irving Place, New York, N.Y. 10003.

The purpose of a book talk is to try to make the children want to read the book you are discussing by giving a short synopsis of the plot, highlighting one or two incidents or characters, or reading a particularly appealing short passage from the book. It is appropriate to focus on anything that will capture the interest of your students so that they will be anxious to read a particular book.

You might pick a theme and choose all of your books accordingly, or you might just present a selection of books that you think will be of interest to a certain grade even if they are not related to each other.

Here are some guidelines for giving book talks:

1. The most important point is that you have read the book and are enthusiastic about it. Your enthusiasm will be contagious and will make the children want to read the book too. (It's very hard to "sell" a book solely from the description on the dust jacket.)
2. Don't tell too much of the story. Stop at a point where you have your listeners' interest.
3. If you are giving a lot of book talks during one week (as you would for Children's Book Week), go to the shelves a week or so before and pull off all of the copies of the books you will discuss. If you have multiple copies (including paperbacks), this is even better. If you are successful in your talks, a number of children will want to read the same book; and the more you can accommodate at once, the more effective the experience will be for them. This in no way implies that having only one copy of a book precludes using it for a book talk.
4. If you have several classes of the same grade, choose different books for each class. This will ensure that each book can be immediately taken out by at least one person in each class.
5. If possible, use eight to ten books per class, taking no more than one minute for each title. If you have ten or twelve classes scheduled that week, this is a great deal of work. However, it is extremely rewarding to capture the interest and enthusiasm of the children and to see them really excited about reading various books. Also, you are probably familiar with most of the titles you have chosen, so there should not be an inordinate amount of time required in getting ready for each class.

6. Keep a list of the books you discuss with each grade level. Looking back at it will help you in the future. Often students will come up to you several months later and ask for a book that you featured in a book talk with their class.

7. If you are not sticking to one theme in your book talks, try mixing the old standbys with some new books that the children might not know about.

8. This is a good opportunity to introduce the children to some poetry. If you have a good collection, consider using one book of poetry for each class. Funny and offbeat poems are an excellent choice.

9. If several children want the same book, be sure to have reserve slips available (see this month's Volunteers section), and try to get the books to the children as quickly as possible.

Your book talks might be such a success that you will have requests from some classes to continue them on a regular basis throughout the year.

WRITING BOOK BLURBS

Activities should add to the students' knowledge and skills. Having the students write blurbs for books in the media center will help not only the students but also the media center.

Blurbs, the capsule summaries that are on the inside flaps of book jackets, are a great help to a student looking for a book. Teachers frequently direct students to blurbs, telling them that this is a good way to discover if they would be interested in the book. Unfortunately, many books do not have blurbs. Some once had them, but the blurbs were discarded along with the book jackets when wear and tear made that necessary; others never had them. These "blurbless" books too often sit on the shelf unread because no one takes the time to find out what they are about.

By encouraging students to write blurbs, you not only offer them an opportunity to do a different type of creative writing but also add new life to books that have not been circulating.

To avoid poorly written, badly spelled blurbs, set the standards early. An excellent method of achieving the quality you would like is to work in conjunction with the classroom teachers. Most teachers are looking for new ideas to spark book reports, and they are very willing to have the students write blurbs instead of the usual reports. The teacher then corrects the blurbs, and the students neatly rewrite or type them on paper provided by the media center.

MATERIALS:

—1 sheet of 11″ × 14″ colored posterboard
—felt markers
—1 sheet of typing paper (optional)
—easel back
—sheets of 4″ wide-ruled paper (The length will vary according to the book. Allow 2 sheets for each blurb, for the front and back covers.)
—rubber cement

PREPARATION:

1. Make a poster that gives the students directions for writing a blurb. (See illustration.)

Take Pen in hand... write a blurb

A **BLURB**

is a short summary inside a book jacket that makes you want to read the book.

Rules for writing Blurbs

1. Read one of the books without a blurb.

2. Write a short summary of the plot.

3. Do NOT give away the ending.

4. Have your blurb corrected for spelling and grammar.

5. Get special paper for final copy from the circulation desk.

6. Type your blurb, or write neatly.

7. Bring the book and the finished blurb to the desk, and. . .

Your BLURB will be pasted into the Book!

a. Draw or copy a cartoon figure in the corner.

b. Use bold letters to announce the activity.

c. Because the directions are long, you can type them and then paste the sheet onto the posterboard.

d. Attach the easel back.

2. Have one of the volunteers pull all of the books without blurbs off the shelves.

3. Set up a display with the explanatory poster and the books. A counter top is sufficient space.

4. Keep the blank paper to be used for the finished blurbs at the circulation desk. Distribute it only when you have seen a corrected copy of the blurb.

PROCEDURE:

1. When the student turns in the final copy of the blurb, check to see that the title and author of the book are recorded at the top and that the name of the student who wrote the blurb is written at the end.

2. While the student watches, paste the blurb into the book.

3. Before reshelving them, display all books that have student-written blurbs.

Storytelling Suggestions

SEASONAL BOOKS AND BEAR STORIES

With fall under way and Thanksgiving approaching, you might want to select books on these subjects. For Thanksgiving, you will have a problem because there is very little material available other than nonfiction books dealing with the history of the holiday and its counterpart in other countries. Some suggestions follow.

Seasonal Books

Devlin, Wende and Harry   *Cranberry Thanksgiving*
                                 Parents, 1971

Thanksgiving dinner becomes very exciting when one of the guests tries to steal Grandmother's prize recipe for cranberry bread. (first to third grade)

Ernst, Kathryn   *Mr. Tamarin's Trees*
                        illus. by Diane de Groat
                        Crown, 1976

Mr. Tamarin gets tired of raking all of the leaves that keep falling off his trees and decides to take drastic measures. (second grade)

Fisher, Aileen   *Where Does Everyone Go?*
                        Thomas Y. Crowell, 1961

This poetic discussion of what happens in the fall follows the sequence of events from chilly weather and changes in nature to the first snow. (second to fourth grade)

Ipcar, Dahlov   *Hard Scrabble Harvest*
                       Doubleday, 1976

A story in rhyme of the problems faced by a farmer planting his fields and defending his crops from the animals until harvest time. (first and second grade)

Lenski, Lois *Now It's Fall*
Walck, 1948

A little girl and boy experience all the joys of fall in this tiny rhyming book. (kindergarten and first grade)

Lionni, Leo *Frederick*
Pantheon, 1967

While all of the other field mice store food for the winter, Frederick, the poet, stores the memories of warmth and color. (kindergarten to third grade)

Bear Stories

Another interest-rousing approach to storytelling is the use of a theme. Choose several books on the same subject, or try the following ''teddy bear'' collection. This particular group of books will easily lead you into a discussion of favorite toys owned by the children.

Alexander, Martha *I'll Protect You from the Jungle Beasts*
Dial Press, 1973

In his dream, a little boy is going to protect his teddy bear. But as they become involved in some scary experiences, the teddy bear grows and protects the boy with the aid of his ''special stuffing.'' (kindergarten and first grade)

DuBois, William Pene *Bear Party*
Viking, 1963

The quarreling koalas return to their usual serenity when the oldest and wisest koala organizes a masquerade party. (first and second grade)

Freeman, Don *Beady Bear*
Viking, 1954

Black-and-white illustrations tell the story of a wind-up bear who tries to be a real bear and finds that he needs his key and love. (kindergarten)

Freeman, Don *Corduroy*
Viking, 1968

A teddy bear on sale in a department store looks for his lost button in order to make himself saleable. He is bought, despite the missing button, by a little girl who loves him for himself. (first and second grade)

Ormondroyd, Edward *Theodore*
illus. by John Larrecq
Parnassus, 1969

Lucy's carelessness causes Theodore to have a dreadful experience getting washed at the laundromat. But in the end she proves, as Theodore has always known, that she really understands a bear. (kindergarten to second grade)

Skorpen, Liesel Moak *Charles*
illus. by Martha Alexander
Harper & Row, 1971

Frankly, this is a sexist account of how Charles the bear is maltreated by his female owner but understood and loved by his subsequent male owner. Boys love the story, so use it. But counterbalance it with *Theodore* and a good discussion. (first and second grade)

Teaching Unit

SAMPLE CATALOG CARDS

This unit is designed to be used in a classroom learning center for grades four through six. However, it can be easily adapted for use in the media center should your situation require it.

Because the unit is for a classroom, all preparation should be done in cooperation with the teacher. The library media specialist prepares all of the materials requiring library skills, notably the sample catalog cards, the oversize cards, and the accompanying questions. The teacher sets up the area in the classroom, transfers the questions to the task cards, rewords the questions for student comprehension if necessary, adds any additional directions the students may need, and checks their work.

This type of classroom unit provides an excellent opportunity to improve your working relationships with the faculty and to improve the library skills of individual teachers. It also helps the teacher gauge the level of library competency to be expected from the students. Another feature of this unit is that it utilizes the extra catalog cards sent with processed books as teaching devices instead of as scrap cards.

OBJECTIVES:

At the conclusion of this unit, students should be able to:

1. Distinguish among author, title, and subject cards.
2. Locate a call number on a catalog card.
3. Look at any type of catalog card and tell the author and title.

   Note: Some students may also be able to use the information on the tracing to locate additional subject headings.

MATERIALS:

—three pieces of posterboard, as close to 9″ × 15″ as possible
—black fine-tip felt markers
—25 to 30 extra catalog cards sent with processed books (Be sure to have at least two cards for each title.)
—yarn
—blank catalog cards (the number depends on how many complete sets you want and how many of the extra cards you have per title.)
—clear self-stick vinyl

PREPARATION (oversize catalog cards):

1. On the three pieces of posterboard, print the information you would find on an author card, a subject card, and a title card for the same book.

- It is not necessary to include the annotation.
- Choose a book that has more than one subject heading, but make only one subject card.
- If possible, let the teacher put the actual book on display in the classroom. It helps to tie the abstraction of a catalog card to the reality of a book.

2. Have a conference with the classroom teacher and explain the three cards. Be sure that the teacher understands what information is presented on the catalog cards and how it is presented. Point out the capitalization used on the cards and what it indicates. You might give the teacher some suggestions for setting up the display.

- When setting up the display, the teacher should label the three cards as author card, title card, and subject card.
- It is helpful if the teacher also lists the main components of the cards and then uses yarn to connect these components (such as author, title, call number, and publisher) to the places where they appear on the cards.

3. Prepare a list of questions relating to the oversize cards. The teacher will use the questions to make task cards. The questions are designed as a drill to teach students how to look at a catalog card to extract information.

Sample Task Card Questions:

1. Card #1 is an author card because _____.
2. Card #2 is a title card because _____.
3. Card #3 is a subject card because _____.
4. The call number is _____.
5. FIC means _____.
6. DUN is the first three letters of _____.
7. You know that the book has pictures because the card says it is _____.
8. Another subject heading for this book is _____.

PREPARATION (extra catalog cards):

1. Take the extra cards and type the necessary information on them to make title and subject cards.

- Reserve some of the cards to use as author cards.
- Include selections from as many sections of the media center as possible.
- Make several complete sets; that is, author, title, and at least one subject card. Use the blank cards to fill in where necessary. Not all of the cards have to be part of a complete set.
- Try to have two or three cards with the same subject heading.

2. Cover all of the sample cards with the clear self-stick vinyl. You can write ''Sample Card'' on the back of each one to avoid any confusion.

3. Analyze the cards and prepare a list of questions that the teacher can use to make task cards. If you wish a group of questions to be on one card for the sake of logic or continuity, indicate this to the teacher. Be sure that you provide the teacher with the answers to the questions.

Sample Task Cards

Card 1   1. Who are the authors of three mystery books? (Subject heading: MYSTERY AND DETECTIVE STORIES)
2. What is the title of the book by Leonard Everett Fisher?
3. What is the call number of the book located in the reference section?
4. What is the subject heading for the book <u>Unidentified flying objects</u> by Gene Gurney?

Card 2   Find three cards with the call number 560 GRE.

1. What is the author's name?
2. What is the title?
3. Why are there three cards for one book?
4. Give the first letter of the three catalog drawers in which these cards would be found.

Card 3   Note: Catalog cards are filed alphabetically according to the top line.

1. How many of these cards would be found in the C drawers?
2. How many in the F drawers?

Card 4   Find the cards with the call number 704.94 FIS

1. Who is the author?
2. Copy the top line of the subject card exactly as it appears on the catalog card.
3. Use the information on the bottom of the card and name the other subject heading, which is not included in the set but is found in the card catalog in the media center.

Card 5   Bonus Task Card

This book has 216 pages.
It is illustrated by Alton Raible.
The publisher is Atheneum. The copyright date is 1976.
A subject heading is FANTASY.
Look at the oversize cards on display. Make an author card, a title card, and a subject card for this book. Use 3" × 5" cards.

Professional Responsibilities

RUNNING A BOOK FAIR

First you must ask yourself, "Should I have a book fair? The media center is a source of free materials. Should it now peddle what has been offered for free?"

No library media specialist would suggest that the media center is a replacement for a home library; yet many students own no books. Those who do own books may have only titles that are considered inferior literature. Also, if you do not run the book fair, it is likely that the parent association will do so. In that case, you will have no control over the quality of materials being offered. There is a mercenary aspect to consider as well. If the media center sponsors the book fair, the media center usually makes the profits. A little extra cash is always helpful.

If you have decided to have a book fair, you will need to find a company that will provide the books. If you have not been buried in multiple mailings from companies begging you to run a book fair, you can survey the choices at state library conventions. More often the problem is deciding which company to choose. Check the following points with the various companies:

1. What percent of the gross sales is your profit? (Expect to receive 20 percent.)
2. Will the company provide publicity? (Usually it does, but the quality is poor.)
3. Does the company provide forms for listing children's selections? Does it provide sales receipts? (If not, you will have to make up your own forms.)
4. Will the company be able to supply you with additional copies in the event that certain titles prove extremely popular?

   Note: This is a key issue. Children should be asked to bring their money on a given day. If a book is sold out and cannot be ordered, they will be disappointed. It is hard enough to tell them that a book must be ordered. As it is impossible to predict which titles will be the biggest sellers, there will always be a number of books for which the demand will exceed the supply. The company should be able to bring the needed titles when it picks up the unsold books.

With these caveats in mind, a book fair can be a smooth operation. Be sure you prepare adequately and know what to expect.

PREPARATION:

Two weeks before the fair:

1. Put up posters around the school announcing the event. Use either the posters provided or those of your own design. (See sample poster on next page.) If the art teacher is willing, he or she can help the students create the posters in class. If you choose the latter alternative, start a month before the book fair in order to get the posters done.
2. Make up a schedule of class visits. Each class needs two visits: one for browsing, one for purchasing. Schedule 30 minutes for each visit. You might take two classes at the same time if there is room in the media center, but do so only with grades three to six. Students in the lower grades need help in writing their selections and later in locating their books, both of which take a

great deal of time. As you prepare the schedule, be careful not to interfere with teacher preparation time. Leave gaps in the schedule. You will need them to catch your breath. The gaps are also helpful when it is necessary to re-schedule a class because of a conflict. Schedule some time for those who were absent when their class was scheduled.

3. Prepare a ditto master of the schedule and distribute it to the teachers. Be prepared to adjust the schedule for any teachers expressing dissatisfaction with a time slot. If you are lucky, any complaints will be voiced when the schedule is first handed out. It is more probable that you will get an urgent message to change a teacher's time the morning of the scheduled day. Do the best you can.

4. Send a letter home to the parents describing how the book fair will work. (See sample letter.)

Dear Parents:

During the week of _____, a book fair will be held in the school media center. The classes will be scheduled to come to the fair twice. The first time the children will look at the books and prepare a list for your approval. The approved list and the money should be brought in when the class returns for the second visit. Checks should be made out to the _____ School. Parents may visit the book fair to browse or purchase at any time. The most convenient time for this would be from 12:00 to 12:30 p.m. and from 2:30 to 3:00 p.m.

Very truly yours,

One week before the fair:

1. Have your library chairperson get coin wrappers from the bank.
2. If the company did not provide order and sales forms, make a ditto master of the necessary forms and run off sufficient quantities. (See sample forms.)

Books I Would Like

Price	Title

Name_____   Room #

Sales Slip

Name_____ Class_____

Price	Title

3. Have a supply of carbon paper cut to fit the sales slip forms.

4. Have a supply of red and black or blue pens.

5. Have your library chairperson contact the volunteers to ask them to give extra time. You will need more than the usual number of persons. Maximum help is needed when the lowest grades come to look and buy.

6. Prepare about 300 2″ × 3″ squares of scrap paper. Mark an X on each piece.

Day the books arrive:

1. Books should arrive on Friday for a fair beginning on Monday.

2. Arrange books in a logical pattern. One arrangement is:

   - Adjoining tables of books for grades kindergarten to two
   - A double table of books for grades three to five
   - A table of books for the most capable readers
   - A table of nonfiction
   - Tables for sports, science fiction, mystery, and animal books (if there are many titles in these categories)
   - A table for craft books, puzzles, riddles, and workbooks

3. Remove any books that do not meet acceptable standards. Inevitably, the selections include titles that have inferior illustrations, unsuitable type face, inappropriate vocabulary, and "supermarket shelf" quality. Occasionally the collection may include material that is too mature for the students. Book selection is a professional responsibility that cannot be ceded to a book fair company. Although more leeway should be allowed since purchases are made by and for individuals and not the school media center, some evaluation must be done.

4. Check to be sure that all copies of a title have the same price. If there are any discrepancies, change all copies to the lowest price.

5. To indicate "last copy—do not sell," place a scrap of paper with an X on it on the top copy of each stack of books and attach it with a small piece of masking tape. (Use cellophane tape if you must, but be careful. Removing the tape can damage the book.) When all of the X's are attached, put the marked books at the bottom of each stack.

Day the book fair begins:

1. Distribute "Books I Would Like" forms to the classroom teachers. It is simpler for them to distribute the forms to students just before they come to the media center. Tell them to have each student bring a pencil.

2. Explain to each class how the tables are arranged.

3. Tell students who are too young to write to bring a copy of any books they want over to you, the teacher, or any of the volunteers to have the title and price recorded. To make things easier for these students, seat all helpers at the tables with the simpler books. Be prepared; these youngsters love to see how many titles they can record! As long as the parents realize that the final choice is theirs, there is no harm other than writer's cramp.

4. If a class is more than five minutes late for a scheduled visit, check with the teacher. Occasionally a teacher does forget that the class is due.

5. Remind the students that on the day they return to purchase books, they must bring their money and the "Books I Would Like" form.

Day before the first sale day:

1. Place a table near the door to the media center.
2. On the table put sales receipts, carbon paper cut to size, blue or black pens, red pens, and a stapler.
3. Obtain four small boxes or cups for keeping coins separated.
4. One small carton or cash box is good for holding checks and cash until it can be counted.

Sale days:

1. Students select the books not crossed off their lists by their parents and bring the books to the table by the door to pay for their purchases.
2. A sales receipt with a carbon is written out. The student receives the carbon copy.
3. Staple together the original sales receipts for all of the students in one class.
4. When a student wants a book that has an *X*:

   • Inform the student that the book will have to be ordered.
   • When writing out the sales slip, circle the title to be ordered in red pen.
   • Keep all sales receipts indicating books to be ordered in a separate location.

5. When the lower grades come to make their purchases:

   • Seat the class.
   • Take the students one at a time and find the books on their lists.
   • Bring students, books, lists, and money to the table for payment.

6. If all of the books on a student's list have *X*'s on them, choose one of the titles and remove the *X*. Tape the *X* to the table and write the title and price on the same piece of paper. This practice is particularly necessary with students in the lower grades. It seems cruel to have a child come in filled with anticipation, pay for whatever is on the list, and go home with nothing. Patience may be a virtue, but so is common sense.
7. Whenever there is a break in the schedule, remove the collected money to a quiet area. If you have time, you can:

   • Wrap coins.
   • Clip all checks together.
   • Separate bills by denomination.
   • Clip single bills together in groups of ten for easy counting.
   • If you have bill wrappers, wrap the appropriate amounts. If not, wrap rubber bands around bills in groups of $50.
   • Keep a running total.
   • Be sure that the money is locked up at night.

Day before unsold books are picked up:

1. Take the receipts for books that have to be ordered.
2. Use 3″ × 5″ cards to prepare the order, one card per title.
3. On the card, record the full title and price. (Check the tables, if necessary.)
4. For each copy that is ordered, place a tally mark on the card.
5. Call the company and read them the list of how many copies of various titles are needed. When the unsold books are picked up, the ordered books will be delivered.

6. If there are any additional purchases after the order has been placed, sell any book, with or without an X, but do not order more books.

Day unsold books are picked up:

1. Carefully remove the X's from the books.
2. Pack the unsold books into the original cartons.
3. Unpack the delivered order and arrange the books on a table.
4. Take the "on order" sales slips and put them inside the appropriate books.
5. If more than one title was ordered by a student, put a rubber band around the order.
6. Put all orders for one class in one pile.
7. Deliver books to students.
8. If the shipment was short, call the company again and make arrangements for a further shipment. Be sure to explain the situation to any students who are still waiting.
9. Make a list by classroom of students' names and titles that they have not yet received.
10. When all orders are complete, deduct your profit and have a bank check made out to the company.

Congratulations! You have finished! It is all over and you can enjoy your justly earned reward.

RENEWALS

Students may renew books as many times as necessary as long as there are no reserves on them.

To renew books, pull the card from the appropriate place in the circulation file. Then have the students write their names and room numbers as usual. If you prefer, the students may write "renewed" and the day's date on the line below their previous signatures instead of resigning their names. They then follow the normal charge out procedure. (See the Volunteers section in the September chapter.) The book cards are filed in the circulation drawer and included in the daily circulation count.

RESERVES

When a student wants a book that is already in circulation, he or she may place a reserve on it.

One way to handle reserves is to design a reserve request form (see sample) and to keep copies of it at the circulation desk at all times. When volunteers have a few minutes to spare, they can search the circulation file for the book card of the requested book. The shelf list card should be checked to see whether there is more than one copy of the book and whether it is also available in paperback. These factors determine which of the following procedures are to be followed:

1. Recheck the shelves. Occasionally a student will be unable to locate the book and will assume it is in circulation.
2. If there is only one copy, slip a red-banded plastic cover over the book card and place the reserve form behind the card. Book card covers are available in various colors from library supply houses.
3. If there are multiple copies of the book, find all outstanding book cards. (The one with the earliest due date is not necessarily the copy that will be returned first.) Slip a red band over each card and place the reserve form in the circulation drawer in a separate file that is arranged alphabetically by name of author.
4. If there are several reserves for a title, they are filed by the earliest request date.

When the book is returned and slipped, the red band on the card immediately identifies the book as being on reserve. It should then be placed on a special reserve shelf pending borrower notification.

Another form is used for notifying students that their books are waiting (see sample on the following page). The notifications can be placed in the teachers' mailboxes. The student's reserve request is then clipped to the top of the book cover, and your initials and the final date for the student to pick up the book are written on the request to denote that notification has been sent.

When the borrower comes to charge out the reserved material, the original request is thrown away. If there are no other reserves, the band is removed from the card. If others are still waiting for that book, the band is retained on the book card.

To _____   Room _____

The book you reserved

_____
                    TITLE

is now in the media center. Please

pick it up before _____
                                    DATE

Open End

CENSORSHIP vs. SELECTION

The most open of open-ended questions is that of censorship and selection. No library media specialist gets through school without having countless discussions and reading numerous articles on the subject. Then why is it discussed here, in a book concerned with on-the-job, practically oriented matters? The reason is because the articles and the discussions are no longer just theory, and what you decide to do is no longer hypothetical but real.

First there is a budget, and a budget automatically sets limits on purchases. There are many excellent books and other materials that create absolutely no problems. They are worthy and they excite no controversy.

As for the small percentage of books that may be open to questions by administrators or community members, your guideline is the district selection policy. Become familiar with it. If there is none, make every effort to see that a selection policy is written and established. Otherwise, you are in a position of ordering materials without any formal administrative support. No matter how strongly you feel about intellectual freedom and the right to read, it is not simple for a nontenured (or even a tenured) library media specialist to order materials that might result in outraged complaints.

For elementary library media specialists, the "moment of truth" does not occur that frequently. Because of today's "relevant" literature, however, decisions must be made more often than in the past. When the moment does come, it is sometimes difficult to balance your ideals with a realistic concern for your job and possibly for your future career. Before you subject yourself to inner turmoil, stop and reevaluate the material to be sure that it is worth it. It is quite possible for a book or other medium to deal with a sensitive subject and not meet the usual standards of selection; a controversial subject is not a guarantee of merit. It is also possible for the material to be of great value in a secondary school yet be inappropriate for the elementary grades. In the attempt to be free of any taint of censorship, a conscientious library media specialist may forget that standards of selection are applied on the basis of need, relevance, amount of material available on the subject, and literary merit. Extra points are not given merely for dealing courageously with a controversial subject.

Until you are confident that you are in touch with the needs, interests, and abilities of the student body, it is reasonable to err on the side of caution. But this is not a brief for self-censorship. To refuse to purchase material because you are fearful of a confrontation is unacceptable and a violation of trust. If you have difficulties, your local education and media associations will provide support and, should the need arise, the state and national intellectual freedom committees will come to your aid.

December

Happy Birthday To . . .

5   **Jim Kjelgaard** (1910)—author
       Animal stories for upper grades, including *Big Red*
      Harve Zemach (Harvey Fischtron) (1933)—author
       Picture books including *The Judge* and *Duffy and the Devil*

6   **Elizabeth Yates** (1905)—author
       Historical fiction for intermediate and upper grades, including *Sarah Whitcher's Story* and biographies such as *Amos Fortune, Free Man*

8   **Padraic Colum** (1881)—author
       Excellent adaptations of folk tales and Greek myths, such as *The Golden Fleece*
      James Thurber (1894)—author and illustrator
       Modern fairy tales such as *The Great Quillow* and *Many Moons*
      Edwin Tunis (1897)—author and illustrator
       Authentic, detailed pen-and-ink drawings illustrating various facets of history, such as *Frontier Living* and *Indians*

9   **Jerome Beatty, Jr.** (1918)—author
       Humorous stories for intermediate grades including *Matthew Looney and the Space Pirates*

10   **Rumer Godden** (1907)—author
       Intermediate fiction including *Diddakoi* and *Dolls' House*

13   **Leonard Weisgard** (1916)—illustrator
       Wide range of illustrated works including *The Little Island* and *Salt Boy*

Joy and happiness abound. The media center takes on a festive air as winter and holiday time approach.

Bulletin Boards

THE TWELVE DAYS OF CHRISTMAS*

A popular display for December (see the illustration) tells the story of "The Twelve Days of Christmas." Adapt the dimensions given here to fit your bulletin board or use available wall space. Begin creating this bulletin board twelve days before school closes for vacation. Start wih the partridge and add one set of figures each day. As word gets around, you will have children, teachers, and even parents stopping by daily to see what has been added to the board. On the last day before vacation, the scene is completed with the twelve drummers drumming.

Primary grade children especially enjoy singing "The Twelve Days of Christmas" while gathered around the bulletin board, pointing to each day's gifts as they sing. Below is a list of the gifts for each of the twelve days:

first day—a partridge in a pear tree
second day—two turtle doves
third day—three French hens
fourth day—four calling birds
fifth day—five golden rings
sixth day—six geese a-laying
seventh day—seven swans a-swimming
eighth day—eight maids a-milking
ninth day—nine ladies dancing
tenth day—ten lords a-leaping
eleventh day—eleven pipers piping
twelfth day—twelve drummers drumming

MATERIALS:

—1 sheet of 22″ × 28″ green kraft paper
—1 sheet of 22″ × 28″ blue kraft paper
—1 sheet of 22″ × 28″ brown construction paper
—1 sheet of 9″ × 14″ yellow construction paper
—1 roll of gold tinsel cord
—rubber cement
—glue stick
—scissors
—ruler
—pencil
—felt markers in various colors
—several sheets of tracing paper
—carbon paper
—1 ditto master
—12 sheets of ditto paper
—1 manila envelope, 6″ × 9″
—1 acetate sheet
—overhead projector
—1 copy of any version of the book, *The Twelve Days of Christmas* (optional)

* Bulletin board conceived and executed by Cynthia Edson.

PREPARATION:

1. Use tracing paper to trace the following figures from the sample illustration:
   - one partridge
   - two turtle doves
   - three french hens
   - four calling birds
   - one goose a-laying
   - one swan a-swimming
   - one maid with cow
   - one dancing lady
   - one leaping lord
   - one piper piping
   - one drummer drumming

2. Place a sheet of carbon paper between the tracing paper and a ditto master and retrace your drawings. Run off twelve copies of the ditto. You will, of course, have extra copies of some items, but that will give you a chance to experiment with various colors and choose your favorite ones.

3. Use felt markers to color in the appropriate number of "gifts" for each day. Cut out the figures you will need. Be sure that all of the figures to be ued on one day are colored identically.

4. Place all of the figures in the manila envelope until they are needed.

5. Use the acetate sheet to trace the sample tree. Omit the leaves, pears, animals, and rings.

6. Use the overhead projector technique described in the October chapter to transfer the tree to the brown construction paper. The size of the finished tree should be approximately 12″ × 25″. Cut out the tree.

7. Take the green paper and cut a hilly horizon line. The high point should be 21″ from the bottom of the bulletin board or wall, and the low point about 15″ from the bottom. Save the leftover green paper for making leaves.

8. Cut out an 18″ × 22″ piece of blue paper. Save the leftover blue paper for making a pond.

9. Attach the blue paper to the top of the bulletin board or wall.

10. Use rubber cement to paste the green paper to the blue paper, overlapping it so that the sky is above and the grass is below. Attach the green paper to the bottom of the bulletin board or wall.

11. Cut 20 to 30 simple leaves from the remaining green paper.

12. Draw a 3″ high pear with a stem on the yellow construction paper. Cut it out and use it as a pattern to make about nine more pears.

13. Use rubber cement to attach the tree to the sky and grass. Be sure to attach the lowest branch only where it meets the trunk, because you will put the rings there later.

14. Use the glue stick to attach the leaves and pears to the tree.

15. Cut a pond shape out of the remaining blue paper.

16. Use rubber cement to attach the pond to the grass near the base of the bulletin board.

PROCEDURE:

1. On the first day, use the glue stick to paste the partridge onto a branch of the pear tree.
2. On each subsequent day, add the next gift from the song, using the glue stick to attach it to the bulletin board or wall.
3. On the fifth day, form five rings from the gold tinsel cord. Place the rings around the lowest branch of the tree.
4. You may want to display one or more copies of the book, *The Twelve Days of Christmas,* alongside the bulletin board.

'TIS THE SEASON TO BE JOLLY

Design a wintry bulletin board such as the one shown here to leave the children laughing as they begin their winter vacation. Instead of promoting the usual holiday books, have a snowman with a pouch filled with a reading list of humorous books.

No bibliography is given with this bulletin board because you should have no problem in preparing one based on your own collection. Include riddle and joke books, books of tongue twisters, and humorous fiction. You can use a star to mark titles that are for middle or upper grade readers. Be sure to include the call numbers; it is good practice for the students. Annotations are helpful, but they can be omitted if you are pressed for time. If space permits, display the titles listed in the bibliography.

MATERIALS:

—1 sheet of 22″ × 28″ light blue posterboard
—2 sheets of 24″ × 36″ white construction paper
—1 piece of 2½″ × 1½″ brown construction paper
—1 sheet of 9″ × 14″ green construction paper
—red construction paper and additional green construction paper if you prefer a holiday look; otherwise use the white construction paper
—black wide-tip felt marker
—scissors
—cellophane tape
—ruler
—rubber cement
—1 ditto master
—enough ditto paper to run off copies for each class
—1 manila envelope, 9″ × 14″ (optional)
—1 small piece of orange construction paper (or a picture of a carrot)

PREPARATION:

1. Cut a gently rolling snow hill out of the white construction paper and paste it onto the bottom of the posterboard. The hill should not be more than 6″ high.
2. Use the felt marker to draw a musical staff at the top of the bulletin board.
3. Cut 3 circles from the white construction paper—4½″, 7½″, and 12″ in diameter. Outline the circles in black marker so that the snowman will stand out against the snow.
4. On the smallest circle, draw two eyes and a mouth with the black marker.
5. Cut out a carrot shape from the orange construction paper, or use the carrot picture. Paste it on the small circle to form the nose.
6. Draw three buttons on the middle circle.
7. Cut a piece of white construction paper to measure 9″ × 14″ and fold it into a pocket. Tape it onto the largest circle. Print ''Books to Make You Laugh'' on the pocket. If you prefer, use a manila envelope and attach it to the side of the bulletin board.
8. Overlap the circles and paste them together.
9. Paste the snowman onto the posterboard. The height of the completed snowman should be approximately 16″.
10. Cut the tree out of green construction paper. An easy way to do it is to cut three triangles of increasing size and paste them one on the other, overlapping to form the tree. The completed tree measures approximately 8″ high and 9″ wide at the base.
11. Use the brown construction paper to make a trunk.

12. Paste the green tree over he brown trunk. The visible portion of the trunk height is only 1″. Paste the completed tree to the bulletin board. Part of the tree should touch the sky and the rest should be on the snow.
13. Draw or copy the letters and the treble clef on white construction paper or on red and green paper. Then cut out the letters. (If you use white paper, outline the letters with black marker.)
14. Position and paste the letters onto the staff.
15. Type the bibliography on the ditto master and run off copies. If you choose to put the bibliography in the snowman's pouch, type the ditto master the long way so that it can be folded into a booklet. This will prevent the snowman from being blocked by the bibliography.

Library Art Activity

HAPPINESS IS . . .

Decorate the media center with drawings by the children that express their ideas of happiness. Most of their wishes will be frankly commercial, others will try to impress the adults, and a few will be genuinely moving. Encourage the children to contribute their drawings by designing a poster such as the one shown on the following page. Have drawing paper and crayons on hand for those who have time to draw their ideas of happiness while in the media center. Although this activity is not directly related to books or other media, it is a nice way to make the room look attractive at holiday time. Also, since the drawings are not particularly tied to the holidays, the pictures will not have to be taken down on the day you return to school in January.

MATERIALS:

—1 sheet of 11″ × 14″ colored posterboard
—felt markers in assorted colors and widths
—white construction paper
—rubber cement

PREPARATION:

1. Use the overhead projector to copy the two cartoon figures and their thoughts about happiness onto the construction paper, or be inventive and draw your own.
2. Cut out the drawings and paste them onto the posterboard. Draw "thought clouds" to accompany the cartoon figures.
3. Use wide-tip markers to print "Happiness Is . . ." in large letters in the middle of the poster. Do not write the letters in a straight line. Allow them to flop around in a happy way.
4. Use narrow-tip markers to write the instructions and to describe the cartoon figures' thoughts under the drawings. Vary the colors to convey a jolly mood.

PROCEDURE:

As the students turn in their drawings, display their ideas of happiness around the media center.

Happiness is a 10 speed bike.

Fill in the sentence and make a picture.
Show what happiness is to you.

Happiness is all the candy I can eat.

Library Enrichment Activity

SCIENCE IN A SHOEBOX

The circulation of science kits that enable children to perform simple science experiments at home is a valuable project in which to involve the media center. A project known as "Science in a Shoebox" was begun about 12 years ago by the Princeton, New Jersey, branch of the American Association of University Women; it was further refined by the Jersey Shore and Berkeley Heights branches, both in New Jersey. Its use has since spread to many other areas.

Five categories of science are covered by the project: heat, forces, air and sound, magnetism and electricity, and optics. A series of experiments has been developed for each category. For example, the optics boxes described below contain instructions for performing eleven experiments. All of the materials and instructions needed for a set of experiments, as well as a book card and pocket, are contained in a shoebox. The box is painted in bright enamel colors and tied with a shoelace, making it simple for a child to carry.

Some of the experiments in the kits are adapted from various science books; others are completely original. The kits are extremely popular with students because of the fact that all of the materials for one set of experiments are included within one box, which makes it easy for students to perform them, either on their own or with parental supervision. The degree of supervision depends, of course, on the child's age.

Since setting up the boxes is time-consuming, it would be a good idea to enlist help from your P.T.A. or from volunteer parents who are interested in science. Five identical boxes are made for each of the five categories, so you'll eventually have a total of 25 science kits available for circulation in the media center. These can be placed in any available space and signed out in the same manner as books, generally for a one-week period. When the boxes are returned, each one must be checked item by item. The checker should make sure that nothing is missing and replace any consumable parts before the boxes are put back into circulation. Several volunteers could be trained to do this job regularly.

Instructions for setting up the Science in a Shoebox kit on optics, directions for performing three of the eleven experiments, the introduction to the kit, and the concluding "Things to Think About" are given in the remainder of this section.

Directions for Setting Up the Kits

MATERIALS (for making the shoebox kits):

- —5 shoeboxes
- —white shellac
- —yellow enamel paint
- —paintbrush
- —5 shoelaces, 36″ long

—1 sheet of 22″ × 36″ posterboard
—1 package of ¾″ wide elastic tape
—5 book pockets
—5 book cards
—stapler
—scissors
—paste
—felt marker

PREPARATION (for making the shoebox kits):

1. Paint the inside and outside of the shoeboxes and lids with yellow enamel paint, after first priming with white shellac.
2. Attach a shoelace to the bottom and sides of the shoebox with a stapler. The unattached ends of the shoelace should be long enough so that they can be used to tie the box shut. (See illustration.)

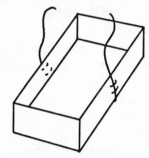

3. Cut the posterboard into two 6″ × 8″ pieces.
4. Cut the elastic into four 1″ long pieces.
5. Form an envelope by attaching the four pieces of elastic to the two pieces of posterboard, stapling near top and bottom. The elastic acts as a hinge. (See illustration.)

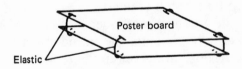

6. Paste the bottom side of the envelope to the inside lid of the shoebox. The bottom edge of the envelope should touch the edge of the lid so that there will be room to put the directions for the experiments into the envelope. (See illustration.)

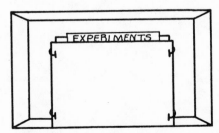

7. Type OPTICS 1 on the book card and book pocket.
8. Paste the pocket onto an inner side of the shoebox. Slip the book card into the pocket.
9. On the outside of the box and on the lid, write OPTICS 1 with a felt marker.
10. Repeat steps 2 through 9 four more times, but number each set consisting of a shoebox and lid, a book pocket, and a book card sequentially.

MATERIALS (for the optics experiments):

Each of the five boxes contains all of the following items:

—1 piece of 12″ × 6″ white cardboard on which you draw three inverted *V*'s with red, blue, and black felt markers. (See illustration.)

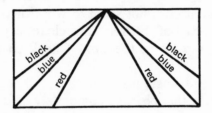

—2 pieces of 2″ × 9″ white paper folded in half lengthwise
—1 piece of 4″ × 4¼″ graph paper
—1 piece of 4½″ × 6″ white paper with an oily spot on it
—1 piece of 4″ × 5″ black construction paper with a 1″ hole in the center
—1 black cylinder (Made by completely covering a toilet paper roll with black construction paper. Seal the ends with black paper and punch a ½″ hole in one end.)
—1 3″ × 5″ card with the word "water" printed on it with felt marker
—1 piece of 3″ × 5″ clear plastic
—1 piece of 3″ × 6″ aluminum foil
—1 metal ring, ¾″ in diameter
—1 pill bottle with cap, any size
—1 popsicle stick
—2 rubber bands
—1 cylindrical glass jar, any size
—1 mirror

PREPARATION (for the optics experiments):

1. Type the following information on a ditto master that is no larger than 2½″ × 6″:

    Contents of Optics Experiments:

    1 piece of cardboard with colored lines
    2 pieces of white paper
    1 piece of graph paper
    1 piece of paper with oily spot
    1 piece of black paper with hole
    1 black cylinder
    1 card with printed word
    1 piece of clear plastic

1 piece of aluminum foil
1 metal ring
1 pill bottle
1 popsicle stick
2 rubber bands
1 glass jar
1 mirror

2. Type the following directions on a ditto master that is no larger than 5″ × 6″:

General Directions for Experiments:

   a. Read the directions for each experiment before you start.
   b. Work with clean hands on a clean counter or table.
   c. If an experiment does not seem to work the first time, try it again.
   d. Make sure that all of the items are clean, dry, and in good shape before you put them back in the box. Check to see that the contents are complete.
   e. Please try not to waste materials.
   f. All materials in this box are completely safe to use <u>if they are handled according to instructions.</u>
   g. Some of the experiments in each box can be performed by children in first grade. Some of the experiments are more appropriate for older children. Do as many as you can by yourself. If you have difficulty, ask someone for help. Have fun!
   h. The future success of this project depends very much on you. Please try to return this science kit to the media center in the same condition as it was when you borrowed it. That way, other students will be able to enjoy it too. Thank you.

3. Run off five copies of both ditto masters, and paste one copy of each to the outside of the envelope on the inside lid of each shoebox.
4. Directions for performing three of the eleven optics experiments are provided on the following pages. Type the introduction to the kit, the experiments, and the concluding material entitled "Things to Think About" on a ditto master. Each part should be no larger than 8½″ × 5½″. Run off five copies of each part, cut them, and laminate them. Place all of the directions inside the envelope on the inside lid of each shoebox.
5. Replace the lids and tie the shoeboxes shut, and they are ready for circulation. Science in a Shoebox kits can be enjoyed by children in grades one through six, although the younger ones will need to be supervised by a parent or an older brother or sister.

THE OPTICS EXPERIMENTS

Optics: An Introduction

Optics is the science of light: its origin, how it travels, and its effect on matter.

<u>Caution: Never look into the sun. It will damage your eyes.</u>

The first two experiments will show how light travels. Light moves along straight lines. Watch the sunbeams breaking through the clouds. They look like straight beams. How is it possible, then, that light reaches our eyes even if we do not look directly into the sun? How is it that even a room with windows facing north is filled with light (but not direct sunlight)? This is through diffuse reflection: if light hits a surface it is bounced off, usually in all directions. Light is diffusely reflected by the wall of a house, the earth, your body, all objects which it hits. This diffusely reflected light travels along straight lines, too, but it has changed direction.

Another process by which light is bounced in all directions is called "scattering." This happens when light travels through a medium filled with tiny particles. Light is scattered, for example, by air; but it is scattered much more effectively by tiny water droplets (clouds or fog). This is the reason that even on a cloudy day we have daylight.

Finally, light beams become slightly fuzzy along their edges. It is because a light beam is truly a wave. Experiments 1 and 2 will show how light travels in straight lines.

EXPERIMENT NO. 2

To prove: Light travels in straight lines.
Materials: glass jar
black paper with hole
two rubber bands
flashlight (you must supply this item)
½ teaspoon milk (you must supply this item)
Procedure:
1. Fill jar with water.
2. Cover one side of the jar with the black paper with hole. Hold it in place with the two rubber bands.
3. Carefully put ½ teaspoon (or 10 drops) of milk into the water. Do not stir or shake jar.
4. Hold a flashlight behind jar and let a beam of light pass through the hole.
5. Look into the water from the uncovered side of the jar.
Observation: You will see the beam of light like a bright pencil in the milky water.

Conclusion: Light travels in a straight line.
Note: Milky water was used because it scattered enough light into your eyes so you could see the beam of light. If you try this experiment with very clear water, you may not be able to see the beam, even though it is there. Try the experiment without the milk and look for the beam of light right after you fill the jar and again later. When water is first drawn from the faucet, it has many tiny air bubbles which scatter the light. These go

away as the water sits undisturbed. The water may also contain tiny particles of dust which will settle out as the water sits in the jar.

Experiments 9 and 11 are designed to show refraction.

When light travels from one medium into another (when it passes from air into glass, for example), it changes its speed because the resistance of the new medium is different. Imagine yourself running from a paved road into sand. Immediately, your speed will be lowered. The same thing happens when light passes from air into water or glass. A result of this change in speed is that the direction of the light ray is changed. This is called refraction because the light ray is refracted or "broken."

EXPERIMENT NO. 9

To prove: Water can act as a magnifying lens.
Materials: glass jar
                  graph paper (paper with squares on it)
Vocabulary: magnifying—increasing the apparent size
                    cylindrical—shaped like the glass jar
                    curvature—a surface that is bent continuously, like a circle
Procedure:
1. Fill the glass jar with water.
2. Place the graph paper upright behind the jar.
Observations:
1. Notice the size of the squares on the part of the paper that sticks out above the jar.
2. Notice the size of the squares as you look at them through the side of the jar.
3. Which squares appear bigger? Why?
4. Do the squares change size up and down and side to side, or do they change size in only one of these directions? Which one?

Conclusion: The water acts as an optical lens, specifically as a cylindrical magnifying glass. The curved shape of the water-filled jar only produces the magnifying effect in the direction of the curvature. Therefore, the squares appear larger from side to side when viewed through the water.

EXPERIMENT NO. 11

To prove: Water can produce different refraction effects, depending upon whether the water surface is flat or curved.
Materials: glass jar
                  metal ring
Procedure:
1. Pour water into the glass jar to a depth of about two inches.
2. Place the metal ring in the center of the bottom of the jar.

3. Place the jar on a table.
4. Look into the jar with your eyes a little <u>above</u> the level of the water surface.

<u>Observation</u>: You will see two metal rings.

<u>Conclusion</u>: Because of the refraction of light at the water surface, the metal ring can be seen twice: once displaced by refraction and once directly. Notice that the ring observed through the sides of the jar below the water surface appears larger. This again shows the magnifying lens effect of the curved water surface.

THINGS TO THINK ABOUT

1. Why is the sky blue? Why are sunsets red?
2. Where do you get tanned and sunburned faster, in the garden or at the seashore? Why?
3. When camping at a lake shore, do you need a glass mirror to look at your face?
4. Do you think you can accurately judge the depth of a pond just by looking at the bottom (if it is visible)? Will it appear deeper or shallower to you? Why?
5. Do you see yourself in a mirror as other people see you? Give the reason for your answer.
6. Try to find out, by making a simple drawing, why your shadow is long in the morning and evening and short at noon.

As stated on the first page, optics is the science of light: its origin, how it travels, and its effect on matter. What is light? Light is an electromagnetic wave which can travel in solids, liquids, air, or empty space. Imagine yourself throwing a pebble into a quiet pond; waves will spread in all directions. They travel with a certain speed, and if the pond is big enough, you will see them fade out before they reach the shore. If there is an obstacle—the shore, a rock—the waves will be reflected, producing interesting patterns. You can also throw in several pebbles at the same time and watch the wave patterns which are produced. This overlapping of waves is called "interference."

Light waves behave similarly. You have a light source—the sun, a flashlight—which sends out light waves. Light waves travel at tremendous speed (it only takes them about 8 minutes to come to us from the sun). Finally they reach our eyes or another receiver (photographic film, for example) and they are "seen." On their way, things may happen to them. They may be reflected (on a mirror, on a water surface); they may be scattered in all directions (by a cloud, by fog); they may be absorbed (by a dark roof); they may be refracted (change their direction by going through glass or water); or they may interact with other light waves (remember the water waves).

What is the wavelength of light? The wavelength of a water wave—or the distance between two neighboring "hills" or crests—is an inch or so. Light waves have a wavelength a hundred thousand times smaller than that. Just as sound waves of different wavelengths produce sounds of different pitches, so light waves of different wavelengths produce different colors of light. White light as it comes from the sun is a mixture of light of all different wavelengths (and therefore, different colors). If we can separate sunlight according to its wavelength, we can see the different colors. A good example of this separation of colors is the rainbow.

Light is also a form of energy that can be converted into other forms of energy. For example, it can be converted into electrical energy with a device called the solar cell which is used in satellites; into chemical energy (plants do this in the process called photosynthesis); or into heat energy (water and other objects are warmed by the sun).

Note: Complete information on all five science kits can be obtained from the Berkeley Heights Branch of the American Association of University Women by contacting Mrs. Jean Ruch, 16 Oak Ridge Road, Berkeley Heights, New Jersey 07922. The information will be forwarded for a nominal fee to cover postage and printing.

REVIEWS ON FILE

Have a ready reference file in your card catalog of student book reviews. This not only encourages reading but also provides a handy tool for children who are searching for something new or different to read. You can create a poster that encourages students to contribute reviews. (See the illustration.)

MATERIALS:

—blank catalog cards
—3" × 5" cards
—1 sheet of 11" × 14" colored posterboard
—felt markers, 1 black and 1 of another color
—rubber cement
—easel back
—overhead projector

PROCEDURE:

1. Draw a card catalog (or trace one using the overhead projector) on the posterboard with any color marker.
2. Print the directions with the black marker.
3. Type a sample review on a catalog card. Choose a familiar title such as *Charlotte's Web*.
4. Paste the sample review on the posterboard with rubber cement.
5. Use the same color marker that you used for drawing the card catalog to write Sample Review on the posterboard near the review card.
6. Attach the poster to the easel back.

Reviews on File

1. Write a short review of a book you read and liked.

2. Use 3 x 5 cards (available at the desk).

3. Completed reviews will be retyped on catalog cards and filed in the last drawer of our card catalog.

Sample Review

Call #	Author
	Title

Review

Student Name   Grade

Storytelling Suggestions

SNOW AND HOLIDAYS

These December book selections reflect the season with its snow and holidays. Depending on the policy in your school (see this month's Open End), you might make your choices from one or both of these categories.

Holiday Stories

Andersen, Hans Christian   "The Fir Tree"
in *Seven Tales by H. C. Andersen*
trans. by Eva Le Gallienne
illus. by Maurice Sendak
Harper & Row, 1959

The bittersweet tale of a fir tree who wished for great things and gave no attention to the beauty of today. Large type for easy reading aloud, a flowing translation, and detailed Sendak drawings make this a perfect choice. (third to sixth grade)

Carroll, Ruth and Latrobe   *The Christmas Kitten*
Walck, 1970

A kitten chooses a home in this story without words. Despite the mother's original objection, the kitten wins everyone over. Children can look for the kitten as it hides and watch the various clocks indicating how much time is passing. (kindergarten to second grade)

Cunningham, Julia   *Onion Journey*
illus. by Lydia Cooley
Pantheon, 1967

Gilly's grandmother leaves him alone for three days at Christmas with an unexplained gift of a red onion. As he meets and befriends a bird, a badger, and a hare, the layers of the riddle unfold into a gift of love. This strange tale is best told in one 30-minute stretch. Prepare the class, set the scene, and let the quiet of the story pervade the room. (fourth to sixth grade)

Epstein, Morris   "The Old Dreidel"
in *My Holiday Story Book*
Ktav Publishing, 1958

In this brief story, a young girl rehearses the narration for a Hebrew school play. She explains simply the historical aspects of Chanukah, skims over the miraculous ones, and concludes with a description of the dreidel and traditional foods. A satisfactory way to introduce Chanukah to non-Jewish children. (kindergarten to second grade)

Hutchins, Pat   *The Silver Christmas Tree*
Macmillan, 1974

Squirrel questions his animal friends as he sees them hiding odd-shaped parcels. He is convinced that one of them must have taken the silver star that shines from the top of his tree at night. (first to third grade)

Janice   *Little Bear's Christmas*
illus. by Mariana
Lothrop, Lee & Shephard, 1964

Little Bear awakens well before spring. It is Christmas Eve. He accompanies Santa Claus and is given a very special present. This simple story will delight the children who feel that a ride in Santa's sleigh is the best Christmas present. (kindergarten to second grade)

Johnston, Tony   *Mole and Troll Trim the Tree*
illus. by Wallace Tripp
Putnam's, 1974

Mole and Troll decide to trim a tree together. After bickering about the best way, they combine ornaments for the most beautiful tree of all. An old theme, but popular at this time of year. (kindergarten to second grade)

Winter Stories

Buckley, Helen E.   *Josie and the Snow*
illus. by Evaline Ness
Lothrol, Lee & Shephard, 1964

In this rhyming story, Josie's cat and dog want to stay inside, but the entire family joins her in an all day frolic in the newly fallen snow. Strong feelings of family togetherness are very appropriate for this time of year. (kindergarten and first grade)

Craft, Ruth   *The Winter Bear*
illus. by Erik Blegvad
Atheneum, 1975

In this rhyming story, three children are bundled up for a walk. As they pass through a winter landscape, they see birds, cows, and seeds. They find an old toy bear and take him home to love him. (kindergarten and first grade)

Holl, Adelaide   *Bedtime for Bears*
illus. by Cyndy Szekeres
Garrard, 1973

Even though it's almost winter, Small Bear doesn't want to go to bed just yet. But when he finds that everyone else is too busy to play with him, he begins hibernating like a proper bear. (first grade)

Keats, Ezra Jack   *The Snowy Day*
Viking, 1962

Peter spends a wonderful day in the snow in this Caldecott Medal book. He dreams that the snow has melted and is delighted to awaken to a fresh fall. Students will enjoy describing their own favorite snow activities. (kindergarten and first grade)

Kellogg, Steven   *The Mystery of the Missing Red Mitten*
Dial Press, 1974

Annie's search for her lost red mitten turns up many other missing items. The mitten is discovered at last as the heart of a melting snowman. Students will empathize with Annie's discovery of all the lost clothing. (kindergarten to second grade)

Welber, Robert   *The Winter Picnic*
                                  illus. by Deborah Ray
                                  Pantheon, 1970

A boy wants a picnic in the snow. Mother is skeptical until he fashions bowls and plates from snow and brings out sandwiches and lemonade. An unusual idea for a story. First ask the children what they eat and where they go for a picnic. Then ask if they have ever gone on a winter picnic. (kindergarten and first grade)

Teaching Unit

CLASSROOM MULTIMEDIA UNIT

One of the most common tasks of the library media specialist is to supply teachers with resource materials for a unit in a specific subject area. This is actually a form of teaching. Teachers who are accustomed to utilizing this service have discovered that classroom collections that come and go with a unit are more actively used than those that sit on the shelf year after year. You can provide teachers with this service by discussing the unit with the teacher, collecting the appropriate material, asking a volunteer to sign it out, and then delivering it. The additional time that you spend in charging out and delivering materials is negligible, and it pays off very well in teacher appreciation.

In order to prepare a thorough multimedia resource list, the library media specialist must know the objectives of the unit and be familiar with the abilities of the class. The following sample unit on deserts does not list all of the materials that would be sent to the teacher. It is instead a selected bibliography that shows the scope of the materials and the criteria for selection. The unit has been designed for about the fourth grade level. Note that certain selections are suggested as enrichment material for academically talented youngsters and that others are considered more appropriate for slow learners. When the materials are delivered, discuss these special features of the selections with the teacher so that he or she can make optimum use of what is presented.

The follow-up questions included here are intended to improve students' library skills and to further their knowledge of the specific subject area. The questions send students to the media center to obtain answers that are not in textbooks and probably not in the additional material sent to the classroom.

BIBLIOGRAPHY FOR DESERTS

BOOKS:

Atwood, Ann. The Wild Young Desert. Scribner's, 1970
      Full color photographs on every page illustrate the effects of water and wind, and the inherent beauty of desert life. Text is minimal but difficult for most intermediate readers. Nonetheless, the pictures make it an excellent resource.

Epstein, Sam and Beryl. All About the Desert. Illus. by Fritz Krebel. Random House, 1957.

Written at the perfect level for intermediate readers. Chapters cover the similarities and differences of deserts. There are separate chapters for the deserts of each of the five continents. Indexed.

Goetz, Delia. Deserts. Illus. by Louis Darling. Morrow, 1956.
Easy-to-read account of desert life. Excellent for slower learning children.

Huntington, Harriet E. Let's Go to the Desert. Doubleday, 1949.
Full of attractive sepia prints. Although the vocabulary is quite simple, each photographic illustration of plants, animals, or the desert environment is carefully and accurately explained. With so much information, this book is of help to the average student as well as the slow learner.

Klots, Alexander. The Community of Living Things in the Desert. Creative Education Society, 1967.
Black-and-white photographs are accompanied by one or two page explanations. The book illustrates plants, animals by family groups, and the influence of man. Text is upper level, but material is usable because the information is organized for easy access and each photograph with explanation is self-contained. Indexed.

Knight, David C. The First Book of Deserts. Watts, 1964.
Black-and-white photographs and drawings are accompanied by a text that is most appropriate for the upper grade reading level. Use at the intermediate level is best for gifted students who are exploring special topics such as classification of deserts by types. Indexed.

Leopold, Aldo Starker. The Desert, Young Readers Edition. Time-Life Books, 1961.
Black-and-white and full color photographs and drawings. The text is more difficult than the Epstein book and less difficult than the Knight book. It has the usual outline, including the origins of deserts, the location of deserts, water problems, plant life, animal life, and the survival of animals and people in the desert. Some of the questions raised about whether or not man has the right to destroy the deserts for the sake of human survival might be of interest to the better student. Most intermediate readers can handle some of the material. Indexed.

FILMSTRIPS:

Desert Life. (silent filmstrip) Scott Education Division, Holyoke, Massachusetts, 1972.
Four color filmstrips with captions that explain the desert environments and the adaptations of plants and animals.

"The Desert" from the Small Worlds of Life series. (sound filmstrip) National Geographic Society, Washington, D.C., 1972.

Color filmstrip on the deserts of North America. Although it is fairly difficult for the intermediate grades, the photographs are so excellent that teachers will stop the filmstrip and explain the difficult sections.

The Ecology of a Desert: Death Valley. (sound filmstrip) Imperial Film Co., Lakeland, Florida, 1973.

Excellent photography in this two-strip series accompanied by detailed explanations of one of the great American deserts. A teacher may assign the strips to a small group rather than show the strips to the entire class.

STUDY PRINTS:

"Deserts of the World." (study prints) Instructional Aids, Inc., Mankato, Minnesota, 1968.

Six full color 18″ × 13″ prints showing various desert environments. Remove the print for polar deserts because it can be very confusing unless the teacher plans to explain it. Using the prints to decorate the classroom can provide the right mood for beginning the unit.

Follow-up Questions on Deserts

1. Why is it repetitive to say "Sahara Desert"?
2. Why don't you need an umbrella for some rainstorms in the Sahara?
3. What cargo does a camel caravan carry to market?
4. Why did traders use caravans instead of going by themselves?
5. What is a one-humped camel called? Where does it live?
6. What is a two-humped camel called? Where does it live?

Suggestions for finding the answers:

1. For questions one and two, see The World Book Encyclopedia.
2. For questions three and four, see Compton's Precyclopedia.
3. For questions five and six, you are on your own.

Professional Responsibilities

USE OF CIP IN CATALOGING

Although most library media specialists order books that come with commercial catalog cards or are completely processed, you should be aware of the Cataloging in Publication (CIP) program begun in the early 1970's and now under the auspices of the Library of Congress.

The CIP program makes available to the publishers who subscribe to it professional cataloging data to be printed in their books. The information generally can be found on the back of the title page; it includes the Dewey and Library of Congress numbers, an annotation, and suggested subject headings. As of July 1974, there were 640 publishers participating in the program, with new ones joining regularly.

What this means to library media specialists is that when you purchase a book directly from a publisher rather than through a jobber, your cataloging may have been done for you if that publisher uses CIP. It takes only a few minutes for you to check the back of the title page, to prepare a sample catalog card using the information contained there, and to have the book ready for processing by one of your volunteers. (See the Volunteers section of the April chapter for how to type catalog cards.)

You should not follow the CIP suggestions blindly, however. Often the Library of Congress will catalog a book in such a way that you know it will never be used in your media center. Also, the subject headings are sometimes not the ones that you would use in your card catalog. If you are alert to these possibilities, it is not too difficult to institute your own changes before the book is cataloged. (See the Professional Responsibilities section in the October chapter for a discussion of the problems that you may encounter in reclassifying commercial catalog cards.)

If you have more volunteers than money, you might find it worthwhile to order most of your books unprocessed. This will save a considerable amount of money, and you can count on the CIP information to help you catalog the books quickly before passing them on to your volunteers for typing and processing.

Unfortunately, some publishers of children's books have not yet joined the CIP program, and this may slow down your cataloging. However, the majority of publishers do print the information in their books. If those who do not use CIP hear an outcry through their mail, they might be persuaded that the program is valuable to library media specialists.

Meanwhile, whether or not you regularly take advantage of CIP, you should be aware that it exists today as a cataloging aid.

ROUNDUP OF HARDWARE

Vandalism seems to have become a fact of life for all schools. During long holiday recesses such as winter vacation, the schools become targets for anything from wanton destruction to calculated theft. Audio-visual hardware is particularly vulnerable. Although overhead projectors are bulky and not worth much money on the open market, 16mm and 8mm projectors, record players, and cassette players pay off very well.

It is a wise precaution to lock up hardware over long vacations. If you lack the space to store all of the equipment, focus your attention on those items that are most attractive to anyone breaking into the building.

Notify teachers at least one week in advance of the procedure that you will be using to safeguard the equipment. Be sure to specify what items are to be locked up and where they are to be delivered. Remind teachers that the equipment is to be picked up immediately after vacation, for you will probably need the space. Try to have most of the hardware locked up the day before school closes. Special arrangements should be made for teachers who need to use a particular machine on the last day. Record players used for class parties are commonly kept in the room until the last possible moment.

Use the equipment control board (see the Professional Responsibilities section in the September chapter) to make a list by room or by teacher of the equipment to be returned. Four months have elapsed since the equipment was first distributed, and this roundup can be used as a rough inventory. Use the list to check off the equipment as it comes in; do not move the pins on the control board. Storing the hardware by teacher rather than by type will allow you to redistribute it more quickly after the holiday.

It is hoped that the teachers will promptly pick up their equipment upon returning to school after the vacation. The control board can be used to ensure that they get the same equipment they had before vacation. If teachers are forgetful, either deliver the hardware personally or send notes to the teachers asking them to have students come to the media center to pick up the equipment.

Volunteers

PROCESSING PAPERBACKS

Paperbacks are purchased because they are an inexpensive way to have multiple copies of popular material. They are not expected to have a long shelf life—twenty circulations is considered very good. Extensive processing causes the real cost of a book to go up, and it is wasted on a book that does not last long. Thus, the processing of paperbacks is kept to a minimum, and no cards are filed in the card catalog.

Paperback books are stamped and their pockets are pasted in the same manner as hard-bound books. (See the Volunteers section in the October chapter.) Consider using a different color book card (such as salmon or green) for paperbacks in order to make it easier to spot them in the circulation drawer and to avoid mix-ups with hard-bound books.

Book pockets and cards should show author, title, copy number, and call number. You may want to use the same call number on the paperback as you do on the hard-bound copy. In that case, a spine label is needed. On the other hand, you may choose to label paperbacks "pb" and to use the first three letters of the author's last name on the card or pocket. This method does not distinguish fiction from nonfiction, and the books do not need spine labels. However, the spines should be reinforced with 2″ or 3″ clear vinyl tape, depending on the size and width of each paperback.

To keep a record of your paperback holdings, prepare a 3″ × 5″ card for each title. The card should include the following information: author, title, publisher, copyright date, number of copies, where purchased, and price paid. A file of these cards can be kept on your desk or on top of the shelf list file for easy access.

PROCESSING PERIODICALS

Magazines arrive regularly throughout the year. They must be processed as rapidly as possible so that the users have ready access to current materials.

Organize the operation by keeping all needed supplies in a box that is the same size as the ones in which book cards are packaged. These materials should include periodical record cards, magazine cards, pockets, a property stamp and stamp pad, glue, tape, and the key for locking vinyl binders for current issues. Processing is more efficient if magazine cards are prepared several months in advance. They are easy to find if you keep them standing up in alphabetical order in the box. Assign one or two volunteers the responsibility of maintaining the periodical collection.

As magazines arrive, they are placed next to the box of supplies. They are first stamped and then checked off on the magazine record cards. These can be purchased from any library supply house.

The volunteers who are processing the magazines should alert you to missing issues. If you act quickly and notify the jobber or the publisher, the issues will be replaced. Be aware that publishers do not maintain an extensive stock of back issues; if you delay, the issues will be unavailable. Also notify the jobber or the publisher if a magazine arrives torn or in otherwise unreadable condition.

Once the periodicals have been checked in, you must prepare them to go on the shelf. If all issues including the current one circulate, a card and a pocket are pasted either on the inside back cover of the magazine or on the last page. If both locations have important information, use tape to hinge the card and pocket. You might use special magazine cards or standard book cards in a color different from the one used for books. Be sure to type the title of the magazine and the date on the card.

If the current issue does not circulate, consider purchasing locking vinyl binders from a library supply house or a periodical jobber. (You can frequently save money by purchasing them from a jobber.) A binder makes an issue look more attractive, adds to its shelf life, and acts as a signal to the person at the circulation desk not to permit the issue to circulate. Another means of preventing the current issue from circulating is to paste the card and pocket in the magazine only when it is removed from the binder and is ready to be charged out.

Professional periodicals are processed in the same way. You may omit cards and pockets for periodicals that are used only by you. However, be sure that the volunteers responsible for maintaining the periodical collection note on the label that the periodical has been checked in.

Open End

THE HOLIDAY SEASON: SECULAR vs. RELIGIOUS

Along with the joy and spirit of good will, the holiday season brings problems to the media center. Any manifestation of religion in a public school can bring out pressure groups who, in turn, can bring out counter-protesters.

Some school districts maintain a firm position against the introduction of items with even the most remote religious connotations. Santa Claus and Christmas trees have no place in these schools. If this is the policy in your district, you have no problem. Use only winter themes for your bulletin boards and story selections.

In the absence of a definite policy, the decision is yours to make. Should you avoid any religious display at all, include only common or commercial themes, or give equal time to all the holidays of the season?

If you decide to avoid all holiday themes, there will be those who bemoan the absence of the Christmas spirit. Some people feel that Christmas is more than a religious observance, that it embodies an attitude that should be encouraged. Many who want some Christmas celebration in the school feel that if you also include some recognition of the other holidays, everyone will be happy.

On the other hand, there are Christians who feel that Christmas is a very religious holiday and who resent any school observance which does not emphasize the holiness of the day. Jewish groups have informed schools that Judaism is not served by the presence of a menorah alongside a Christmas tree. Atheist and agnostic groups also have rights in a democracy; they argue that any religious holiday has no place in a public school. Unfortunately, no matter what you decide to do, someone will be dissatisfied.

All of these conflicting opinions leave the library media specialist without a clear-cut answer to the problem. In order to reach a decision, you will need to analyze your own attitudes and those of the community you serve. In the course of this analysis, it may be helpful to remember that our professional organizations have always held strong views on the freedom of all people. We have a responsibility to be as fair to all groups as we possibly can. This posture would suggest that the best approach is the absence of any religious observance.

On the other hand, you cannot ignore community habits and beliefs. Should you choose to lead in this area, remember that a leader who is too far ahead of the group is walking alone. Know where your school stands. Know the elements that comprise the faculty and student body. If only Christmas is traditionally represented, you might go as far as explaining the significance—or in some cases, the existence—of non-Christian holidays by reading a story that shows how others celebrate. Perhaps you will wish to display books that explain the various holiday symbols. You may decide that in your school sufficient time is given to the seasonal religious observances in the classrooms and that you do not need to add to them. You will, of course, have material available in the media center on all of the holidays.

Try to remember that this is a joyful season, and then do your best not to offend the sensibilities of anyone. Good luck.

'Tis the Season to be Jolly

January

Happy Birthday To . . .

2   **Isaac Asimov** (1920)—author
      Science fiction including *Fantastic Voyage* and *Foundation Trilogy*; nonfiction such as *The Human Body, Words of Science,* and *The Shaping of England*

      Crosby Newell Bonsall (1921)—author and illustrator
      Easy-to-read books including *And I Mean It, Stanley* and *Case of the Cat's Meow*

3   **Joan Walsh Anglund** (1926)—author and illustrator
      Tiny picture books such as *A Friend Is Someone Who Likes You* and *Love Is a Special Way of Feeling*

      Carolyn Haywood (1898)—author
      The Betsy series for upper primary readers, including *B is for Betsy* and *Little Eddie*

      J. R. R. Tolkien (1892)—author
      Intermediate and upper grade fantasy, notably *The Hobbit* and *The Lord of the Rings* trilogy

4   **Jakob Grimm** (1785)—author
      Elder of the two famous Grimm brothers, collectors of fairy tales

6   **Carl Sandburg** (1878)—author
      Biographies of Abraham Lincoln, *The Rootabaga Stories,* and many books of poetry for children and adults

7   **Kay Chorao** (1936)—author and illustrator
      Funny picture books such as *Molly's Moe* and *Albert's Toothache* (illustrator only)

9   **Clyde Robert Bulla** (1914)—author
      Short, simple fiction including *Eagle Feather* and *Sword in the Tree*

10   **Remy Charlip** (1929)—author and illustrator
      Picture books with unusual format, such as *Thirteen, Hand Talk,* and *Fortunately*

11   **Mary Rodgers** (1931)—author
      Humorous fiction for intermediate grades, such as *Freaky Friday* and *A Billion for Boris*

Get away from winter's gloom with folk and fairy tales and a favorite book contest.

━━

12   **Jack London** (1876)—author
      Adventure stories for upper grades, including *Call of the Wild*
      Charles Perrault (1628)—author
      French collector of fairy tales including *Cinderella* and *Puss in Boots*
13   **Michael Bond** (1926)—author
      Series for intermediate grades, about Paddington Bear and Olga da Polga
14   **Hugh Lofting** (1886)—author
      Creator of the Dr. Dolittle series
18   **A. A. Milne** (1882)—author
      Creator of Winnie-the-Pooh
19   **Edgar Allen Poe** (1809)—author
      Poems and tales of terror for upper grades
22   **Blair Lent** (1930)—illustrator
      Picture books including *Funny Little Woman* and *Tikki Tikki Tembo*
      Brian Wildsmith (1930)—author and illustrator
      Bold, vibrant illustrations in books such as *The Lion and the Rat* and *Brian Wildsmith's Circus*
25   **James Flora** (1914)—author and illustrator
      Tall tales in picture book format, such as *The Day the Cow Sneezed* and *Stewed Goose*
26   **Mary Mapes Dodge** (1831)—author
      Author of *Hans Brinker and the Silver Skates*
27   **Lewis Carroll** (**Charles L. Dodgson**) (1832)—author
      Creator of Alice in Wonderland
      Jean Merrill (1923)—author
      Fiction for intermediate grades, such as *Pushcart War* and *Toothpaste Millionaire*
29   **Bill Peet** (1915)—author and illustrator
      Amusing picture books such as *The Wump World* and *Kermit the Hermit*
30   **Lloyd Alexander** (1924)—author
      Fantasy series about Prydain for intermediate and upper grades

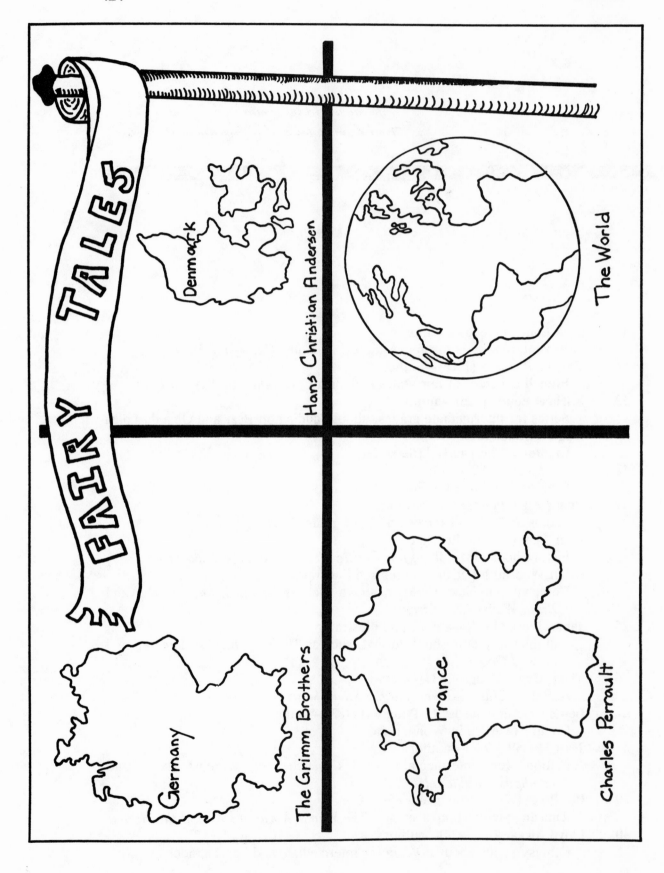

Bulletin Boards

FAIRY TALES

The purpose of the fairy tale bulletin board is to illustrate that fairy tales originate from countries all over the world. As shown in the illustration, the bulletin board features the most famous storytellers of Germany, Denmark, and France. After you've constructed the bulletin board, use the accompanying Library Art Activity to broaden the students' awareness of fairy tales.

MATERIALS:

—1 sheet of 28" × 22" light blue posterboard
—3 sheets of fluorescent poster paper, in any 3 colors
—1 sheet of white poster paper
—1 strip of 1" × 50" black construction paper
—1 strip of 1½" × 25" purple construction paper
—1 sheet of 12" × 36" yellow tissue paper
—rubber cement
—felt markers
—scissors

PREPARATION:

1. Cut the strip of black construction paper into 22" and 28" lengths. Attach the strips to the posterboard so that they divide it into four equal sections.
2. Draw and cut out outlines of Germany, Denmark, and France using the fluorescent paper. Paste the maps onto the posterboard. Denmark is cut into four pieces and should be placed carefully on the posterboard.

Note: If you have difficulty drawing the maps, use the overhead projector techniques described in the October chapter.

3. Sketch an outline of the earth on the white sheet of poster paper.
4. Use a blue felt marker to fill in the water areas of the globe.
5. Use colored felt markers to letter the names of the countries and the famous storytellers on the posterboard.
6. Cut a knob shape on the top of the strip of purple construction paper. This will form the staff of the banner.
7. Fold the yellow tissue paper in four lengthwise, making a 3" × 36" band.
8. Cut one end of the tissue paper to form a fringe.
9. Wrap the other end of the tissue paper loosely around the staff to see how paper will fall.
10. Lightly sketch the letters for "Fairy Tales".
11. Color the letters with a purple felt marker.
12. Attach the banner to the staff.
13. Attach the banner to the right side of the posterboard.

FAVORITE BOOK CONTEST*

Announce a Favorite Book Contest and call attention to the upcoming school-wide balloting with the eye-catching bulletin board shown in the illustration. This month's Library Art Activity and Library Enrichment Activity give directions for holding the contest and for encouraging students to participate in it.

MATERIALS:

—1 sheet of 22″ × 28″ white posterboard
—5 sheets of fluorescent poster paper (light orange, dark orange, lime green, medium green, shocking pink)

_____

* Bulletin board conceived and executed by Cynthia Edson.

—1 sheet of white poster paper
—10 black pipe cleaners
—black felt marker
—rubber cement
—scissors
—stapler
—shoebox
—paper to cover shoebox

PREPARATION:

1. Sketch five different book shapes, one on each of the five colors of fluorescent paper.
2. Cut out the books.
3. Paste them onto a sheet of posterboard.
4. Staple two pipe cleaners onto each book for use as arms.
5. Cut ten hand shapes out of the white poster paper.
6. Staple the hands to the unattached ends of the pipe cleaners.
7. Cut out the letters *V*, *O*, *T*, and *E*, each letter from a different color fluorescent paper.
8. Make four 1½″ × 6″ strips from the fifth sheet of fluorescent paper. Staple a strip to the bottom of each letter.
9. Staple the strips and letters to the top of the posterboard.
10. Use a black marker to outline the book shapes and hand shapes to make them stand out. Letter the books with slogans that encourage students to vote.
11. Cover a shoebox with fluorescent paper or wrapping paper and make a slit in the top. Place this ballot box near the bulletin board.

Library Art Activity

DRAW A SCENE FROM A FAIRY TALE

MATERIALS:

—100 pieces of 6″ × 3½″ light-colored construction paper, folded in half to form 3″ × 3½″ booklets
—1″ wide strips of black construction paper
—1 sheet of 8½″ × 11″ yellow posterboard
—rubber cement
—purple felt marker

PROCEDURE:

1. Use the purple felt marker to write directions to the students on the posterboard. (See illustration for student directions—on following page.)
2. Place the poster next to the fairy tale bulletin board or by the circulation desk.
3. Have the folded sheets of construction paper available at the desk. If there is great interest among the students, you will need more than 100 pieces.

Draw a scene from a

Fairy Tale

To add to the Fairy Tale Bulletin Board:

1. Read a fairy tale. See 398.2.

2. Check preface or blurb to discover country of origin.
    Or ask at the circulation desk.

3. Ask at desk for special paper for illustrating story.

4. Write the name of the tale on the outside of
    the booklet.

5. Draw a scene from the fairy tale on the inside.
    Add your name and room number in the corner.

6. Paste your picture on section of bulletin
    board showing the country the fairy
    tale comes from.

    ASK FOR HELP IN PASTING!

4. Show the students where to write the title and where to draw the illustration. The title goes on the outside front cover, the illustration on the inside right page.
5. All areas of the bulletin board may be covered with students' illustrations except the names of countries, the black strips dividing the bulletin board into sections, and the fairy tale banner.
6. Use the 1″ wide black construction paper pieces to lengthen the dividing strips so that they continue onto the surrounding wall as the bulletin board becomes covered. The students' work can then spill over to cover a wide area.

POSTERS FOR THE FAVORITE BOOK CONTEST

Students can make posters to be placed around the school to promote the Favorite Book Contest.

MATERIALS:

—sheets of 22″ × 28″ posterboard
—colored felt markers
—slips of paper giving the students directions for making the posters

DIRECTIONS TO STUDENTS:

1. Posters should contain the following information: name of contest, date, location where voting takes place.
2. Printing should be large enough to be legible at a distance.
3. No specific book titles should be mentioned on the posters.
4. Posterboard and felt markers can be obtained in the media center for use during free periods or lunch.
5. All posters must be turned in at the circulation desk by January 10, 19—.

Library Enrichment Activity

WRITING ORIGINAL FOLK AND FAIRY TALES

Students in the intermediate grades frequently study folk and fairy tales as part of the language arts curriculum. Even when it is not part of the required curriculum, many teachers would be interested in a folk and fairy tale unit if the library media specialist provided a fresh approach and support from the media center.

Be sure to give teachers advance information of the fairy tale bulletin board. (See this month's Bulletin Boards and Library Art Activity.) Suggest that this is a good time for a coordinating activity. The students' monthly book report can be on a folk or fairy tale collection. Teachers can also discuss with their classes the elements common to folk and fairy tales. For example:

1. Stories follow a narrative form and involve an adventure.
2. Frequently there are two siblings in addition to the hero or heroine.
3. The youngest child is the hero or heroine.
4. The hero or heroine is good natured, but not necessarily smart.
5. The fortune of the hero or heroine is the result of magical intervention.
6. There is always a happy ending.

Students can then use these elements and any others that emerge from the class discussion to write an original folk or fairy tale. Each class can compile its tales in a book designed by a student and display the book in the media center for others to read.

RECORDING AN ORIGINAL FOLK TALE NARRATIVE

Folk tales can be further explored by recording an original narrative to a folk tale filmstrip. This learning center activity for more advanced students involves sending them in pairs to the media center to select a sound filmstrip of a folk tale that they have never heard before. Indian legends and the folk tale series produced by Guidance Associates are good choices.

The students see the filmstrip without listening to the accompanying cassette or record. After frequent viewings, they are ready to write a tale to accompany the filmstrip. When the text is completed, the classroom teacher may review it and make suggestions, or the students may be allowed to develop the original folk tale on their own.

Next, the students prepare a tape from their script. When all is complete, the finished product is shown to the class. For contrast, the commercial tape that accompanies the filmstrip should also be played. Classes have often pronounced the students' work superior to the original.

The children involved in this production learn to organize their ideas according to the pattern of the frames of the filmstrip. Creativity is required to rise to the challenge of fitting new ideas into a prescribed format. In addition to writing a new tale, the students must devise a method of signaling frame advance and find and record suitable background music and sound effects. They must also pace their story so that the frames are not advanced too rapidly.

In the course of this activity, students learn the importance of clear speech. The first playback of their tape is invariably garbled, full of unintentional pauses, and too fast to be listened to comfortably. After three or four attempts, a satisfactory tape is achieved.

At the conclusion of the activity, file the students' recording with the original filmstrip. Teachers may use it as an example for future classes. The filmstrip and student tape can also be shown without comment to an unsuspecting class to see what kind of reaction results.

HOLDING THE FAVORITE BOOK CONTEST*

One stimulating way to overcome the January doldrums is to have a contest in which students choose their favorite books. This enjoyable contest will provide many students with added motivation for reading. It is not a contest in which literary excellence is necessarily a factor. Unlike the Newbery and Caldecott awards, which are chosen by adults for children, these titles are chosen by the children themselves. The only requirements are that the book is available in the school media center and that the child really likes it.

---

* Based on an article by Ruth Toor that appeared in *School Media Quarterly* 5:55 (Fall 1976).

MATERIALS:

—posters prepared by students in this month's Library Art Activity
—ballots run off on different colored ditto paper
—notices to classrooms announcing the contest (on ditto paper)
—medals made of 3¼″ round paper discs, three different colors of foil, rubber cement, and self-stick stars
—a 13″ × 33″ × 9″ foil-covered shadow box with a 3″ × 13″ sign stapled to the top
—notices to students announcing the winners (on mimeo paper)
—letters to the award-winning authors (optional)

PREPARATION:

About two weeks before the contest:

1. Decide how to divide the students in your school into groups. One way is to divide them by grade level into three teams: first and second grades (primary team), third and fourth grades (middle team), and fifth and sixth grades (upper team). Then run three separate contests. The teams will use different colored ballots. They can therefore vote in the same ballot box yet remain easily distinguishable.

2. Run off the ballots on your ditto machine. The ballots should contain spaces for the title of the book and the name of the author. Send the correct number of ballots to each classroom teacher so that each student gets only one vote.

My favorite library book is:
Title
Author

3. Along with the ballots, send out notices to each classroom telling when and where voting will take place and when results will be announced. (For sample notice, see next page.) Balloting should last an entire week, with an extra day at the beginning of the following week for make-up voting by students who were absent. Announce the results as soon as possible while the students' interest is still high.

4. Set up a bulletin board in the media center calling attention to the contest. Attach a ballot box to the bulletin board or place one nearby. (See this month's Bulletin Board section.)

5. Take time to discuss the contest with each class in the school. This way you will know that every child is aware of the contest and is thinking about it.

6. Collect the posters made by students to advertise the contest and place them throughout the school.

7. Arrange with the art teacher to work with the fifth and sixth grade students to make Book Award medals that will be placed on all copies of the winning books. These medals should be 3¼″ round discs that bear the legend "School Name Book Award, 19—." The students should decorate them with original

Notice Announcing the Favorite Book Contest

January 14, 19—

It's almost time for our third annual Southern Boulevard Book Award Contest in which each student votes for his or her favorite title.

There will be a separate contest for each team, and voting will take place in the media center during the week of January 24 to 28 on special ballots (green for the upper team, blue for the middle team, and yellow for the primary team) to be distributed to the classes beforehand. Any student who is absent during that week can vote on Monday, January 31.

Ballots will be counted, and the winning titles will be announced on February 4. They will be on display in the media center with their very own 19— Southern Boulevard Book Award Medals designed by our upper team students.

Since children will be voting for their favorite books, the list of winners, which will be distributed to everyone after the contest, should encourage additional interest in reading.

I would like to speak to each class about the contest for just a few minutes next week, and I will be contacting you individually to set a time convenient to you and to find out whether you would like your class to vote individually or as a group.

Thank you for your cooperation in making this contest a pleasant experience for all our students.

Ruth Toor

artwork. (See facing page.) Try to get approximately three medals from each upper grade student. You and the art teacher can choose the best ones, making sure that everything is spelled correctly. You will need about forty, depending on how many copies of each winning book you have. The medals are then mounted with rubber cement on slightly larger discs. Use a different color for each team, such as gold for primary, blue for middle, and green for upper. A star can be pasted on a medal to denote that a book has won first place.

PROCEDURE:

During the week of the contest:

1. Students cast ballots throughout the week.
2. You should remove ballots from the ballot box each day and keep a private running total. This is a good time to pull possible winners off the shelf. Be sure to keep this operation top secret.
3. At the close of the make-up voting day, prepare the final tally and ready the winning titles for display.

Spotlighting the winners:

1. Compile a list of winning titles, runners up, and books receiving more than one vote. Make a separate list for each team. Duplicate each list, making enough copies so that there is one for each child on the team. The lists should be distributed to the classrooms promptly. Students can learn about the winners and can refer to their lists for additional reading suggestions.

2. Affix the medals beneath the clear vinyl jacket covers of all copies of the winning books. (Generally, there are three or four winning titles for each team.) This is a good time to re-cover the books. If a book does not have a dust jacket, place the medal on top of the cover and put transparent tape over it for protection. If you have any paperback copies of the winning titles, affix medals to them and put them on display with the other books.

3. Set up a display of the winning titles in the media center. Place the first place winners in the shadow box (see illustration) and arrange the other winners around the box. Let the books remain on display for one week so that all of the children can see the winning books and discover if their medals are on any of them. At this point you can begin taking reserves (see the November Volunteers section) for the books that are likely to be extremely popular. Try to have multiple copies of the winning titles on hand.

Additional suggestions:

1. You might write to the author of each winning book in care of the publishers and ask if he or she will autograph the winner if you send a copy. Most authors will graciously comply.

2. Use the letters and responses as the subject of a follow-up bulletin board.

Storytelling Suggestions

FOLK AND FAIRY TALES

Folk tales and fairy tales are assigned the same Dewey decimal number. The distinctions between them are frequently hazy; yet we would not think of *The Jack Tales* as anything but a folk tale and *Cinderella* as anything but a fairy tale. Folk tales are usually part of an oral tradition; they have evolved through many years and many tellers. Fairy tales often have a single known author and may be populated with fairies, elves, and gnomes.

Folk Tales

Before beginning a folk tale, talk about its origins—what country it came from and how it was passed down from generation to generation. After the tale has been read, ask the children if it reminded them of any special characteristics of the country and its people.

Here are some favorite short folk tales that you might enjoy sharing with your classes. Each one takes about ten minutes to read aloud. Be sure to allow time for discussion.

Aardema, Verna *Why Mosquitoes Buzz in People's Ears*
illus. by Leo and Diane Dillon
Dial Press, 1975

This West African folk tale tells how a chain reaction is set off when Mosquito tells Python a silly tale. It is the 1976 Caldecott Medal winner. (first and second grade)

Bernstein, Margery and *The First Morning*
Janet Kobrin illus. by Enid Warner Romanek
Scribner's, 1976

A mouse, a spider, and a fly must perform three very complicated tasks before they can bring light to earth from the sky king. This African myth is accompanied by stunning black and white illustrations. (first and second grade)

Bang, Betsy *The Old Woman and the Red Pumpkin*
illus. by Molly Garrett Bang
Macmillan, 1975

In this Bengali folk tale, an old woman outwits a bear, a tiger, and a jackal who all want to eat her. (first to third grade)

De Paola, Tomie *Strega Nona*
Prentice-Hall, 1975

In this Italian folk tale, big Anthony fools with Strega Nona's magic pasta pot, and the village is inundated with pasta when he doesn't know the secret words to shut it off. (second and third grade)

Domanska, Janina *The Turnip*
Macmillan, 1969

A classic Russian folk tale about an enormous turnip that proves to be almost impossible to harvest. (first and second grade)

Maestro, Giulio *The Tortoise's Tug of War*
Bradbury, 1971

A tortoise tricks a whale and a tapir into believing that he is the strongest animal and can pull them into the sea in this folk tale from South America. (second grade)

Mosel, Arlene *Tikki Tikki Tembo*
illus. by Blair Lent
Holt, Rinehart & Winston, 1968

This Chinese folk tale demonstrates why Chinese firstborn sons are no longer given "grand long names." (first and second grade)

Say, Allen   *Once Under the Cherry Blossom Tree*
                                    Harper & Row, 1974

A wicked old landlord swallows a cherry pit, and a cherry tree grows through
the top of his head in this folk tale from Japan. (third and fourth grade)

Stalder, Valerie   *Even the Devil Is Afraid of a Shrew*
                                    adapted by Ray Broekel; illus. by Richard Brown
                                    Addison-Wesley, 1972

A peaceful man who has a complaining and shrewish wife loses his patience,
and his wife ends up with the devil. This folk tale from Lapland is accompanied
by stylized illustrations. (second and third grade)

Wolkstein, Diane   *Lazy Stories*
                                    illus. by James Marshall
                                    Seabury, 1976

Three tales about lazy people from Japan, Mexico, and Laos—plus tips for
storytellers—can be found in this book. (third and fourth grade)

Fairy Tales

Andersen, Hans Christian   *The Nightingale*
                                    trans. by Eva Le Gallienne
                                    illus. by Nancy Ekholm Burkert
                                    Harper & Row, 1965

Mention that Hans Christian Andersen told his stories to groups of Danish
children, occasionally holding one or two of them on his lap. Explain some of
the unusual words, such as chamberlain and courtiers, and describe what a
nightingale looks like and its reputation as a singer. Three sessions are needed
to complete this tale. During the first session, read until the nightingale is
invited to the court. During the second session, read until the nightingale is
banished. Complete the tale during the third session. Ask the children if they
think Andersen believed that mechanical things were not good? Also ask them,
"What is the great gift that the nightingale gives the Emperor of China?"
(fourth grade and up)

Grimm, Jakob   *The Fisherman and His Wife*
                                    adapted and illus. by Margot Zemach
                                    Norton, 1966

This classic tale of a woman who was not satisfied is illustrated in brown and
blue. Ask the students who was at fault in the story. After they tell you "the
wife," ask if anyone else was at fault and why. New responses will include
"the husband" (he knew it was wrong and still asked) and "the fish" (he led
them on). (first to fourth grade)

Johnson, A. E. (translator)   *Perrault's Complete Fairy Tales*
                                    illus. by W. Heath Robinson
                                    Dodd, Mead, 1961

Before beginning this fairy tale, tell the children you will read a story that they
all know but that they do not realize is really a French fairy tale. Explain that
the tale has been changed and adapted for movies and cartoons and that, as
a result, they do not really know the story. Then read "Cinderella." At the
conclusion, have the students discuss differences between the version just
read and the version with which they are familiar. (first to fourth grade)

Segal, Lore (translator)   *The Juniper Tree*
                                illus. by Maurice Sendak
                                Farrar, Straus & Giroux, 1973

The pen-and-ink illustrations are marvelous but small, which makes it difficult to use them with large groups. Select one or two tales for your storytelling session; many students will quickly borrow the book and be able to enjoy the stories and illustrations on their own. Try "The Golden Bird" since few students are familiar with it. If the students are familiar with fairy tales, ask them, "What are some of the traditional elements in this tale and what are some of the variations?" Ask classes without this background if it is fair that the fox continued to help the youngest brother. While listening to the students' opinions, you can point out traditional elements in the story. (third grade and up)

Teaching Unit

BASIC LIBRARY SKILLS

This unit is taught in six weeks and is designed for about the third and fourth grade levels. Each session lasts approximately 45 minutes and should be attended by the classroom teacher if possible. This is a particularly successful unit. Everyone enjoys it immensely and has such a good time that both teachers and students have commented that they are sorry to see it end. Since the same unit can be adapted to several grade levels, you can reassure children in the lower grades that they will have the chance to do it again. It may seem somewhat unbelievable when students stop you in the hall and beg for another book scavenger hunt, but that is the usual overwhelming reaction to this unit. Even students who are discipline problems respond well.

OBJECTIVES:

At the conclusion of this unit students should be able to:

1. Distinguish between fiction and nonfiction.
2. Explain the difference between the shelf arrangements for fiction and nonfiction.
3. Explain the Dewey Decimal Classification System in terms of its subject arrangement.
4. Identify a call number on a book spine.
5. Use a call number to locate a book on the shelf.
6. Know the location of a call number on a catalog card.
7. Use the card catalog as a source of information on books in the media center.
8. Distinguish among title, author, and subject cards.

MATERIALS:

—ditto master and copies of pretest
—filmstrip on organization of a media center, for example:
   Using the Elementary School Library "Exploring the Library" (Society for Visual Education)

Books and More: Library Media Center "Getting to Know the Library Media Center" (ACI Media)
—transparency of fiction arrangement
—transparency of nonfiction arrangement
—transparency of catalog card with two overlays
—60 strips of 11" × 2" posterboard
—ditto master and copies of scavenger hunt
—ditto master and copies of post-test

PREPARATION:

Two weeks before session 1:

1. Run off copies of pretest. (See sample pretest below.)

LIBRARY SKILLS PRETEST

Matching

1. _____ Fiction
2. _____ Nonfiction
3. _____ Biography
4. _____ Dewey Decimal System
5. _____ Card Catalog
6. _____ Call Number
7. _____ Audio-Visual Materials
8. _____ Author
9. _____ Title
10. _____ Illustrator
11. _____ Reference Books
12. _____ Alphabetical Order
13. _____ Numerical Order
14. _____ Subject Card
15. _____ Title Card
16. _____ Author Card

A. Someone who writes a book
B. Arranged in number order
C. Filmstrips, Records, Tapes, etc.
D. Books that are true
E. Name of a book
F. Books that are not true
G. Someone who draws pictures for a book
H. Catalog card with title on the top line
I. Arranged according to the ABC's
J. Catalog card with author's name on the top line
K. Letters and numbers that give a book's location
L. Catalog card with subject on the top line
M. Books that may not be borrowed from the media center (encyclopedias)
N. Way of arranging books on shelves to keep subjects together
O. Book about someone's life
P. Index to what is in the media center

2. Send filmstrip to classroom teacher, allowing time for teacher to become familiar with the material in it.
3. Begin preparation of posterboard strips for the catalog card game. It is a time-consuming process and is best begun early.

a. On each strip, write an author, a title, or a subject as it appears on the top line of a catalog card. (See illustration below.)
b. Be sure that all selections are actually in your card catalog.
c. Include examples of special library problems, such as authors' names beginning with *Mc* and titles beginning with numbers or with the words *A*, *An*, or *The*.

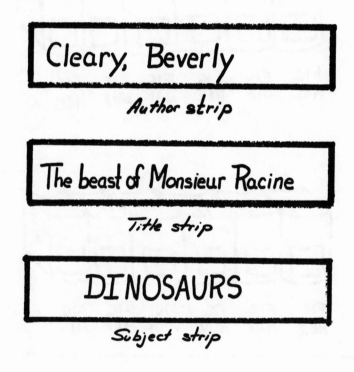

Cleary, Beverly

Author strip

The beast of Monsieur Racine

Title strip

DINOSAURS

Subject strip

One week before session 1:

1. Make a transparency showing the shelf arrangement of fiction books. This need not be a permanent transparency. Simply sketch two shelves of six books each on a sheet of acetate. Below each shelf write six call numbers in incorrect order. (See illustration at top of page 140.)
2. Make a transparency showing the shelf arrangement of nonfiction books. This, too, need not be permanent. (See illustration at bottom of page 140.)
3. Make a transparency of a catalog card with two overlays. On a sheet of 8½" × 11" unlined paper draw a 3" × 5" catalog card. Type or write the information that is found on an author card. Choose a card that lists at least two subject headings and an illustrator. Lay a second sheet of 8½" × 11" paper over the first and place the sheets on an overhead projector. Write the title of the book as it would be found on a title card on the top sheet of paper. This will be the first overlay. Lay another sheet of paper over the first and prepare one subject entry. All three sheets should then go through a thermal copier to form permanent transparencies. Mount the author card transparency and hinge on the overlays, one on each side. (See illustration on page 141.)

Fiction Shelf Arrangement

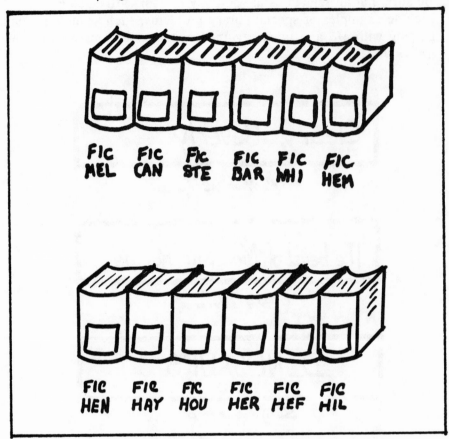

FIC
MEL   FIC
CAN   FIC
STE   FIC
BAR   FIC
NHI   FIC
HEM

FIC
HEN   FIC
HAY   FIC
HOU   FIC
HER   FIC
HEF   FIC
HIL

Nonfiction Shelf Arrangement

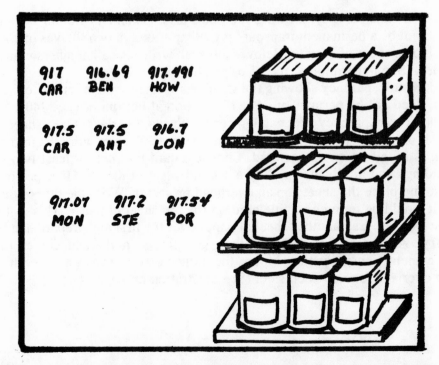

917
CAR   916.69
BEN   917.491
HOW

917.5
CAR   917.5
ANT   916.7
LON

917.07
MON   917.2
STE   917.54
POR

CATALOG CARD TRANSPARENCY
WITH TWO OVERLAYS

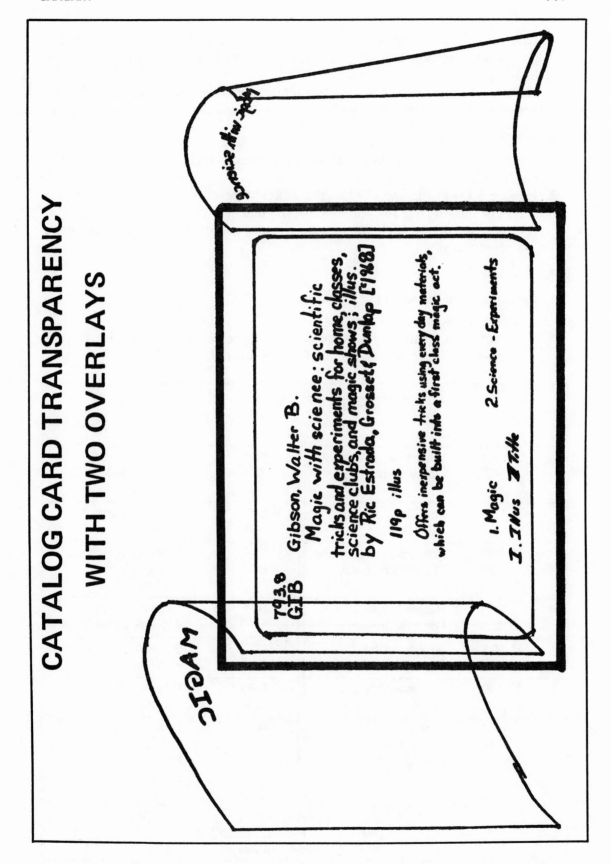

with my science

MAGIC

793.8
GIB

Gibson, Walter B.
Magic with science: scientific
tricks and experiments for home, classes,
science clubs, and magic shows; illus.
by Ric Estrada, Grosset & Dunlap [1968]

119p   illus

Offers inexpensive tricks using every day materials,
which can be built into a first class magic act.

1. Magic   2. Science - Experiments
I. Illus   II. Title

4. Give the teacher the pretest to distribute to the students. The pretest is usually given immediately before the first class, but it can be given as much as a week in advance.

5. Have an overhead projector and transparency markers ready for use with the fiction shelf transparency.

Before session 2:

1. Choose ten to twelve fiction shelves and rearrange them so that the books are not in order.

2. Prepare a list of the shelves and the difficulty level of each shelf. Make two copies of the list: one for you, one for the teacher.

3. Have the nonfiction shelf transparency, transparency markers, and overhead projector ready.

Before session 3:

1. Begin work on the scavenger hunt.

   a. Pull 45 books from the shelves.
   b. Select books carefully so that lists of three levels of difficulty can be prepared. (See following sample lists for levels I, II, and III.)

LIBRARY SKILLS SCAVENGER HUNT			
Level I			
1. FIC WOO	Woolridge, Rhoda Hannah's brave year	8. 581 ZIM	Zim, Herbert S. What's inside of plants
2. 172 LEA	Leaf, Munro Fair play	9. 677 ADL	Adler, Irving Fibers
3. 292 HAW	Hawthorne, Nathaniel The golden touch	10. 736 ROT	Rottger, Ernst Creative wood design
4. 389 BER	Berger, Melvin For good measure	11. 811 UPD	Updike, John A child's calendar
5. 397 HOR	Hornby, John Gypsies	12. 920 SUL	Sullivan, George Hockey heroes
6. 400 ALE	Alexander, Arthur The magic of words	13. 985 BLE	Bleeker, Sonia The Inca
7. 540 FRE	Freeman, Mae The story of chemistry	14. B FERMI	Epstein, Sam Enrico Fermi; father of atomic power
BONUS			
598.1 HAR	Harris, Louise Dyer Slim Green		

LIBRARY SKILLS SCAVENGER HUNT					
Level II					
1.	FIC SMU	Smucker, Barbara C. Wigwam in the city	8.	629.2 STE	Stevens, Leonard The trucks that haul by night
2.	133.4 WIL	Wilkins, Frances Wizards and witches	9.	634.9 HUR	Hurd, Edith Thatcher This is the forest
3.	292 TUR	Turska, Krystna Pegasus	10.	791.3 FEN	Fenner, Mildred Sandison The circus, lure and legend
4.	353.2 COO	Cooke, David C. Your Treasury Department	11.	895.6 BAR	Baron, Virginia Olsen The seasons of time
5.	420.7 GLA	Glaus, Marlene From thoughts to words	12.	918.1 SEE	Seegers, Kathleen Brazil
6.	551.3 POO	Poole, Lynn Danger! Icebergs ahead	13.	979.4 DOL	Dolan, Edward F. Disaster, 1906
7.	591.1 POD	Podendorf, Illa Toby on the move	14.	B SEATTLE	Montgomery, Elizabeth Chief Seattle
BONUS					
	636.59 WHI	Whitehouse, Arch Heroic pigeons			

LIBRARY SKILLS SCAVENGER HUNT					
Level III					
1.	001.6 JON	Jones, Weyman Computer: the mind stretcher	4.	384.09 FOS	Foster, G. Allen Communication: from primitive tom-tom to Telstar
2.	154.6 KET	Kettelkamp, Larry Dreams	5.	551.4 GOE	Goetz, Delia Grasslands
3.	294.3 SER	Serage, Nancy The prince who gave up a throne	6.	591.973 STO	Stoutenburg, Adrien Animals at bay

7. 595.79 MYR	Myrick, Mildred Ants are fun	11. 915.96 TOO	Tooze, Ruth Cambodia: land of contrasts
8. 621.909 LIB	Liberty, Gene The first book of tools	12. 973.75 PRA	Pratt, Fletcher The Monitor and the Merrimac
9. 796.33 NEW	Newcombe, Jack The game of football	13. B DOUGLASS	Davidson, Margaret Frederick Douglass fights for freedom
10. 821.08 BRE	Brewton, Sara Laughable limericks	14. REF 453 CAS	Cassell's Italian dictionary Italian- English, English- Italian

BONUS

915.694 RUT   Rutland, Jonathan
Looking at Israel

BOOK SLIPS FOR SCAVENGER HUNT

FIC SMU	Smucker, B C Wigwam in the city	133.4 WIL	Wilkins, F Wizards and witches	292 TUR	Turska, Krystna Pegasus

353.2 COO	Cooke, D C Your Treasury Department	420.7 GLA	Glaus, M From thoughts to words	551.3 POO	Poole, Lynn Danger! Icebergs ahead

c. Prepare ditto masters of the lists. Run off enough copies for the students.

d. Prepare about eight ditto masters containing six 2½″ × 4″ "book slips" each. (See illustration on facing page.) Run off copies of book slips and include blank slips in case you run out during the hunt. The book slips (containing author, title, and call number) will be placed in the appropriate book pockets before the scavenger hunt. There should be enough slips in each book for all students working at that level.

2. Choose ten to twelve nonfiction shelves with books that are relatively simple to arrange. Rearrange the shelves so that the books are not in order.

3. Prepare a list of the shelves and the difficulty level of each shelf. Make two copies of the list: one for you, one for the teacher.

Before session 4:

1. Choose ten to twelve more difficult nonfiction shelves and rearrange them. See Procedure: Session 4 for suggestions on choosing the shelves.

2. Prepare a list of the shelves and the difficulty level of each shelf. Make two copies of the list: one for you, one for the teacher.

Before session 5:

1. Run off copies of the three scavenger hunt lists.

2. Cut out the book slips and insert them in the book pockets of the appropriate books. (See illustration below.)

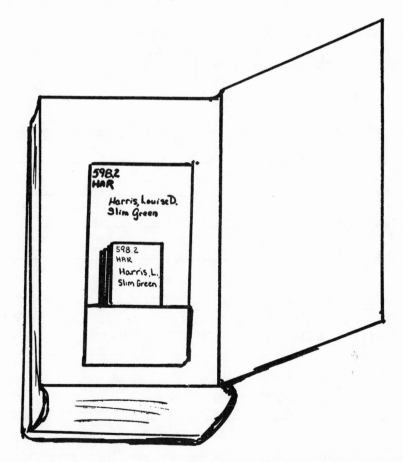

3. Have the 60 posterboard strips ready for the catalog card game.
4. Have permanent transparency on the card catalog, transparency markers, and overhead projector ready.

Before session 6:

1. Run off copies of post-test. Page one of the post-test can be the same as the pretest. A second page gauging proficiency in use of the card catalog should be added. (See sample post-test below.)

LIBRARY SKILLS POST-TEST

```
                 BRIDGES
      624        Goldwater, Daniel
      GOL            Bridges and how they are built; illus by
                 Harvey Weiss. Young Scott Books
                 c1965

                 72p illus maps

                     1.  Bridges   2.  Building, iron and steel
                 I.  Illus   II  Title
```

Use the above catalog card to answer the questions.

1. The call number of this book is [   ]

2. The author is _____.

3. The title is _____.

4. The illustrator is _____.

5. The publisher is _____.

6. The copyright date is _____.

7. Illus means _____.

SUPER TOUGH QUESTIONS

8. The above card is (choose the correct letter) _____, a. a title card   b. an author card   c. a subject card because _____
_____.

9. Another subject heading for this book is _____
_____.

2. Shelve all 45 books named on the scavenger hunt lists about one hour before the class meets. You can then be reasonably certain that the books are in order.

After session 6:

1. Give teacher copies of post-test to administer to the class.
2. Give posterboard strips used in catalog card game to the classroom teacher to be used in follow-up activities.
3. Plan to meet with the teacher for an informal evaluation session. Discuss ways of making the unit more effective. This might involve suggestions for continuing library skill activities.

PROCEDURE:

Session 1—Introduction:

In this introduction you will find out what students remember from previous teaching units and what knowledge they have acquired through use of the media center. Since this first session does not require much in the way of active participation by the students, it is the most difficult. Try to communicate the excitement of unlocking the mysteries of the media center. You can tell the students that in six weeks they will know where everything is and will understand why the shelves are arranged the way they are.

Discuss the following terms with the students:

fiction	nonfiction	reference	biography
autobiography	call numbers	spine labels	media

Bring the name of Melvil Dewey to the attention of the class and discuss the problem of how to arrange books so that you can find them when you want them. Melvil's system—which brought forth order from chaos—should be simply but dramatically explained. This way, the Dewey Decimal Classification System will remain part of the students' awareness. The one point you must stress is that the Dewey Decimal Classification System is a method of arranging books in numerical order to keep them together according to their *subject*.

Follow this explanation with a brief discussion of fiction shelf arrangement and then show the students the fiction shelf transparency. The transparency is divided into two sections. The first section requires single letter alphabetizing. The second section, in which all of the call numbers begin with the same letter, is more complicated.

Both of the shelves shown in the transparency have books with blank spine labels. The call numbers of the books are given below each shelf in incorrect order. Have the students use transparency markers to fill in the labels so that the call numbers are arranged in correct sequence. Obviously, students will have a little more trouble with the second part. But even those who seem to understand alphabetical order will get confused when they work with the actual books during the next session.

Conclusion: Explain that the students will rearrange some fiction shelves next week. Inform them in all seriousness that their assignment is to study the alphabet. Respond to the resulting laughter by gravely reminding them that they have been warned.

Follow-up: The teacher shows the class the filmstrip on how the library is arranged.

Session 2—Fiction arrangement:

Before the students arrive, rearrange ten to twelve fiction shelves of various levels of difficulty. The teacher divides the class into groups of two or three students of similar abilities. Be sure to give the teacher a list indicating the shelves to be assigned to the students and their level of difficulty. It is now the students' task to arrange the shelves in the correct sequence. Those who have finished their shelves early and have had them checked may look at magazines or borrow books from their shelves.

Conclusion: Congratulate the students and briefly review some of the problems encountered. Discuss the nonfiction shelf arrangement. This segment takes about 15 minutes. Since the students have yet to learn decimals, the following points should be stressed:

1. The numbers on the books are arranged column by column, starting with the hundreds column. For example, first check to see if all books on the shelf are 500's. That is the first column. Then see if all books are 520's. Stress that this rule also applies to numbers after the decimal point.
2. Read a number such as 535.92 as "five thirty-five point nine two" (*not* ninety-two).

Now show the students the nonfiction shelf transparency. As with the fiction transparency, the spine labels are blank and the call numbers of the books are given in incorrect order. Use a transparency marker to fill in the call numbers in correct sequence as the students give you the answers. As they call out the answers, be sure that they read the decimals correctly. Remind the students again that the Dewey Decimal Classification System keeps books together by subject.

Explain next week's activity and tell the students that their assignment is to review the alphabet and to count from one to ten!

Session 3—Nonfiction arrangement (part 1):

Group the students the same as during the previous session. The rearranged nonfiction shelves should be fairly simple, and only a few call numbers should have more than one numeral after the decimal point. Again, there should be several levels of difficulty. Before the students go to the shelves, quickly review nonfiction arrangement and remind them of the column-by-column rule. Also remind them that the Dewey Decimal Classification System keeps books together by subject.

Conclusion: Congratulate the group on a job well done and discuss any problems encountered. Usually several students forget the column-by-column rule when it comes to putting it into practice. If there is time, ask several students what kinds of books were on their shelves. This reinforces the subject orientation of the Dewey System. Explain that next week they will again rearrange nonfiction shelves, but that the shelves will be much more difficult.

Session 4—Nonfiction arrangement (part 2):

Students are grouped as before. Again give a short review of nonfiction shelf arrangement. This time the students' responses will be quicker because they know what is expected. They will still make errors when they get to the shelves, which is why this "hands-on" approach is so successful. The shelves should be more difficult, with the hardest shelves having six-digit numbers. Shelves in the 620's and the 910's are good choices.

Conclusion: Discuss the problems encountered, and congratulate the students on mastering a difficult skill. Briefly mention the next week's activities.

Session 5—Introduction to the card catalog:

This can be a difficult lesson. The students are excited by the activities of the three previous weeks and are not eager to sit and listen. In order to calm them, hint that they will be playing a game at the end of the discussion. Highlight the fact that the card catalog is an index to the media center, that media are listed as well as books, and that the arrangement is alphabetical. You can show the catalog card transparency with two overlays so that students see how an author card "magically" becomes a title card or a subject card. Place emphasis on the fact that a top line made up entirely of capital letters indicates a subject card.

The parts of a catalog card are then explored. Ask questions rather than lecturing. For example, ask what "illus." and "c.1968" mean. You can tell students that you are going to teach them a trick for finding additional subject headings and then point out the tracing on the bottom of the card. Give a transparency marker to a student who has figured out a second heading. Have the student print the proper heading above the author card. This accomplishes two things: it reinforces the concept of the main entry and the fact that subject headings are written entirely in capital letters. After this brief introduction to the card catalog, end the class on an upbeat by playing the catalog card game.

Catalog card game: The students are divided into three groups and seated in three circles. The author, title, and subject posterboard strips are shuffled, and 20 assorted strips are placed face down in the center of each circle. Silently, the students take turns reading a strip and placing it in an author, title, or subject pile. At the end of the game, discuss the errors made by each group.

Conclusion: Explain the next week's activities

Follow-up: The classroom teacher gives one posterboard strip to each student. Students who have a title strip will go to the media center and find the author and call number. Those who have an author strip will find one title by the author and give its call number. Those who have subject strips will choose one card with that subject heading and give the author, title, and call number. By doing the follow-up activity, students will learn how to actually use the card catalog.

Session 6—Scavenger hunt:

Begin your preparation in advance by pulling the 45 books from the shelves and by preparing scavenger hunt lists and book slips. Just before the class comes in, shelve all of the books.

With slower classes, the scavenger hunt can take as long as an hour. If you cannot schedule that much time, reduce the number of titles in the hunt to ten. Then have a list of "Super Puzzlers" available for the early birds.

The students are divided into groups, and each student is given a list at the appropriate difficulty level. Each child must silently locate the books on his or her list. As soon as a book is located, the student removes one of the book slips and replaces the book on the shelf in the proper location. (This is where you will have to supervise. If it is reported that a book is not where it should be, stop the activities of the appropriate group and send those who have already located the title to search for it.) After collecting 15 book slips, the student shows them to the library media specialist or the teacher. A prize may be given to the first child in each group to complete the scavenger hunt.

> *Note:* Avoid having students in the same group crowd around one of the shelves. If this occurs, quietly move some of the group members to other areas of the room. There is no reason why students should have to find their titles in any particular sequence.

Conclusion: Congratulate all of the students on a job well done. Now that they have learned the fundamentals, all that is needed is practice. Let the class know that you, too, are sorry the unit is over, but that you are looking forward to the students continuing to use the media center in the course of their class work. Remind them that you expect that they will never shelve any books incorrectly since they are now all experts.

Follow-up: The classroom teacher should follow up this session with the two-part post-test described earlier.

Professional Responsibilities

PREVIEWS OF MEDIA

Most library media specialists must operate within a limited media budget. Despite the increasing demands made upon the library to function as a *media* center, finances do not always take into account the prices of filmstrips, loops, multi-media kits, and the accompanying paraphernalia. If you are one of the fortunate library media specialists who may order at will, it is a simple matter to make decisions and order materials. If the materials are not what you expected, most companies will exchange them for something that will prove more satisfactory.

Selections for purchase will be based on curriculum needs, reviewing tools, and producers' catalogs. To minimize the number of exchanges you need, it is helpful to order material for preview or "on approval" whenever possible. On approval orders follow the same procedures as those discussed for previews, except that you must send a purchase order with the on approval request. If you decide the material is a good addition and wish to purchase it, you simply keep it and the company bills you as usual. Should your ordering policy permit you to order this way, you can frequently take advantage of money-saving offers and have needed material on hand long before any reviews of it appear.

If you cannot purchase on approval, getting material for preview is an excellent idea. Producers often send special order cards announcing their most recent releases. In addition, producers' catalogs often indicate if previews are available. Materials can generally be previewed for a period of thirty days. If your teachers are going to use these materials with a class, remind them to take proper care of them. It is essential that preview materials be returned in salable condition; for financial reasons (you are responsible for the condition of the material) as well as out of common courtesy, extra precautions should be taken.

If previews are to be of service when you prepare your orders, you must keep a record of the reactions of the evaluators. A simple Media Evaluation Form should be given to the teacher along with the material to be previewed. (See sample form.)

MEDIA EVALUATION FORM

Type (Filmstrip, Tape) _____ Producer _____

Title _____ Length _____

Grade Level _____ Subject Areas _____, _____, _____

	Poor	Fair	Good	Excellent
Accuracy				
Technical Quality				
Student Response				
Currency				
Relevance to Curriculum				
Quality of Manual				
Overall Rating				

Comments: _____

_____

_____

_____

Check One:

_____ We must have this!!

_____ It would help.

_____ Forget it!!

Evaluator's Signature _____

Date _____

_____

Date returned to producer _____

Purchase Priority _____ Funding under which purchased _____

Catalog No. _____ Price _____

To make things as easy as possible, the title, copyright date, catalog number, and price should be entered on the form before it is given to the teacher.

At the end of the thirty days, check to be sure that everything is in proper condition. It is thoughtful to include a thank you note when you return the materials. (See sample note.) Although the producers are very understanding if material is kept slightly longer than the alloted time, it is not professional to abuse the terms to which you agreed. One cautionary note: Do insure the preview material when you ship it. You are liable for the cost if it is lost in the mail.

Gentlemen:

Thank you for giving us the opportunity to see this material on approval. We will certainly consider it when we prepare our purchase order.

Very truly yours,

Hilda K. Weisburg
Library Media Specialist

Volunteers

OVERDUE MATERIAL

Material borrowed by students is generally filed behind the date that it is due, so it is easy to tell by a glance at the calendar when something is overdue. It is usually a week or two from the date the book is due before the student receives an overdue notice. Generally, fines are not charged. Charges are incurred only in the case of lost or excessively damaged books.

To prepare overdue notices, remove all cards behind the week-old date. The shelves are then checked against the cards to be sure that the material has not been accidentally shelved without the cards. Once it has been established that these books are still missing, lists are made by classes. The names of the students in the class, the books they have borrowed, and the date the books were due are listed. The lists are sent to the appropriate teacher who then informs the students.

An alternative to this plan is to send individual notices to each student involved. This way, the teacher can simply pass out the notices to students in his or her classroom. If this is done, a master list of students by grade and room is kept at the circulation desk. This enables you to quickly inform any student who wants to know if he or she owes any overdue books without having to check through the entire card file.

You may want to file the book cards behind a card labeled "first notice." Second notices are sent to the classrooms one week later if any materials have still not been returned. The same procedure of checking the shelves and compiling class-room lists or individual notices plus a master list is followed. The book cards are then filed behind a card labeled "second notice." One week after the second notice, third notices are sent. The same procedure is followed as before.

As overdue books come in, volunteers should pull out the master list and cross off the titles and the names of the students who charged them out. The names can be easily located by checking the student's homeroom on the book card as it is slipped. Keeping this list as up-to-the-minute as possible until a new one is compiled is helpful to both the library media specialist and the students, for everyone concerned can tell at any time who owes what overdue books.

There are several methods for dealing with students after third notices are sent. In some cases, the principal becomes involved; in others, parents are notified. Sometimes the student may be asked to pay for the missing book. The resolution of this problem is for you and your principal to decide.

ACCESSIONING BOOKS

To accession or not to accession is something that you will have to decide. Accession numbers are used to identify and to keep a record of books. Every book has its own accession number that keeps it from getting mixed up with other copies of the same title.

In general, if you have a large number of multiple copies and the books in your media center have been accessioned in the past, you have nothing to lose by continuing to accession. On the other hand, if you are starting a new media center and you don't wish to accession your books, you can differentiate multiple copies by labeling them "copy 1," "copy 2," and "copy 3."

If you decide to accession, first type the author and title of a new book in the accession book next to the first blank accession number. Use an automatic numbering machine to stamp this accession number four times—on the book pocket, on the book card, on the top of the page where the pocket is pasted, and on the shelf list card. Your book is now accessioned, and the automatic numbering machine has saved a great deal of time.

Open End

SHOULD YOU DIVIDE YOUR COLLECTION?

As was noted in the October Professional Responsibilities section, most library media specialists try to limit the amount of original cataloging they must do by ordering commercially processed books. But sometimes commercial processing means dealing with cataloging decisions made by catalogers who are removed from the problems of running a media center. Books below third grade come through classified as *E*. No distinction is made between an easy reader and a picture book. You will find many of these disparities between your needs and commercial processing methods, and there are various approaches to dealing with them.

An easy or beginning reader has a limited vocabulary, follows a specific format regarding size of book, size of type, and number of words to the page, and is designed to be read by children who are just learning to read. Some beginning readers are at the preprimer level; others are at the second grade level. In either case, the intent is to present the children with something they can read and enjoy on their own.

Picture books are less simple to describe. They are primarily designed for children to look at while an adult or older child reads the text. The illustrations are usually the major concern, although there are notable exceptions. Many have complicated plots that are of interest to children in second or third grade. Picture books with very simple vocabularies are meant to be read to very young children. By the time a child can read the text in a picture book, it is below his or her interest level. The dimensions of a picture book vary from the miniscule to the cumbersome. Type size is chosen for its appearance on the page, not necessarily for easy reading.

Obviously, there are several differences between picture books and beginning readers. The question is, what are the library media specialist's alternatives in cataloging and shelving them?

If a decision is made to have separate collections of picture books and beginning readers, an added burden is placed on you and your volunteers. Each book classified as *E* by the jobber must be carefully evaluated. If it is to be shelved with the picture books, corrections must be made on cards and labels. If you request it, many jobbers will send *E* books without any classification. This way, either *E* or *PIC* will have to be added to each book, but erasing is eliminated.

On the positive side, if picture books and easy readers are shelved separately, children can be easily directed to the section where they will find books suited to their reading level. On the negative side is the extra work caused by relabeling. The corrected classification requires a new label that must be typed or printed by hand. Typed labels are difficult to read; hand-printed labels require a volunteer who can print neatly, and a neat printer is not always an easy person to find. Because the new label is put on the outside of the plastic jacket, it must be covered with white paste to prevent it from becoming dirty and illegible.

There is another way in which you might divide your collection. Many beginning readers can be classified as nonfiction. Some catalogers designate these as *E*; others assign the appropriate Dewey decimal number. Another approach is to use both *E* and the Dewey number. This distinction is helpful to children who, from the very beginning, do not enjoy fiction. Slow readers are also helped; many reject the regular *E* books because the illustrations portray children much younger than them selves. Compensatory education teachers are pleased because this method of labeling pinpoints areas in which they can direct students to parallel class work with simpler material. On the other hand, you might reasonably question whether the book collection should be so fragmented that the patron must look in several places to find the material he or she is seeking.

Of course, there are advantages to shelving all books as a single, unified collection. With picture books and beginning readers alongside such titles of 150 to 200 pages as *Treasure Island* or *Johnny Tremain*, there is no stigma attached to the older child who is a poor reader and needs a 30-page easy book while others in the class are tackling 120-page books without illustrations. Anyone can go to the unified shelves for any book without worrying about peer pressure. Older children may want to browse through the titles, read a picture book that they enjoyed at an earlier age, or just reread a Dr. Seuss rhyme. If the collection were separated, these students would hesitate to search among the shelves where the "little children" get books.

One disadvantage of a unified collection—that it is hard for a new reader to find a suitable book among the thousands facing him on the shelves—can be offset if you spotlight a number of picture books and beginning readers daily and display them on a special table or shelf. This way, young children will have some preselected books to look through, and older children will also be able to choose any book that catches their eye.

You must weigh the alternatives. Which approach is best suited to your needs and those of the students? Are the benefits to the various users of the media center sufficient to justify the time, effort, and expense it takes to change classifications already assigned and paid for? Should your collection be split or unified? The ultimate decision is yours.

February

Happy Birthday To...

2   **Rebecca Caudill** (1899)—author
Upbeat stories with a rural setting for third graders, including *Did You Carry the Flag Today, Charley?*

4   **Russell Hoban** (1925)—author
Creator of Frances, a badger whose problems young children identify with

5   **Patricia Lauber** (1924)—author
Intermediate nonfiction books with a science orientation, including *The Restless Earth* and *Earthquakes*

7   **Charles Dickens** (1812)—author
Younger children can be introduced to this noted English writer through *A Christmas Carol* and *The Magic Fishbone*
Laura Ingalls Wilder (1867)—author
Creator of the partly autobiographical Little House series

8   **Jules Verne** (1838)—author
Classic science fiction writer whose books are still enjoyed by upper grade children. Popular titles include *Twenty Thousand Leagues Under the Sea* and *Journey to the Center of the Earth*

9   **Hilda Van Stockum** (1908)—author
Primarily World War II fiction set in the Netherlands and written for upper grades, including *The Winged Watchman*

10   **E. L. Konigsburg** (1930)—author and illustrator
Contemporary stories with suburban and urban settings for upper grade children, including *From the Mixed-Up Files of Mrs. Basil E. Frankweiler* and *About the B'nai Bagels*

Trim the room with red for Valentine's Day and Chinese New Year.

Charles Lamb (1775)—author
Represented on the shelves by *Tales from Shakespeare*

12 **Judy Blume** (1938)—author
Very popular writer of books with relevant contemporary themes about the doubts and problems of preteen boys and girls, including *Are You There God, It's Me, Margaret* and *Blubber*

15 **Norman Bridwell** (1928)—author and illustrator
Creator of Clifford, the pet dog who is bigger than a two-story house. This is for the picture book set.

19 **Louis Slobodkin** (1903)—author and illustrator
Simple illustrations for books by other authors as well as his own picture books, including *Magic Michael*

24 **Wilhelm Karl Grimm** (1786)—author
Younger of the two famous Grimm brothers, collectors of fairy tales

25 **Frank Bonham** (1914)—author
Fiction for upper grades, including *Mystery of the Fat Cat*

27 **Henry Wadsworth Longfellow** (1807)—poet
His works are still used by many teachers as examples of 19th century American poetry.

Uri Shulevitz (1935)—author and illustrator
His different types of illustrated works range from the soft colors of *The Fool of the World and the Flying Ship* to the bold primary colors of *Oh, What a Noise*, which he also wrote.

28 **Sir John Tenniel** (1820)—illustrator
Famous illustrator of *Alice's Adventures in Wonderland*

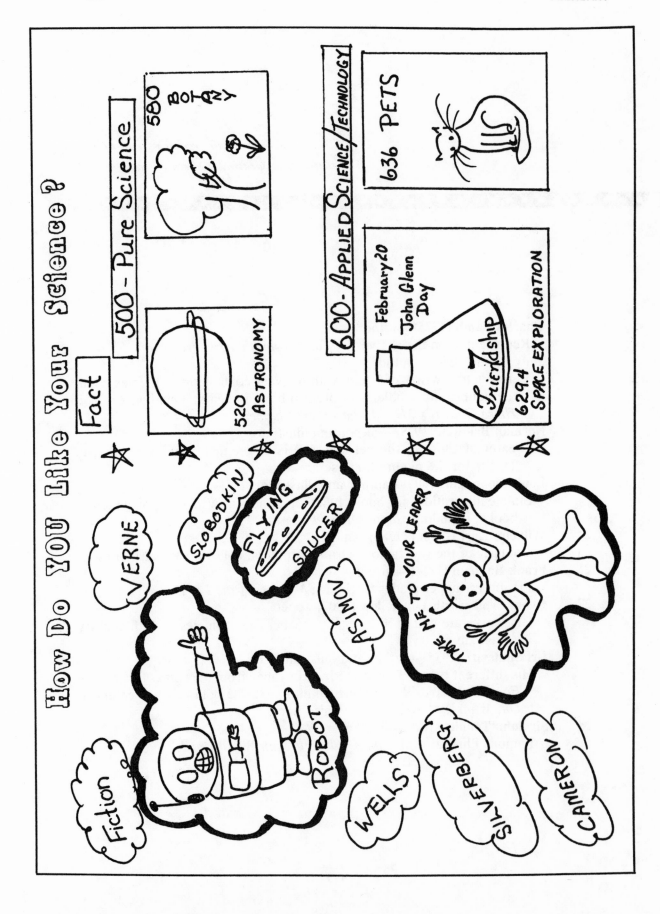

Bulletin Boards

HOW DO YOU LIKE YOUR SCIENCE?

This month's cluttered bulletin board draws attention to science as both fact and fiction. (See illustration.) February marks the birthday of two of the science fiction writers featured on the bulletin board, Jules Verne and Louis Slobodkin. This month is also the anniversary of John Glenn's historic flight in *Friendship 7* on February 20, 1962.

Do try to obtain black posterboard. It suggests outer space and provides a strong contrast for all of the colored cutouts. If it is unavailable, substitute black construction paper.

MATERIALS:

—1 sheet of 22″ × 28″ black posterboard
—1 box of large silver gummed stars
—construction paper in assorted colors including white and light green
—wide-tip and narrow-tip felt markers in assorted colors
—scissors
—rubber cement

PREPARATION:

1. Cut out 1½″ high letters for the title of the bulletin board from the white construction paper.
2. Use felt markers to print "Fact" and "Fiction" on the white construction paper. The letters should be approximately 1¼″ high.
3. Cut out "Fiction" in a balloon shape. Cut out "Fact" in a rectangle.
4. Draw or trace an 8″ tall robot on colored construction paper. Label the drawing "robot." Draw a wavy, broad line in any color but black around the robot and cut it out.
5. Use a dark green marker to draw an 8″ tall Martian on the light green construction paper. Letter "Take Me to Your Leader" above the drawing. Surround the drawing with a wavy, broad line. Cut out the illustration.
6. Draw a flying saucer about 6″ wide and 2″ long. Label it, draw a wavy, broad line around it, and cut it out.
7. Print the names of some of the science fiction authors represented in your collection in 1″ high letters on assorted colors of construction paper. Cut them out in cloud shapes.
8. Print "500-Pure Science" and "600-Applied Science/Technology" in 1″ high letters on white construction paper. Cut these labels out in rectangles.
9. Draw a ringed planet on a 5″ square of construction paper. Label the drawing "520-Astronomy."
10. Draw a simple tree and flower on a 5″ × 7″ piece of construction paper and label it "580-Botany."
11. Draw a model of *Friendship 7* on a 7½″ square piece of construction paper. Be sure to include the date of John Glenn Day and the Dewey decimal number for space exploration.

12. Draw a simple cat or dog on a 7½" × 5" piece of construction paper. Label it "636-Pets."
13. Divide the bulletin board in half by pasting the silver stars down the middle.
14. Arrange the letters, labels, authors, and pictures to your satisfaction and paste them to the black posterboard.

VALENTINE'S DAY

A touch of the poet is always appropriate for Valentine's Day. Make a giant valentine to books and reading. Copy the sentiment from the sample shown or write your own. Follow up the bulletin board with this month's Library Art Activity, and you'll have a literary Valentine's Day.

MATERIALS:

—1 sheet of 22" × 28" red posterboard
—1 large sheet of pink construction paper
—1 large sheet of white construction paper
—1 package of white paper doilies
—large pieces of scrap paper for patterns
—narrow-tip and medium-tip red felt markers
—pencil
—rubber cement
—scissors

PREPARATION:

1. Fold a scrap sheet in half, draw half of a heart along the fold, and cut it out. The completed heart should measure 25″ wide and 20″ long down the middle.
2. Use the heart pattern to cut out a valentine from the pink construction paper.
3. Fold another scrap sheet, draw half of an open book along the fold, and cut it out. The completed book should measure 17″ wide and 14″ long.
4. Use the pattern to cut a book shape from the white construction paper.
5. Use a felt marker to draw a cover and pages on the book.
6. Lightly draw curved lines at the bottom of the book to suggest the open pages.
7. Print the poem lightly with a pencil, using capital letters with curlicues for a romantic effect.
8. Go over the letters with a red marker. Erase the pencil lines.
9. Paste the book onto the heart and the heart onto the posterboard.
10. Cut lace from the doilies. Fold it to fit and paste it around the edge of the heart.

Library Art Activity

A VALENTINE TO AN AUTHOR

Cover the walls of the media center with children's valentines to favorite authors. The display is colorful and will grab the attention of students, suggesting to them new authors and titles. Make a poster such as the one shown on the following page that will encourage the children to design valentines. Be sure that the students realize that it is not necessary for them to prepare a rhyme, but that you are willing to help them compose one. Upper grade students might be introduced to a rhyming dictionary.

Distribute the hearts only after you or the volunteers have seen the completed valentines. Otherwise you will be handing out hearts that will be used for valentines with less "literary" themes.

MATERIALS:

—1 sheet of 11″ × 14″ white posterboard
—scrap paper for use as patterns
—red felt markers
—red and pink construction paper
—scissors

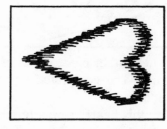

PREPARATION:

1. Fold a sheet of scrap paper, draw half of a heart along the fold, and cut it out. The completed heart should measure 10″ across and 6″ long down the middle.
2. Place the heart on the posterboard. Rub a red marker up and down around the entire outline of the heart, allowing the marker to go off the edge of the paper pattern. (See sketch above.) When you lift the paper heart, there will be a distinct heart shape with a fuzzy edge.

3. Fold another piece of scrap paper, draw half of a heart along the fold, and cut it out. The completed heart should measure 5″ wide and 3½″ long down the middle.

4. Use this heart as a pattern to draw the two hearts at the bottom of the poster.

5. Letter the directions to the students with a red felt marker. If you feel whimsical, make all of the *a*'s and *o*'s in heart shapes.

6. Use another scrap sheet to cut a heart that measures 7¾″ wide and 5″ long down the middle.

7. Have a long-suffering volunteer use the pattern to cut 50 to 75 hearts from pink and red construction paper. This will give you enough hearts to start with, and you can cut more as they are needed.

Library Enrichment Activity

CELEBRATE THE CHINESE NEW YEAR

Add an exotic element to the media center by welcoming the Chinese New Year. How much you get involved in this activity is up to you, your resources, and the interest of the faculty. This can be solely a media center activity consisting of stories (see this month's Storytelling Suggestions) and posters (see illustrations in this section), or it can be expanded to include additional hall decorations, classroom art activities, and experiments in foreign cuisine.

Here is a brief overview of the Chinese New Year. The Chinese, whose noisy celebrations in the Chinatowns of San Francisco and New York attract thousands of tourists, mark the New Year on the second new moon after the winter solstice. Usually this occurs during the first two weeks of February; occasionally the date is in late January. Check the date before you plan the activities. Other Asians such as the Vietnamese also celebrate the New Year at this time. The Chinese calendar follows a 12-year cycle, and each year is designated by a particular animal. Thus, each person was born in the Year of the Rat, the Dragon, or one of the other animals.

The Chinese New Year festivities are exceedingly colorful and are explained in detail in the standard books on customs and holidays as well as in books on China and Hong Kong. There is enough material to enable you to plan the activity completely around Chinese themes, or you might broaden the scope to cover various Asian countries. Ask any Chinese, Vietnamese, or Japanese students in your school to help you with authentic details. In most schools, Asian students are a minority and the curriculum pays little or no attention to their magnificent heritage.

For a simple Chinese New Year activity, you will need a lot of red art materials for posters and long streamers. Red is the color of good luck. It would be helpful to have at least one dragon to frighten away evil spirits. A streamer or poster reading *Gung Hay Fat Choy* (Happy New Year) should be prominently displayed. (See the illustration on page 165.) Exhibit books on Chinese history, geography, and customs. Set up an area for showing filmstrips on China. Do not forget Chinese crafts and fine arts.

One of the major customs associated with this holiday is the giving of red envelopes containing money to children. It is too expensive to have students enjoy this custom, but you can decorate the media center with large red luck envelopes made from folded red construction paper. Instead of money, insert one fact about the Chinese New Year or about another aspect of Chinese culture. This is not as exciting for the children as money would be, but it is educationally sound!

If teachers are interested, plan ahead by beginning preparations in January. Children can decorate the classrooms and halls with Oriental themes. It is likely that at least one teacher will teach students Haiku at this time. Although Chinese calligraphy is a difficult art form as well as a system of writing, interested upper grade students may enjoy copying some words. Felt markers capture the feeling of the brush stroke and are much simpler to use than brushes and ink. Sources for words include general encyclopedias and Kurt Weise's book *You Can Write Chinese* (Viking, 1945).

An excellent culminating activity, to be scheduled at a convenient time during the two week celebration, is allowing the students to cook and eat Chinese food. In the simplest form, all you need are rice, soy sauce to flavor the rice, and chopsticks. An older or more venturesome class can make a stir-fry vegetable dish to accompany the rice.

Stir-Fry Vegetable Recipe

INGREDIENTS:

2 cups fresh bean sprouts (or 1 can)
3 cups bok choy or celery cabbage
1 5 oz. can water chestnuts
1 5 oz. can bamboo shoots (optional, since it is more expensive than the other ingredients)
2 tbsp. vegetable oil

½ tsp. salt
½ tsp. sugar
1 tbsp. soy sauce
2 tbsp. water

PREPARATION:

One hour is needed for a class to prepare this dish.

1. You will need the following kitchen tools: knives, cutting board, strainer, spatula, and a wok or a 10″ skillet.
2. If the bean sprouts are canned, soak them in cold water for a half-hour and drain; if fresh, cover them with cold water, remove the green hulls that float to the surface, and drain.
3. Cut stalks of celery cabbage in half lengthwise, then crosswise diagonally into 1½″ lengths. Separate the stalks from the leafy tops.
4. Drain and slice the water chestnuts.
5. Drain the bamboo shoots.

COOKING:

Four minutes of cooking time is required.

1. Heat the wok or skillet for 30 seconds on a hot burner. Add the oil and swirl it around in the pan for another 30 seconds. Cooking should be done at a high temperature; if the oil begins to smoke, the heat should be lowered.
2. Add the celery cabbage stalks and stir them in the hot oil for two minutes.
3. Add the remaining ingredients and stir-fry them for one more minute. If softer vegetables are preferred, cover the pan for an additional minute or so of cooking. Turn the ingredients every 30 seconds.
4. This recipe yields 20 very small portions. If more food is desired, cook it in two batches. Cooking a double batch at one time will prevent the food from cooking properly.

If students use chopsticks to eat the dish, the atmosphere will be more authentic. If occidental fingers are unable to overcome the complexity of eating with chopsticks, a simple device will allow them to easily use the unfamiliar utensils. Take a paper towel and fold it several times. Put the folded paper between the tops of the two chopsticks. Secure the chopsticks and the towel by tightly wrapping a rubber band around them several times.

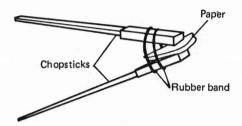

The chopsticks are now in an open position and can function as Oriental tweezers. Pinching the lower ends of the device together with thumb and forefinger will allow the students to eat the meal down to the last grain of rice. If you can find the short Japanese chopsticks, the results will be even more satisfying.

Happy New Year Poster

Try your hand at Chinese and create a Happy New Year poster similar to the one shown. You can use the overhead projector technique described in the October chapter to copy the Chinese letters and the dragon, as well as the English words if you wish. Using felt markers to draw the letters will help to capture the feeling of brush strokes. If you want to try drawing your own dragon, observe that Oriental dragons, unlike Wesern ones, are generally bearded and have flowing manes.

You may decide to convert this poster into a full bulletin board.

MATERIALS:

—1 sheet of 11″ × 14″ red posterboard
—white construction paper
—red and black felt markers
—overhead projector
—crayons or pastels (optional)
—scissors
—rubber cement
—easel back

PREPARATION:

1. Copy the characters for *Gung Hay Fat Choy* on white construction paper. Cut the paper in a strip that measures 3¼″ × 11″ and paste the strip onto the posterboard.
2. Copy or draw a dragon and cut it out. If you wish, color the dragon with vibrant shades of crayon or pastel. Paste it onto the posterboard.
3. Write the letters for Happy New Year on the poster.
4. Attach the posterboard to the easel back and display it alongside the other Oriental materials that you have gathered.

What Is Your Year Poster

Students enjoy discovering in which Chinese year they were born. Make a poster that allows them to look up their own birth year on a Chinese zodiac. (See illustration.) Although many children have some knowledge of the Western zodiac, they are completely unfamiliar with the Chinese one. Note that the name of the animal for the current year is written on a card. This permits you to easily change the animal and use the poster in a future year.

MATERIALS:

—1 sheet of colored posterboard
—1 construction paper circle, 6″ in diameter
—black and red felt markers
—1 paper fastener
—1 piece of 3¼″ × 2″ construction paper
—masking tape
—easel back

PREPARATION:

1. Divide the circle into 12 segments.
2. Print the names of the animals around the circle in the correct sequence. For each animal, fill in a current year as well as the previous year of that animal so that students can find their birth years. The 12-year cycle is as follows:

1. rat	7. horse
2. ox	8. sheep
3. tiger	9. monkey
4. hare	10. rooster
5. dragon	11. dog
6. serpent	12. boar

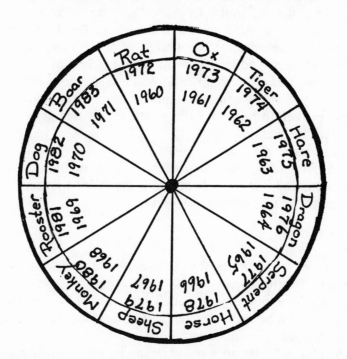

3. Punch a small hole in the center of the circle.
4. Punch a hole in the center of the posterboard.
5. Put the paper fastener through the two holes so that the wheel can spin.
6. Print the remainder of the information on the posterboard.
7. Print the name of the current year's animal on the 3¼″ × 2″ piece of construction paper.
8. Put masking tape on the back of the 3¼″ × 2″ construction paper and attach it to the posterboard.
9. Attach the easel back.
10. Display the poster near the desk where you or a volunteer can keep an eye on it. The wheel will not survive too exuberant a spin. Encourage the children to turn it gently.

READING COUNTDOWN

To get your students into the habit of reading regularly at home, try a reading countdown. Children are asked to read for pleasure at home for a designated number of hours during an entire month. The number of hours varies according to the grade level. Each student is given an entry blank that includes a set of rules, a completion date, and a calendar on which to mark the time spent reading. (See sample on facing page.) When the children return their completed entry blanks to you at the end of the month, they receive certificates of achievement and add their names to the reading road displayed in the media center. (See the illustration on page 171.)

Parents are encouraged to help children keep a record of their reading time and to sign the entry blank when the required number of hours has been achieved. Parents have proven to be very enthusiastic about this activity and are pleased to participate with their child.

This activity takes place over a whole month and there is no pressure or competition. The habit of setting aside short periods of time daily to read for fun is being reinforced, and it is to be hoped that this habit will become strong enough to continue after the reading countdown ends.

MATERIALS:

—stencil
—enough paper to run off copies of the entry blanks for every child in the school, plus about 50 extra copies
—enough blank reading award certificates for all of the children in the school (Certificates can be ordered from any library supply house.)
—several packages of gold stars
—enough colored kraft paper or wrapping paper to cover a door
—1 sheet of 20″ × 72″ brown kraft paper or wrapping paper
—sheets of brown and green construction paper
—2 pieces of 12″ × 18″ yellow construction paper
—enough sheets of yellow construction paper to cut out a 2″ × 3″ piece for every child in your school
—scissors
—black felt marker
—paste
—glue stick
—masking tape

PREPARATION:

Before the month of the countdown begins:

1. Order the blank reading award certificates far enough in advance for you to have them when the countdown begins.
2. A week or two before the month begins, decide what rules you want to use for the reading countdown.
3. Have the entry blanks typed on a stencil, duplicated, and ready for distribution.
4. Talk to all of the teachers, asking them to "spread the word" about the reading countdown among their students. Also discuss with them how they would like the certificates to be distributed to the children.

OFFICIAL ENTRY BLANK FOR
READING COUNTDOWN

Rules
Complete by February 28, 19

1. Every time a student spends time at home reading for fun (not for schoolwork), that time is recorded on this sheet. Cooperation between parent and child is helpful in recording and totaling the time on the calendar below. When the student accumulates the target time for the appropriate grade level, he or she returns the bottom of this entry blank to the media center and is awarded a certificate.

2. Children are encouraged to select their own books on any topic or interest level. (Note: Independent reading level is often approximately one year below the child's reading level.)

3. First grade children should be given credit for "reading" picture books by themselves.

4. The child should read just for pleasure. Oral reading and comprehension checks should be discouraged.

   Good luck to everyone!!

Ruth Toor, Library Media Specialist

Target times: Grade 1: 5 hours (approximately 15 minutes per session)
Grade 2: 6 hours (approximately 20 minutes per session)
Grade 3: 7 hours (approximately 20–25 minutes per session)
Grade 4: 8 hours (approximately 25 minutes per session)
Grade 5: 9 hours (approximately 25–30 minutes per session)

Student's Name

F E B R U A R Y						
1	2	3	4	5	6	7
8	9	10	1	12	13	14
15	16	17	18	19	20	21
22	23	24	25	26	27	28

Student's signature _____ Total time _____

Parent's signature _____

5. Talk to as many classes as you can about the reading countdown. Stress that it involves reading just for fun and answer any questions that the children might have.
6. If your school has a newsletter, you might submit an article about the count-down, alerting the parents to the fact that it will take place soon.
7. Be sure that entry blanks are distributed to all students on the last day of the month preceding the start of the reading countdown.

During the month of the countdown:

1. Begin preparing the certificates. If you or someone else can do calligraphy, the certificates can be lettered that way. If not, start printing them. Leave only the space for the name blank. This will save you from having to prepare 300 or more certificates overnight!
2. Prepare the reading roads as follows:
   a. Cover a long, narrow space such as a door with the colored kraft paper, attaching it at the top and bottom with masking tape.
   b. Cut the brown kraft paper to look like a winding road and paste it onto the background. In order to give the proper perspective, be sure that the bottom of the road is much wider than the top.
   c. Cut out two trees of brown and green construction paper and paste them onto the background.
   d. Cut the two pieces of 12″ × 18″ yellow construction paper into two large cobblestones.
   e. Use the black felt marker to letter "How high can we go?" and "Add your stone to the reading road" on the large cobblestones. Attach these signs to the background with paste.
   f. Cut out a 2″ × 3″ piece of yellow construction paper to resemble a stone. Outline it with black felt marker. Make enough of these blank stones for all of the children in your school.

PROCEDURE (when the entry blanks are returned to you):

1. When children start bringing in their completed and signed blanks, congratulate them and give each of them a blank cobblestone on which they print their names. Use the glue stick on the backs of the stones and have the children paste their stones onto the reading road.
2. Depending on the procedure that has been worked out between you and the teachers, either give the children their certificates immediately (be sure to write in their names) or tell the children exactly when they will receive their certificates. These might be presented in the classrooms or during class visits to the media center.
3. If some children complete their blanks fairly early in the month, suggest that they may want to keep reading all month anyway. Say that if they agree to do so and bring in a note signed by a parent together with the certificate, you will add a gold star to the certificate to show that they continued reading. You may want to add another cobblestone to the reading road for each additional unit of reading time completed by a student.

At the end of the month, it is interesting to see how many of the children in your school actually participated and submitted their entry blanks. If the reading road gets too full of names, consider extending it onto a nearby wall.

Storytelling Suggestions

ORIENTAL TALES

Continue your celebration of Chinese New Year by introducing the children to these selections.

Flack, Marjorie   *The Story about Ping*
                                     illus. by Kurt Wiese
                                     Viking, 1933

Ping, a young duck who lives on a "boat with two wise eyes on the Yangtze River," hides to avoid a spanking and gets separated from his mother and father, his 2 sisters and 3 brothers, his 11 aunts and 7 uncles, and his 42 cousins. He is captured by a boy, narrowly escapes being cooked for dinner, and finally is reunited with his family. (first to third grade)

McDermott, Gerald   *The Stonecutter*
                                     Viking, 1975

A Japanese folk tale about Tasaku, a stoncutter who aspires to ever greater power. He is first transformed into a prince, then the sun then a cloud, and finally into a mountain—only to discover that a mountain is prey to the chisel of a lowly stonecutter. (first and second grade)

Matsuno, Masako   *Taro and the Bamboo Shoot*
                                     adapted from the Japanese by Alice Low
                                     illus. by Yasuo Segawa
                                     Pantheon, 1964

A young Japanese boy picking bamboo shoots for his birthday dinner is lifted into the sky by a rapidly growing shoot. A two page horizontal drawing illustrates how high he goes. Children love to hear how long it takes for the cut shoot to fall. Explain that bamboo shoots eventually grow into bamboo trees, but the young shoots are eaten as a vegetable. (kindergarten to second grade)

Matsutani, Miyoko   *The Crane Maiden*
                                     trans. by Alvin Tresselt
                                     illus. by Chihiro Iwasaki
                                     Parents, 1968

A classic among Japanese children, this is the tale of a poor childless couple who adopt a young girl whom they find on their doorstep. She adds delight to their days, but when they listen to a meddling neighbor and watch the girl at her weaving, she returns to hr natural form of a crane. (second to fourth grade)

Mosel, Arlene   *The Funny Little Woman*
                                     illus. by Blair Lent
                                     Dutton, 1972

A funny little Japanese woman who likes to laugh and make dumplings is captured by the wicked oni who put her to work cooking rice with a magic paddle. Using her wits, she flees with the paddle at an opportune moment and becomes the richest woman in Japan. (first to third grade)

Tresselt, Alvin and   *The Legend of the Willow Plate*
Nancy Cleaver   illus. by Joseph Low
                           Parents, 1968

Koong-se, the beautiful daughter of a wealthy mandarin, is loved by Chang, a poor man. Fleeing a marriage arranged by her father, the two find happiness on a small island. When the jilted suitor finds and kills Chang, Koong-se immolates herself. Kwan-yin, goddess of mercy, is touched and turns the two into doves. The endpapers show a Chinese blue drawing similar to the one that appears on the popular willow pattern dinnerware. (second to fourth grade)

Van Woerkom, Dorothy   *The Rat, the Ox, and the Zodiac*
                           illus. by Errol Le Cain
                           Crown, 1976

A Chinese legend tells how a decision was made in the case of the rat and the ox, who both wanted to rule over the other animals in the newly created zodiac by being named Beast of the First Year. If you make the zodiac poster shown in this month's Library Enrichment Activity, bring it to your storytelling session. (second and third grade)

Wiese, Kurt   *Fish in the Air*
                           Viking, 1948

Little Fish asks his father, Big Fish, to buy him the biggest fish kite in the market. Both the kite and Little Fish are lifted by a gust of wind. Little Fish comes down in the river and is "fished" out, whereupon he asks his father to buy him the smallest fish kite. (kindergarten to second grade)

Williams, Jay   *Everyone Knows What a Dragon Looks Like*
                           illus. by Mercer Mayer
                           Four Winds, 1976

Gold-toned illustrations imitating Chinese silk-screens create a perfect background for this story. Of course, everyone *knows* what a dragon looks like, but only Han the gatekeeper sees him for what he truly is. The little old man is really the dragon who saves the city. (first and second grade)

Yashima, Taro   *Crow Boy*
                           Viking, 1955

Throughout his years of schooling, a young Japanese boy is ignored and regarded as dull by all of his classmates. Only in his sixth and final year does a sympathetic teacher uncover his hidden talents and their source, making those who scorned him quite ashamed. (first to third grade)

———————————

Here's a special suggestion in honor of Abraham Lincoln's birthday:

Waber, Bernard   *Just Like Abraham Lincoln*
                           Houghton Mifflin, 1964

A neighbor who not only looks like Abraham Lincoln but also shares his occupation and interests takes part in a student assembly. His move to Washington leaves a void that is filled by a new neighbor who looks just like George Washington. It is difficult to find a story for Presidents' birthdays that is not syrupy sweet. This one more than fills the bill. (kindergarten to third grade)

Teaching Unit

HOW TO USE AN ENCYCLOPEDIA EVEN IF YOU CAN HARDLY READ

This simple unit is more than an introduction to encyclopedias; it is also an introduction to research methods. The skills that are taught to beginning readers are the same skills that are needed by students at higher reading levels who must sift through greater quantities of material. The teaching is done in one 45-minute period or two 30-minute periods. The learning, however, occurs only as the students apply what was taught to writing a report.

If you wish to expand the teaching time, you can teach the overhead projector techniques described in the October chapter. Students can use the techniques to make maps and report covers and to illustrate whatever is of interest or importance to them.

To obtain the best results, work with the classroom teacher. Discuss areas that students would benefit from exploring. Countries such as Japan, Mexico, or Morocco with interesting foods, dress, and housing are good subjects. Another subject that might be selected is food, with individual reports on different grains, fruits, and dairy products.

OBJECTIVES:

At the conclusion of this unit, students should be able to:

1. Identify an encyclopedia as an alphabetically arranged set of books containing information on all subjects. (This is obviously a rudimentary explanation.)
2. Select one volume from a multi-volume encyclopedia set that contains information on the topic to be researched.
3. Locate an article within a volume.
4. Scan an encyclopedia article and extract the needed information.
5. Explain that a bibliography is a list of books that were used in research.
6. Make a simple bibliography.

Some students will also be able to use an index in an encyclopedia or other book to find additional information.

MATERIALS:

—at least three ditto masters
—enough paper to run off copies for every student in the class
—3 sheets of acetate—2 sheets to make permanent transparencies and 1 sheet to be used during class (Be sure that a thermal copier that makes permanent transparencies is available in your school.)
—at least one set of encyclopedias (Additional sets are helpful.)
—overhead projector
—transparency pens

PREPARATION:

1. Use the ditto masters to prepare at least three work sheets, each containing a list of specific topics on a different country. The classroom teacher may do

this, but you should review the topics to be sure that the students will be able to research them in the available encyclopedias. Since only encyclopedias are to be used, having the entire class research one country would be too much of a drain on the resources of the media center. (See the sample work sheet designed for students at the second grade level.)

Work Sheet on Japan

Do a report on Japan.

Your report should have a cover.

In your report you should have:

1. the name of two big cities in Japan
2. the name of a big river in Japan
3. some foods eaten by the Japanese
4. information about the language and how it is written
5. a picture of a Japanese house
6. the name of a Japanese holiday and how it is celebrated

The last page of your report will be a bibliography.

---

2. Make a permanent transparency of one of the work sheets.
3. Make a permanent transparency of a page in an encyclopedia. Be sure to select a page that uses various type sizes to set off sections. You can make a transparency from a sample page sent by the publisher or from a photocopy of a page in an encyclopedia.

PROCEDURE:

1. Have the students sit in or near the reference section. Briefly discuss with them the kinds of books found in this section. For younger children, it is sufficient to define reference books as dictionaries, encyclopedias, and atlases.
2. Inform the students that you know they are doing a research project and that you are impressed with what they are about to undertake.
3. Explain that it is necessary for them to use encyclopedias to do this research. At this point, some students are bound to tell you that they have encyclopedia sets at home. Acknowledge that this may prove helpful, but explain that the students will have enough time to use the encyclopedias in the media center. Pick up one volume and flip through the pages so that the class can see the text. Agree with the students if they voice the fear that an encyclopedia is a difficult book for them to read.
4. Now reassure them by telling them that you are about to teach the class some "tricks" that make using an encyclopedia simple.
5. The first thing for them to realize is that they do not have to read an entire set of encyclopedias. All they need to begin their project is one volume. Go through the following steps to help them realize this for themselves.
   a. Put the transparency of the work sheet on the overhead projector. (The work sheet on Japan will be used as an example.)

    b. Ask the students, "What is the subject of this report? What will it be about?"

    c. Once they have responded, ask for the first letter of the subject.

    d. Point to a set of encyclopedias and ask which volume will be needed.

    e. Have one student select the correct volume.

    f. Congratulate the student and point out the letter or letters on the spine. Also show the letters on the volumes before and after the one chosen.

6. Give an audible sigh of relief because the class has now isolated the one book that is needed. But even one book is far too much to read. Show the children the first and last articles in the volume. Ask what has to be done to locate the article on Japan. Ask questions that will help the students realize that they must go to the second letter. Turn to the *Ja* section. Be sure to show the class the guide words at the top of each page. Show them that you go to the third letter and fourth letter and so on until Japan is found.

7. Distribute the encyclopedia set (one volume per group of three or four is usually sufficient) to allow some practice. Tell each group to look for a different country in its volume.

8. When the article on Japan has been located, the first step of the research project is complete and the children know how to find an article on their own. Now slowly turn the pages in the article and express dismay at the number of pages.

9. Go back to the transparency of the work sheet. Note that the first topic is the name of two large cities. Pick up the *J* volume again. Ask the students if they know what special picture has names of cities and rivers. If no answer is forthcoming, give them a clue by suggesting that their families might use one before going on an automobile trip. Once you have elicited the word *map*, flip through the pages until you come to a map of Japan.

Note: If you have an unusually alert class, you may introduce atlases at this point.

10. Refer to the volumes that are being shared by several students, and have the students find maps of various countries.

11. Explain to the students that the size of the type indicates the size of the city. Ask them to read or spell the name of a big city on the map at which they are looking. Select a student to repeat this procedure with the map of Japan. Question 1 is now answered.

12. Next ask what color is used to show water. Tell the children that the squiggly blue lines indicate rivers. Let them find rivers on their maps. Ask how they can tell a big river from a small one. You are, of course, looking for "length of the line" as the response.

13. Point out to the students that they have answered two questions of the assignment and that almost no reading has been required. Now they need only copy the information.

14. Put the transparency of an encyclopedia page on the overhead projector. In order to answer the next questions, the class will have to learn how encyclopedia articles are divided. Remind the students that the larger and darker type face on maps showed the more important cities. The same idea is used within the article itself. The larger or bolder type is used to set off sections. They need only look for key words and phrases such as **Way of Life, People,** or **Food** printed in bold type. Encourage them to check the volumes in front

of them to locate similar key words. By now, you have isolated one paragraph on food that the students can read since it is only a sentence or two long. If some students cannot read the paragraph, remind them that you or any of the volunteers would be more than willing to read a few lines to them, especially since they have done all of the work in locating the material.

15. The same techniques can be applied to the question about language.

16. Additional information—on housing, holidays, or whatever else is important about a particular country—can be found by using the methods just learned or by looking at pictures.

17. Point out to the students that the articles they have been looking at have many pictures. If they see one that shows something special about the country, they can try to read the caption aloud. You can use the word *caption*, but explain it immediately. Again, if the caption proves too difficult to read, they can ask for help. The important thing is that they have found the information; they have done research.

18. One more item needs to be covered. The children should be told that whenever they do research and write down information, they must also list where they found the information. This list is called a bibliography. Let them feel impressed with themselves for being responsible for such a grown-up requirement. Use the acetate sheet to make a very simple bibliographic citation. All you need to list are the underlined name of the encyclopedia and the volume number. The form of the bibliography is not important; you are teaching it to set an example that all researchers must acknowledge the sources they used.

19. When the students come to the media center to do research, gifted students can be directed to the regular nonfiction shelves and taught to use an index to obtain further information. The titles of the books they used would also be included in their bibliographies. These would be more extensive than the one, two, or three volumes listed by the majority of the class.

Professional Responsibilities

PREPARING MEDIA BIBLIOGRAPHIES FOR TEACHERS

Library media specialists consider one aspect of their jobs to be keeping teachers informed of new materials they have purchased. There are different ways to do this. One way that has proven to be very effective is to prepare several annotated bibliographies each year of all non-book materials acquired by the media center. This is not a difficult task to do if you plan ahead.

1. Keep a scrap catalog card of each new item as it is processed. Generally, an annotation is already on the card. If not, you can jot down a few words describing the material and the grades for which it is suitable. Do this while the information is still fresh in your mind, either at the time you preview it or when you check it for processing. Each card should contain the following information: call number, titles of the set, producer, copyright date, number and type of items in the set (for example: 4 filmstrips, 2 cassettes, 1 teacher's guide), a brief annotation, and the suggested grade levels. If there is something particularly outstanding about a set of materials, add this information to the card.

2. Keep all of these annotated cards in a specially marked envelope on your desk.

3. Periodically go through the cards in the envelope, sorting them by type (records, kits, loops, and other kinds of media). You will probably want to do this about twice a year depending on the size of your budget and how often you order audio-visual materials.

4. When you have separated the various kinds of media, put the cards in order by their Dewey decimal numbers or according to whatever filing system you use for your audio-visual materials. This will make it easier for teachers to locate the materials described in the bibliography and for you to find something quickly without having to refer to the card catalog.

5. After all the cards have been arranged, you will have a rough draft of your media bibliography ready for typing.

6. Include a date at the beginning of the bibliography. You might start follow-up bibliographies with a note such as this one: "Here is a list of new audio-visual materials received in our media center since last (insert month here)."

7. List materials under headings such as Cassettes, Sound Filmstrips, and Kits. Arrange the materials within each group by call number.

8. If you have recently purchased any unusual types of encyclopedias, reference books, or professional books you feel the faculty should know about, note these at the end of your bibliography.

9. The entire bibliography should not take up more than two or three typed pages. Anything longer than that becomes a chore to read.

Your teachers will be pleased to be informed of new acquisitions in this way. Many of them will save these bibliographies in a folder, mark materials of special interest to them, and use the lists as a reference source for several years. You will be able to gauge the effectiveness of your bibliography almost immediately by the number of requests you have from teachers for the materials you have listed.

If your school buys all of its audio-visual materials after they have been previewed by teachers, this bibliography can still be of use to those teachers who did not have an opportunity to preview the materials. Even the teachers who recommended the purchase are glad to have a list in hand as a reminder.

Your principal should always receive a copy of the bibliography as well as any other notices that originate from the media center. He or she may forward additional copies to your superintendent and school board to show them how your funds are being spent.

WRITING MONTHLY REPORTS

Many library media specialists are required to prepare monthly reports. Even if you are not required to do so, you might consider writing reports to inform the administration of both the activities you have organized and the problems you have encountered in the media center.

Throughout the month, jot down special occurrences on your desk calendar. These should include teaching activities, multi-media units you have prepared, new services you have begun, and projects undertaken by volunteers under your supervision. It is amazing how much you may forget without these notes to serve as a reminder.

Begin the report with the month's statistics on circulation and student use (see the Volunteers section in the September chapter) as well as data on the number of books and other materials processed. Compare the current statistics with those of the previous month or the previous year, whichever seems preferable. Characterize the month, indicating any unusual teaching load or heavy clerical responsibilities. Highlight some of the important features that distinguished the month. Refer to the notes you made and describe the events of the month. Try to present the broad scope of your activities, showing your interaction with teachers, students, and volunteers.

Occasionally there are problems that you wish to bring to the attention of the administration. Discussing the problem in the monthly report gives you the opportunity to put the matter in writing the way you wish to present it. Surrounding the issue with positive happenings makes it clear that you are not needlessly complaining.

Conclude the report with a brief description of what is anticipated for the next month. Generally, a monthly report should not exceed two typed pages.

Volunteers

READING SHELVES

Shelf reading means checking the order of materials on the shelves to see if they are arranged in proper sequence. Since locating books is impossible if they are misshelved, this job is a very important one. At the same time, it allows the volunteer to become familiar with the books in the collection.

It is necessary for you, the library media specialist, to prepare an outline of the way that shelves are arranged and organized in the media center. Be sure to include distinctions among the filing systems for fiction, nonfiction, and biography. Explain how paperbacks are arranged and point out any special area shelving such as reference books, professional books, pamphlets, periodicals, and audio-visual materials.

Once this is done, your volunteers can follow an outline that will help them read the shelves properly. "Lost" books are often found when the shelves are read because they have merely been shelved in the wrong places.

Although shelf reading is not a very popular job, it must be done regularly. One way to solve the problem of who will read the shelves and when is to make a diagram of your media center that designates sections of shelves. Have each volunteer choose one section and "read" it for the entire year. Try to work this out so that no one has more than five or six shelves to read.

Volunteers need spend only a few minutes reading and straightening a section of shelves. This may be done at the beginning or end of their work time. Scheduling shelf reading in this manner should keep the task from being too time-consuming or boring. Furthermore, each volunteer will get used to scanning the same shelves regularly and will spot a misplaced book much more quickly than someone who has never checked that section before.

RELABELING

Spine labels often come off or become illegible after much use. When a label is difficult to read, it should be replaced. All volunteers should be aware of the problem. As they are slipping or shelving, the volunteers should pull any books that need relabeling. To relabel a book, check the book pocket to get the proper call number and then type or print a new label. Apply it to the book's spine and cover it with white library paste. It will dry clear and protect the new label.

Open End

SCHEDULED vs. OPEN MEDIA CENTER

Should your media center have scheduled classes or should it be open to anyone at any time? Many factors enter into this decision, and in some cases your feelings may have very little effect on the outcome.

Teachers' contracts usually spell out the number of free periods that they will have, and one of these may be the weekly library period for their class. If this is the custom in your district, you will have to schedule weekly classes regardless of your wishes. If you have a choice, however, there are factors to be considered on both sides.

With scheduled weekly classes, you will see every child in the school every single week. You can plan various activities and lessons to familiarize the children with the media center and with library skills. You will know that the children are charging out books every week, and you may be able to influence their choices. When a class is in the media center, you can devote your time strictly to them and their needs.

On the other hand, a media center with an open schedule is available to individual children and to classes at any time the need arises. You may see some children every day, even several times a day. You may hardly ever see others because they do not avail themselves of the opportunity to come to the media center on their own. Instead of teaching formal lessons on library skills, you can deal with children on a "need to know" basis, catching them at the optimum moment for learning when, for example, they must look up something in the card catalog to get the information they need. Conversely, some of them may never learn certain library skills because you are not aware of their needs.

With an open schedule your time is fragmented because many children call for your attention at once for many different reasons. You do not know at the beginning of the day what to expect; you do not know in advance whether there will be 70 children or no children in the media center at any given time. Often a teacher does plan ahead with you and schedules a class for a specific time and purpose, but sometimes a teacher and class just come in without warning. During a period in which you have scheduled a class, other children may come to the media center on their own and want you to recommend a good book or help them with an assignment. You have to learn how to juggle priorities and maintain your sense of humor.

With an open schedule you may have more time to check through new books, prepare bibliographies, and consult with teachers than you would with a regular weekly schedule of classes. On the other hand, your periods of relative freedom contrast sharply with the times when you feel that there are 100 children all needing your personal guidance at the same moment. The faculty will also assume that you are always "free" and will make requests at inconvenient times.

You might consider a compromise between a scheduled and an open program by scheduling a weekly story hour for your primary classes (kindergarten to second grade) but still keeping the media center open to anyone else who needs to use it during that time. You could also occasionally schedule intensive library skills units (see the Teaching Units throughout the *Almanac*) yet avoid scheduling your entire week.

Neither system is perfect; both have large but surmountable problems. Whichever you decide to use, try to avoid scheduling all of your time, or you will become a classroom teacher whose room is the media center. How your program finally develops will depend on a number of factors: your feelings, the feelings of the principal and teachers, your district's philosophy of education, what has been done at your school in the past, and what is currently being done in the other schools in your district.

March

Happy Birthday To . . .

2   **Richard Cuffari** (1925)—illustrator
        Highly versatile illustrator whose work is represented in all areas of the media center

        Theodor Seuss Geisel (1904)—author and illustrator
        The well-known Dr. Seuss, creator of the Random House Beginner Books and forerunner of all easy-to-read books for primary grade children

4   **Meindert De Jong** (1906)—author
        Fiction for upper grades, including *House of Sixty Fathers*

8   **Kenneth Grahame** (1859)—author
        Noted author of *Wind in the Willows*

11   **Wanda Gag** (1893)—author and illustrator
        Especially remembered for the old favorite *Millions of Cats*

12   **Virginia Hamilton** (1936)—author
        Fiction about blacks for upper grades, including the Newbery Medal winner *M. C. Higgins, the Great* and *The House of Dies Drear*

13   **Ellen Raskin** (1928)—author and illustrator
        Picture books and books for upper grades that convey a delightful sense of humor, notably *Nothing Ever Happens on My Block* (picture book) and *The Tattooed Potato and Other Clues* (upper grades)

14   **Marguerite de Angeli** (1889)—author and illustrator
        Fiction for middle and upper grades, including the Newbery Medal winner *The Door in the Wall* and *Thee, Hannah!*

*Decorate your media center for spring
highlighting famous illustrators and Caldecott winners.*

16   **Sid Fleischman** (1920)—author
  Humorous tales for the middle grades, including *McBroom Tells the Truth*

17   **Kate Greenaway** (1846)—illustrator
  Sweet illustrations typical of the artist's era

20   **Ellen Conford** (1942)—author
  Lightly humorous fiction on contemporary subjects for middle and upper grades, including *Me and the Terrible Two* and *Felicia the Critic*

22   **Randolph Caldecott** (1846)—illustrator
  Noted Englishman who ushered in a new era of illustrations for children and is commemorated by the Caldecott Medal given to the best picture book of the year

23   **Eleanor Cameron** (1912)—author
  Creator of the Mushroom Planet books for middle grades as well as good fiction for upper grades, including *The Court of the Stone Children*

24   **Mary Stolz** (1920)—author
  Fiction for middle and upper grades, including *Noonday Friends* and *The Dog on Barkham Street*

26   **Robert Frost** (1874)—poet
  Many of Frost's simpler themes can be appreciated by elementary school students.

31   **Beni Montresor** (1926)—illustrator
  Montresor's background as a set designer can readily be seen in *May I Bring a Friend?* and *Cinderella*.

Bulletin Boards

LOOK WHAT THE WIND BLEW IN

As the March winds begin to blow, construct a "windy" bulletin board such as the one shown here. It focuses on things that go up in the air and directs students to one of the sections of the media center where they can find material on flight. You might also include the Dewey decimal numbers for the history of kites, for other types of recreational flight such as hang gliding, and for space satellites and rockets.

MATERIALS:

- —1 sheet of 22" × 28" blue posterboard
- —white construction paper
- —felt markers in assorted colors, including black
- —cotton or cotton balls
- —overhead projector
- —scissors
- —pencil
- —rubber cement

PREPARATION:

1. On white construction paper draw or trace (using the overhead projector) a kite, a balloon, and other objects that fly. Fill in the drawings with brightly colored felt markers.
2. Cut out the objects in cloud shapes.
3. Outline the cloud shapes with a wide-tip felt marker for dramatic effect.
4. Label the drawings.
5. Draw a cloud that directs students to books labeled 629.133. Outline the cloud.
6. Draw or trace the cloud face shown in the illustration on white construction paper and cut it out.
7. Paste cotton on the cloud face for additional puffiness.
8. Position all of the drawings on the posterboard.
9. Print "Look What the" and "Blew In" with a colored felt marker.
10. Use the black marker to write "Wind" in letters that resemble clouds. Paste cotton within the outlines of the letters.
11. Paste all of the drawings on the posterboard.

THE CALDECOTT MEDAL

Salute Randolph Caldecott, born in March 1846, with a bulletin board devoted to the medal named for him. (See illustration on following page.) Use a copy machine to make pictures of both sides of the medal. Pictures can be found in various encyclopedias or in *Caldecott Medal Books, 1938–1957* edited by Bertha Mahony Miller and Elinor Whitney Field (Horn Book, 1957).

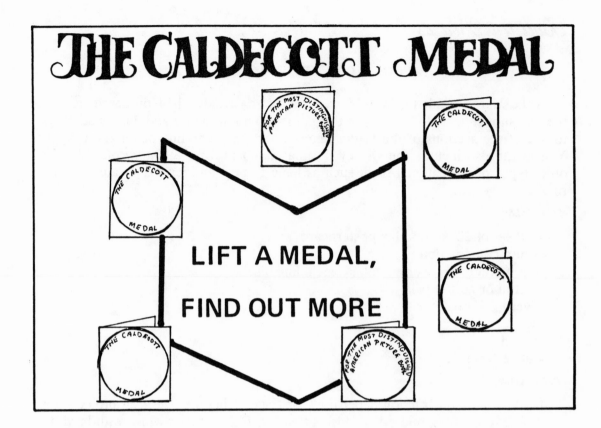

MATERIALS:

- —1 sheet of 22″ × 28″ light-colored posterboard
- —several small sheets of construction paper in assorted colors
- —typing paper
- —felt markers in assorted colors
- —rubber cement
- —pictures of the Caldecott Medal, about 4″ in diameter
- —scissors

PREPARATION:

1. Photocopy pictures of Caldecott Medal. You should have four pictures of the front of the medal and two of the back.
2. Cut six 8″ × 4″ pieces from assorted colors of construction paper. Fold each piece in half so that it resembles a book.
3. Paste a photocopy of the medal onto the front of each piece of folded construction paper.
4. Type six facts about the medal, keeping the information to a 3½″ square area. (Facts about the medal are listed below.)
5. Cut out the typed information and paste one fact onto the inside of each medal book.
6. Cut a sheet of construction paper to resemble an open book that measures about 11″ × 14″.
7. Use a felt marker to print "Lift a Medal, Find Out More" on the open book.
8. Write "The Caldecott Medal" in free-form letters on construction paper. The letters should be about 2½″ high.

9. Cut out the letters and paste them onto the bulletin board.
10. Paste the open book onto the bulletin board.
11. Paste the six medals around the bulletin board.

FACTS ABOUT THE MEDAL:

1. The first Caldecott Medal was given in 1938. The winner is announced each year in January.
2. Randolph Caldecott, for whom the award is named, was a famous English illustrator of children's books.
3. The face of the medal shows Caldecott's illustration of John Gilpin's ride from the poem "The Diverting History of John Gilpin" by William Cowper.
4. The reverse side of the medal shows Caldecott's illustration of "four and twenty blackbirds baked in a pie" from the well-known nursery rhyme.
5. The engraving reads "For the Most Distinguished American Picture Book for Children."
6. The medal is awarded annually by the Association for Library Service to Children of the American Library Association.

Library Art Activity

NEW BOOK JACKETS

People do judge a book by its cover. When confronted by shelves of books, the eye is drawn to new and bright covers. Here is an art activity that will give a lift to tired books. The students design new covers for jacketless books to given them a fresh, new look. In the process, they read the books and encourage others to read them through the new jackets.

Note: You might combine this activity with the section on writing book blurbs in the November chapter.

MATERIALS:

—kraft paper or heavy wrapping paper (Light shades are best, but brown will do if nothing else is available. You need enough to cover all of the books selected.)
—approximately 20 sheets of drawing paper (The number of sheets depends on how many books are used and how many students prefer not to draw on kraft paper.)
—felt markers or crayons in assorted colors
—plastic book jackets (The adjustable ones, available in packages of 100, are most convenient if you normally buy books that are completely processed and therefore have little regular need of covers.)
—rubber cement
—spine labels
—materials for poster
  • sheet of 11" × 14" colored posterboard
  • felt markers in assorted colors
  • easel back

PREPARATION:

1. Make a simple poster announcing the activity and giving directions to the

students. The one shown here resembles an artist's palette. Make the poster as colorful as you can.
2. Pull 25 to 30 jacketless books off the shelves and put them on display near the poster.
   • Concentrate on titles in the fiction and picture book areas, since that is where most of the browsing occurs and where a new cover is apt to spark interest.

- Try to balance the selection to include a range of reading and interest levels.
- More titles can be added if necessary.

3. Cut kraft paper or wrapping paper to fit the books chosen.
   - Be sure to allow for flaps.
   - Draw lines where the flaps will be.
   - Mark the author and title in pencil.
4. Have drawing paper and other materials ready.

PROCEDURE:

1. Students choose books from the display that pique their interest or spark their creative urge.
2. After reading the books, the students make drawings that relate to the plots.
   - Drawings may be made directly on the kraft paper or on drawing paper.
   - Students using kraft paper can use the entire surface of the cover, including the part that covers the back of the book, to make one large drawing, or they can make a second drawing on the back.
   - Pictures made on drawing paper that has been cut to the size of the book are pasted onto the kraft paper.
3. Be sure students include the author and title on each book cover.
4. When the new dust jackets are completed, attach a spine label to each of them.
5. On an inside flap, print ''New Jacket Illustration by'' and fill in the student's name and room number and the year.
6. Put the new jackets in plastic covers and shelve the books.

Library Enrichment Activity

WRITING TO ILLUSTRATORS

A good way to follow up this month's ''Caldecott Medal'' Bulletin Board and ''Learning about Illustrators'' Teaching Unit is to have children write to their favorite illustrators.

MATERIALS:

—ditto master
—enough paper to run off one copy for each child
—small poster giving directions to students (see illustration on following page)

PROCEDURE:

1. Compile a list in alphabetical order of all the illustrators you have covered in the ''Learning about Illustrators'' Teaching Unit.
2. To help the children remember, add to the list the titles of one or two books for which each artist is known.
3. Add the name and address of each illustrator's publisher. If an illustrator has worked with several different publishers, choose the publisher of the book that you have spotlighted on your list.
4. The addresses of the publishers can be found in the back of *Children's Books*

in Print (published yearly by R. R. Bowker) or in the book catalogs that publishers send to every media center.

5. Have the list typed in three columns: name of illustrator, titles, publisher and address. The list should then be run off on the ditto machine.
6. Distribute a list to each child.
7. Explain to the children that this list will remind them of all the illustrators they have studied and that they may write to their favorite illustrators if they wish.
8. Stress that illustrators are very busy people and that they may not respond. If they do respond, it may take some time until their letters are received.
9. Tell the children that you would like to see any responses they receive. They will naturally want to keep their letters, but they will be proud to share them with you and the rest of their class.

ART REFERENCES

Unfortunately, students and adults usually think only of encyclopedias and dictionaries when they consider reference materials. Library media specialists work hard trying to broaden the user's awareness of the many resources that comprise the reference section. One way to do this is to spotlight a specific reference area.

Since so many of this month's activities deal with illustrators, continue this theme by focusing on the art reference materials. Set up a table within the reference section, or use a window nook. You can make a poster like the one shown below to draw students to the display. Keep at least one of the art books open to a vivid painting that will quickly attract attention.

The bibliography of art references given below is a brief one. It includes reference material on illustrators and exposes students to something they may never have seen—boxed illustrations. Some biographies of illustrators that are not reference books are also included. You might expand this display to spotlight art books in general and include works about various painters or styles of art. As with many activities, how involved it gets depends on what you wish to do with it.

Once you have gathered the materials, look through the books and prepare a list of about twenty questions related to art. Put each question on a separate 3″ × 5″ card. Make the cards attractive by using different colored felt markers. Find a small box to hold the cards. The purpose of the questions is to provide a focus for the students' attention when they look through the reference materials. Without these questions, children will merely flip through the books and retain very little of the information in them. Although there is no compulsion to answer the questions, some direction is offered. By having something to look up, the students become familiar with the works on display. If they are interested, they can borrow the books in the display that are allowed to circulate.

SAMPLE QUESTIONS:

1. What is cubism? (pronounced kew-biz'm)
2. What is collage? (pronounced ko-lazh)
3. Who painted the ceiling of the Sistine Chapel?
4. Who painted "View from Toledo"?
5. Look at some "impressionist" paintings. Which one do you like best? Why?

BIBLIOGRAPHY:

Reference books

Chase, Alice Elizabeth. Famous Artists of the Past. Platt & Munk, 1964.
Craven, Thomas. The Rainbow Book of Art. World, 1956.
Miller, Bertha M., and Elinor W. Field. Caldecott Medal Books, 1938–1957. Horn Book, 1957.
Mahony, Bertha E., and others, eds. Illustrators of Children's Books, 1744–1945. Horn Book, 1947.
Ruskin, Ariane. The Pantheon Story of Art. Pantheon, 1964.
Shepard, E. H., ill. Pooh, His Art Gallery. A. A. Milne, author. Dutton, 1966. 8 boxed color prints, 11″ × 14″.
Viguers, Ruth, and others, eds. Illustrators of Children's Books, 1946–1956. Horn Book, 1958.
Ward, Martha E., and Dorothy A. Marquardt. Illustrators of Books for Young People. Scarecrow, 1970.

Circulating books

Ardizzone, Edward. The Young Ardizzone. Macmillan, 1970.
Greenaway, Kate. The Kate Greenaway Treasury. World, 1967.
Linder, Enid, and Leslie Linder. The Art of Beatrix Potter. Rev. ed. Warne, 1972.

Storytelling Suggestions

CALDECOTT MEDAL WINNERS

Continue to explore this month's artistic theme by making your storytelling selections from Caldecott Medal winners. Remember, an award does not guarantee children's interest, so make your selections carefully. You may find some of the honor books more to your liking than some of the medal winners. Older medal winners frequently represent a style that looks dated to contemporary children's eyes. As always, evaluate the materials carefully. The titles listed below are considered sure-fire storytelling hits, but of course you will want to add your own favorites.

DeRegniers, Beatrice Schenk   *May I Bring a Friend?*
illus. by Beni Montresor
Atheneum, 1965

In this rhyming story, the hero is invited to visit the King and Queen on six succeeding days. Each time he brings an unusual friend. On the seventh day, the King and Queen return the visit, joining him and his friends at the city zoo. (first and second grade)

Emberley, Barbara   *Drummer Hoff*
illus. by Ed Emberley
Prentice-Hall, 1967

Succeeding ranks of soldiers and officers prepare a cannon for firing. As each does his part, the whole rhyme is repeated with the new line added. "But Drummer Hoff fired it off." (kindergarten)

Haley, Gail E.   *A Story, a Story*
Atheneum, 1970

In order to pay the Sky God for his stories, Ananse the spider man must capture a leopard, hornets, and the fairy who men never see. With great ingenuity, he succeeds, and this is why stories today are called spider tales. (kindergarten to second grade)

Hogrogian, Nonny   *One Fine Day*
Macmillan, 1971

When a fox laps up the milk in an old woman's pail, she cuts off his tail, telling him that he can reclaim it if he returns her milk. In order to get the milk, he goes from cow to field to hen and performs various other tasks until a kindly miller comes to his rescue. The fox then repeats the chain of tasks in reverse and finally gets his tail. (first and second grade)

Joslin, Sesyle   *What Do You Say, Dear?*
illus. by Maurice Sendak
Addison-Wesley, 1958

Children love this Caldecott honor book on etiquette. By setting up ridiculous situations that require correct social responses, the author gently reminds children of proper behavior. (kindergarten to second grade)

Lionni, Leo   *Swimmy*
Pantheon, 1963

A small black fish is the sole survivor when his school of red fish is eaten. He wanders in an exquisitely drawn ocean world. After finding another school of red fish, he teaches them to swim in a giant fish formation with himself as the eye, and they frighten the larger fish away. A Caldecott honor book. (first to third grade)

Sendak, Maurice   *Where the Wild Things Are*
Harper & Row, 1963

When Max is punished, he dreams that he journeys to the island where the wild things are and becomes their king. He returns home when he feels lonely for "someone who loves him best of all." (kindergarten to second grade)

Steig, William   *Sylvester and the Magic Pebble*
Simon & Schuster, 1969

Sylvester the donkey finds a shiny red pebble that fulfills his wishes. While running from a hungry lion, he wishes he were a rock and becomes one. Sylvester's parents, not knowing why he has disappeared, try in vain to find him. One spring day they picnic on the very rock that Sylvester has become, and their wish to have him back is answered. (first to second grade)

If you would like to read a St. Patrick's Day story, try this suggestion:

Calhoun, Mary   *The Hungry Leprechaun*
                                 illus. by Roger Duvoisin
                                 Morrow, 1962

A starving leprechaun, caught by an almost equally hungry young man, causes one disaster after another while trying to recall enough of his magic to make gold. He finally tries changing rocks into gold—and instead creates the potato! (kindergarten to second grade)

Teaching Unit

LEARNING ABOUT ILLUSTRATORS

This "eye-opening" unit is directed toward children at the primary reading level. It teaches them to see illustrations as art as well as vehicles to explain, expand, and enrich the printed word. A greater visual awareness is developed by discussing the illustrations in familiar picture books. If the art teacher is interested, discuss the unit with him or her about one month in advance. A companion art program could be developed to give students a chance to work with some of the techniques used by the illustrators covered in the unit. Student art work could then be displayed, accompanied by explanations of the techniques used.

This unit is highly flexible, ranging from a minimum of 10 sessions to as many as 25. Allow about 25 minutes for discussing each illustrator and his or her style, for reading one book, and for showing other books done by the same illustrator.

OBJECTIVES:

At the conclusion of this unit, students should:

1. Be familiar with the names and styles of many popular illustrators of children's picture books.
2. Be aware that there are a number of different techniques used in illustrating.
3. Know many of these techniques by name.

MATERIALS:

—one or more reference books with pictures and biographies of famous illustrators such as the *Something about the Author* series edited by Anne Commire (Gale Research Co., published regularly since 1971) or Lee Bennett Hopkins' *Books Are by People* (Citation Press, 1969)
—books by each illustrator
—background on different styles of illustration (Look through a book such as Patricia Cianciolo's *Illustrations in Children's Books* [William C. Brown, 1970] or check standard works on children's literature.)
—sound filmstrip "How a Picture Book Is Made" (Weston Woods, 1976) (optional)

PREPARATION:

1. The preparation for each lesson is similar, and these steps can be adapted from session to session.
2. Choose an illustrator of picture books whose works are available in your media center. You should have a minimum of five different books by that person; the more you have, the more the children will enjoy the lesson.
3. Check your card catalog to see if the illustrator has also done other books, including nonfiction, of which you may not have been aware. Pull all books by the illustrator off the shelves, including any multiple copies, and look at the style of the illustrations so that you will be able to discuss it with the children. Choose one book to read to the class.
4. Look at your reference books to see if there is a page and picture about the illustrator you have chosen. If so, put a marker in the book and place it on top of your pile of picture books. If not, check the dust jackets of the books you have pulled for pictures and information about the illustrator.
5. A sample list of illustrators who have proven to be popular with children is given below. It is by no means all inclusive, and whether or not you use these illustrators depends on personal preferences and on how many books by each illustrator are available in your media center. If you have a strong liking for other artists, by all means discuss them.

Aliki	Mercer Mayer
Jose Aruego and Ariane Dewey	Robert McCloskey
Marcia Brown	Gerald McDermott
Remy Charlip	Beni Montresor
Tomie de Paola	Bill Peet
Leo and Diane Dillon	Beatrix Potter
Roger Duvoisin	Alice and Martin Provensen
Ed Emberley	Ellen Raskin
Don Freeman	Maurice Sendak
Paul Galdone	Uri Shulevitz
Dahlov Ipcar	Peter Spier
Blair Lent	Brinton Turkle
Leo Lionni	Tomi Ungerer
Arnold Lobel	Brian Wildsmith
Giulio Maestro	Margot Zemach
James Marshall	

INTRODUCTORY LESSON:

A good illustrator to discuss in the introductory lesson is Brian Wildsmith. His bold and brilliant illustrations, using many shades of bright colors, are easy to recognize and are generally liked by children. Pull all of your Wildsmith books off the shelves and check your reference book on illustrators before the class comes in.

1. When the children arrive, tell them that you will be talking about and showing them examples of many different types of illustrations in picture books. Ask if they have any favorite illustrators and discuss these illustrators. Explain that illustrators sometimes write their own stories and sometimes they work with stories made up by other authors.

2. Mention some of the techniques and materials illustrators use such as wood-cuts, collage, watercolor, gouache, scratchboard, monochrome, pen and ink, and pen and crayon. Explain that the children will become familiar with most of these terms by the end of this unit. (They have probably already used or seen several of these techniques.)

3. Talk briefly about Brian Wildsmith:

- Include the fact that he is British and talk about his background and family.
- Show the children his picture.
- Read the class one of his books, possibly *The Owl and the Woodpecker* or *The Little Wood Duck* (both published by Franklin Watts).
- Suggest that the children look closely at the illustrations so that all of you will be able to discuss them later.

4. After you have finished the story, have the children describe their reactions to the illustrations. Ask how they feel about the colors Wildsmith uses and ask them to identify the subject of most of his drawings (animals). Show them other books by Wildsmith, paging through each one so that the children can see the similarity of the illustrations. Tell them that Wildsmith paints with gouache (an opaque, water-base paint). After the children have seen several Wildsmith books, they will be able to readily recognize his work.

5. Be prepared to let the children charge out any of the books you showed them, including the story you read. Multiple copies will come in handy, because many children will want to charge out a book by the illustrator of the week.

CONTINUING THE UNIT:

Start future sessions by briefly mentioning the illustrators that you have previously discussed. Often the children will astound you by spouting off a long list of names of now familiar illustrators. Remember that in some cases (Marcia Brown, for instance), an illustrator's style will vary from book to book. Others (such as Robert McCloskey) will be instantly recognizable once you have pointed out a few examples to your class.

At the end of this unit, have the children discuss the illustrators that they especially enjoyed. Consider compiling a list of all of the artists you have studied in case the children want to write to their favorites. (See this month's Library Enrichment Activity.)

During the final session, you could show the class the Weston Woods sound filmstrip "How a Picture Book Is Made." If it is not available or if you are short of time, this session can be omitted.

Professional Responsibilities

INTERLIBRARY LOANS

Even if it is equipped to meet or exceed A.L.A. standards, the modern media center cannot fulfill all of the demands placed on it. Today's curriculum can send students in directions that could not have been anticipated by even the most clairvoyant library media specialist. When such situations arose in the past, the student would be told, "Sorry, but we cannot help you."

Today the picture has altered. The current trend toward library networks and federations permits you to have access to vast facilities in meeting student and faculty needs. Frequently a simple telephone call can answer the question. At other times interlibrary loans are arranged. In order for your patrons to get this assistance, you must become familiar with the services available in your area. Make contact with the larger libraries that provide these services. Find out what help you can expect and how you can obtain it. This involves attending workshops and rap sessions arranged by the umbrella library.

Interlibrary loans can also be made within a school district. All of the media centers in one school district should be able to work cooperatively for the benefit of students and faculty. Even if there is no district media coordinator, the individual library media specialists can develop informal ties to facilitate the interchange of materials. Thus, an elementary school student reading on a high school level can be supplied with suitable books of sufficient difficulty. A foreign student in a junior or senior high school can use materials from the elementary school media center and be able to function in the classroom while gaining competence in English. A special project launched at one school can be enriched if more copies of materials or a greater variety of materials are obtained through interlibrary loans from other schools.

In districts where interlibrary loans are an established procedure, faculty members can borrow material from any media center and be responsible for its return. Where interlibrary loans are still a novel concept, arrangements can be made through the library media specialist. This will help keep circulation records accurate and losses to a minimum, since there will be one person per school responsible for seeing that borrowed materials are returned.

It is not necessary to begin on a large scale. Just work to maintain sufficiently good relations among the library media specialists so that each of you feels free to call when help is needed and is willing to respond to someone else's call.

Volunteers

SNAGS AND DUPLICATE CARDS

"Snags" are books and other media for which book cards or charge out cards cannot be found. Rather than making new cards for these materials immediately, the volunteer should put them aside on a special shelf until a careful search can be made for their cards.

When a volunteer has time to search, the entire circulation file should be checked, including the sections for parents' and teachers' cards. The next step is to go to the shelves to see if the wrong card was placed in another copy of the book. This is the place where many snags are straightened out.

If the cards have not been found after several weeks, new ones should be typed. Each card must be marked "duplicate card." The materials can then be shelved. A typed list of all duplicate cards should be kept in the drawer containing the circulation file for easy reference.

If the original card turns up at a later date, the duplicate card should be destroyed and the title crossed off the duplicate card list. If a duplicate card is used up and the original has not been located, the replacement card need not say "duplicate." Just assume that the original has been irretrievably lost.

THE VERTICAL FILE

A vertical file can contain pictures, maps, newspaper clippings, magazine articles, and pamphlets on many different subjects. These materials are placed in folders that are arranged in alphabetical order according to subject. They provide a source of information for students and teachers that supplements books and audio-visual materials. Often the vertical file contains up-to-the-minute information that cannot be found elsewhere.

If you do not have a vertical file, try to get one started. Although it is a time-consuming job, you will quickly discover that a vertical file is an invaluable addition to your media center collection.

To start a vertical file:

1. Send a notice to faculty members explaining that you are planning a vertical file and asking them to suggest subjects that they would like to see included.
2. Compile an alphabetical list of these suggestions.
3. Add any subjects that you feel are necessary.
4. Poll your volunteers to see which ones are interested in working on the vertical file. This entails such tasks as looking through old magazines for relevant material. Some people have a knack for this; others don't care to do it at all. If possible, find one person who can take charge of this project. This person should be able to make up the folders, look over the material that has been gathered, decide where to file something that has multiple subjects, and create additional subject headings when necessary.
5. Check the current edition of *Sears List of Subject Headings* edited by Barbara M. Westby (Wilson) for the proper subject headings.
6. Have your list of subject headings typed and duplicated for use as a reference.
7. Sources for vertical file material include old magazines, current newspapers, travel brochures, third-class mail, and U.S. Government publications from the Superintendent of Documents. Several books of sources are also available, including *A Guide to Free and Inexpensive Materials,* published annually by Educators Progress Service, Randolph, Wisconsin.
8. Materials should be selected on the basis of interest, timeliness, and relevance to the needs of students and teachers.
9. As materials are compiled, mark the top right-hand side of the first page of each item with the notation "VF—" followed by the subject heading.
10. Try to obtain hanging files for vertical file material. Regular manila folders get battered quickly, and although the initial cost of the material is negligible, the time spent organizing the folders is considerable and it would be depressing for so much effort to be wasted. If a file cabinet is impossible because of space or money, try large, heavy-duty document envelopes.
11. Have a volunteer type subject cards similar to the one shown. File the cards in the card catalog.

```
┌─────────────────────────────────────┐
│            WEATHER                   │
│                                      │
│   See folder on "Weather" in the     │
│   Vertical File.                     │
│                                      │
│                   ●                  │
└─────────────────────────────────────┘
```

12. Be sure to tell the children and teachers about the vertical file and its uses during orientation, reference lessons, and other appropriate times so that they will learn to refer to the vertical file as a resource.

Here is one method of circulating vertical file materials:

1. Type one book pocket for each subject heading and paste it onto the front of the folder.
2. Type several book cards for each subject heading. Vertical file cards should be a different color from book cards. Put cards in the pocket.
3. Save all large brown envelopes received in the mail and use them for circulating vertical file materials.
4. Divide a ditto master into the five columns shown here.

Date Due	Subject	# of Items	Student's Name	Room #

5. Run off the ditto master and paste one copy onto each envelope. Keep the envelopes at the circulation desk.
6. When students borrow vertical file materials, they remove one card from each subject folder they are using and bring the cards and materials to the circulation desk.
7. When the materials are placed in the envelope, enter the necessary information on the attached sheet. Remind students to return all of the materials in the envelope.
8. On the book card, students write the usual information plus the number of items borrowed on the subject. This number should be circled.
9. When the materials are returned, match the subject *and the student's name* on the sheet to the circulation card.
10. Check to be sure that the correct number of items has been returned.
11. Cross the student's name off the sheet and replace the envelope under the desk.
12. Refile the card and vertical file materials.

Open End

UNIFIED vs. DIVIDED CATALOG

At first a unified catalog seems so simple and so logical—a complete index to the media center filed in alphabetical order. Then the complications begin; for example, what is alphabetical order? As library media specialists, we know what we mean. It is word-by-word filing (except for historical dates and periods, which are filed chronologically). Of course, some of us believe in strict alphabetical order, while others believe that commas and dashes represent stops that must be taken into account when filing. The author, title, subject sequence must also be considered. A great deal of time is spent mastering all of the rules for filing. The reasons for these rules are logical, and when fully understood, the rules themselves make excellent sense. Unfortunately, most of the filing is done by volunteers who need to be instructed in the many rules and exceptions. What makes this system even more difficult is that the principal users of the media center are young children who have only recently mastered the alphabet. They assume that alphabetical order simply means ABC and do not dream of the numerous ways of interpreting this term. In other words, you have an excellent system, but most of your users find it difficult and confusing. As always, there are several ways of dealing with this problem.

You can strictly follow Anglo-American filing rules. Keep the book of rules handy so that your volunteers can become familiar with them. Design a learning center that teaches the average student how to use the catalog and illustrates some of the problems that he or she might encounter. If you set up a learning center, keep in mind that sequence—not complex entries—is the student's main problem.

Another alternative is to file strictly alphabetically, word by word. This may cause you some anguish when some key subjects are split by intervening authors or titles; however, the nonprofessional user will be pleased. You will still need to decide how to file historical periods. You might even decide to dispense with filing "Mc" as "Mac."

A third approach is the divided catalog, which means that the subject catalog is filed separately from the author and title catalog. Authors and titles are rarely involved in the problem of what comes first. The students do not have to worry about whether the card they are looking at is a title or subject card. Of course, the user does have to stop and think about which catalog is needed. Without the distraction of author and title cards, the problems of filing subject cards become easier to cope with. You can still choose between strict alphabetical order and the more traditional method. If you choose the latter and have difficulty teaching volunteers and students the rules, borrow an approach used by many college and university libraries. They place the Library of Congress list of subject headings where patrons can use it. Do the same with the *Sears List of Subject Headings*. Volunteers can be taught to follow Sears list, and students can use it for checking filing sequence and for finding an assigned subject heading. With the current edition of the Sears list, the user might even find the Dewey number and go straight to the shelf. Although this method leaves out steps that might need to be retaught later, it fosters an understanding of how the media center is structured and helps people feel comfortable using it.

Which approach you decide to use should depend on considerations such as the sort of catalog that the students will use later in their schooling and the arrangement of the public library catalog. If you wish to divide, you should ask yourself if you really have the space for two catalogs and for double cards when title and subject are the same. Can you handle the heavy traffic that will build up around the subject catalog? How much difficulty are students and volunteers experiencing with your present system? Do you have the time and staff to make the change? Although a divided catalog at first seems to be a simple and obvious solution, it may turn out to be too complex and time-consuming when all of these points are considered.

April

Happy Birthday To . . .

2 **Hans Christian Andersen** (1805)—author
Denmark's beloved storyteller, known for *The Little Mermaid, The Emperor's New Clothes,* and many other great fairy tales

3 **Washington Irving** (1783)—author
Still loved for stories such as ''Rip Van Winkle'' and ''The Legend of Sleepy Hollow''

7 **William Wordsworth** (1770)—poet
A favorite of compilers of anthologies. Some of his shorter poems such as ''I Wandered Lonely as a Cloud'' can be understood and enjoyed by many elementary school children.

9 **Joseph Krumgold** (1908)—author
Fiction for upper grades including Newbery Medal winners *And Now Miguel* and *Onion John*

Leonard Wibberley (1915)—author
Historical fiction for upper grades, notably the Treegate series

10 **Clare Newberry** (1903)—author and illustrator
Picture books about cats including *Mittens* and *Marshmallow*

12 **Beverly Cleary** (1916)—author
Consistently popular writer of fiction. Her Henry Huggins series is an excellent choice for the young reader's transition into full-length books.

Hardie Gramatky (1907)—author and illustrator
Long, heavily illustrated stories with anthropomorphic heroes such as *Little Toot* and *Hercules*

The medium is the message for National Library Week, featuring movies, television, and, of course, books.

██

13   **Marguerite Henry** (1902)—author
     Horse stories, fiction, and nonfiction including *Misty of Chincoteague*

14   **Robert Lopshire** (1927)—author and illustrator
     Easy-to-read books including *Put Me in the Zoo*

19   **Ursula Moray Williams** (1911)—author
     Upper grade fiction including *Tiger Nanny* and *Castle Merlin*

20   **Ruth Adler** (1915)—author and illustrator
     Works with husband Irving Adler on science books such as *Your Eyes*

22   **Kurt Wiese** (1887)—author and illustrator
     Noted for primary grade books with Chinese themes such as *Fish in the Air* and the illustrations for *Story about Ping*

23   **William Shakespeare** (1546)—dramatist and poet
     Although difficult for the elementary grades, his works can be introduced to gifted students.

24   **Evaline Ness** (1911)—author and illustrator
     Picture books including *Sam Bangs and Moonshine*, a Caldecott winner

25   **Water de la Mare** (1872)—author
     Reteller of fairy tales, giving them the same lyric quality as his poetry, such as *Peacock Pie*

      Larry Kettelkamp (1933)—author and illustrator
     Nonfiction for middle grades in all subject areas including *Haunted Houses* and *Kites*

27   **Irving Adler** (1913)—author
     Writes science books with his wife, Ruth Adler, including *Time in Your Life*

Bulletin Boards

APRIL SHOWERS

A spring theme, filled with bright, cheerful colors and fanciful creatures charac-
terizes the April Showers bulletin board shown here. Any bulletin board or activity
should have some educational purpose, and this month is appropriate for bringing
gardening, flowers, and small animals to the attention of students. Meanwhile, the
pastel colors and whimsical cartoons will bring an early spring into the media center.

MATERIALS:

—1 sheet of 22″ × 28″ yellow posterboard
—light green kraft paper
—construction paper in white, dark green, light brown, pink, and yellow
—felt markers in black, blue, red, and green
—rubber cement
—scissors

PREPARATION:

1. Cut a sheet of dark green construction paper into a right triangle. The short
   leg of the triangle is 7″, and the long leg is 12″. The hypotenuse is a wavy
   line.

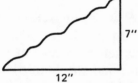

2. Paste the dark green triangle along the right-hand side of the posterboard
   with the right angle 5½″ from the bottom edge of the board.
3. Cut a 28″ wide sheet of light green kraft paper. The height should descend
   from 10″ on one side to 7″ on the other in a gently rolling line.
4. Paste the kraft paper onto the posterboard with the 10″ height on the left.
   The paper will cover the bottom of the dark green triangle.
5. On white construction paper, print "April Showers . . ." in 2″ high letters
   with a blue felt marker. Use the marker to outline a large cloud around the
   words. Cut out the cloud and paste it onto the posterboard.
6. On white construction paper, print "Discover seeds and plants, see 580's"
   in ¾″ high letters with a blue felt marker. Use the marker to make a cloud
   around the words. Cut out the cloud and paste it onto the posterboard.
7. On light brown construction paper, draw a large mushroom and cut it out.
   The cap measures 10½″ at the widest and is about 3½″ high. The stem is 1″
   wide and 4″ high.
8. Outline the mushroom with a black felt marker. Use the marker to draw gills
   on the underside of the mushroom, to shade the stem, and to print ". . . bring
   mushrooms and flowers" in ¾″ high letters.

9. Paste the mushroom onto the kraft paper and the posterboard. The center of the stem is 13″ from the left side of the posterboard. The base of the stem is 8″ from the bottom.
10. Use dark green construction paper to cut out the stem and leaves of the flower. The stem is 10½″ high.
11. Cut the full blossom and the bud from pink construction paper. Use red or black marker to outline the petals. The blossom measures 3½″ × 1½″; the bud is about ¾″ long.
12. Paste the blossom and bud onto the stem and paste the entire flower onto the bulletin board. The bottom of the stem is 1½″ from the left side and 1¼″ from the bottom.
13. Print "Get your garden growing, see 635" and "Find nature in your backyard, see 574" on pink construction paper with black or red felt marker. The letters are 1″ high. Draw a 6″ wide cloud around each group of words, cut out the clouds, and paste them onto the bulletin board.
14. Draw about six small mushrooms on light brown construction paper. Outline them with a black felt marker. You can add dots to some of the mushrooms for variety.
15. Draw the frog (2″ high) and the worm (4″ long) on dark green construction paper. Outline them and fill in the details with a black felt marker.
16. Draw the bird (3½″ high) on yellow construction paper with a black felt marker.
17. Draw the bumblebee (1½″ wide) on yellow construction paper with a black felt marker. Cut it out and paste it onto the large mushroom. Draw the feet and antennae with a black felt marker after the bee is pasted in place.
18. Draw the snail (2¼″ high) and the butterfly (5″ high) on pink construction paper with a black or red felt marker.
19. Cut out the mushrooms, frog, worm, bird, snail, and butterfly. Paste them onto the bulletin board.
20. Use a black felt marker to draw the ant at the bottom of the bulletin board.
21. Use dark green and black felt markers to draw blades of grass where the stems of the mushrooms and flowers are pasted onto the bulletin board.

YOU SAW THE MOVIE, NOW READ THE BOOK

For the nonreader and the occasional reader, familiarity with a subject may be an incentive to pick up a book about it. Many students have seen movies based on books. You might celebrate National Library Week (the first full week of April) by suggesting that students read the books that inspired their favorite movies. Use as many titles as you can remember. You might even include books that were adapted for television shows. Of course, the ABC Afterschool Specials and Mr. Magoo cartoons are sources of different quality, but students do learn something from both types of programs, and you can build from there. Display all available copies of the selected titles and watch them disappear. Advertise the books by constructing the bulletin board shown here.

MATERIALS:

—1 sheet of 22″ × 28″ black or red posterboard
—large sheet of gray construction paper

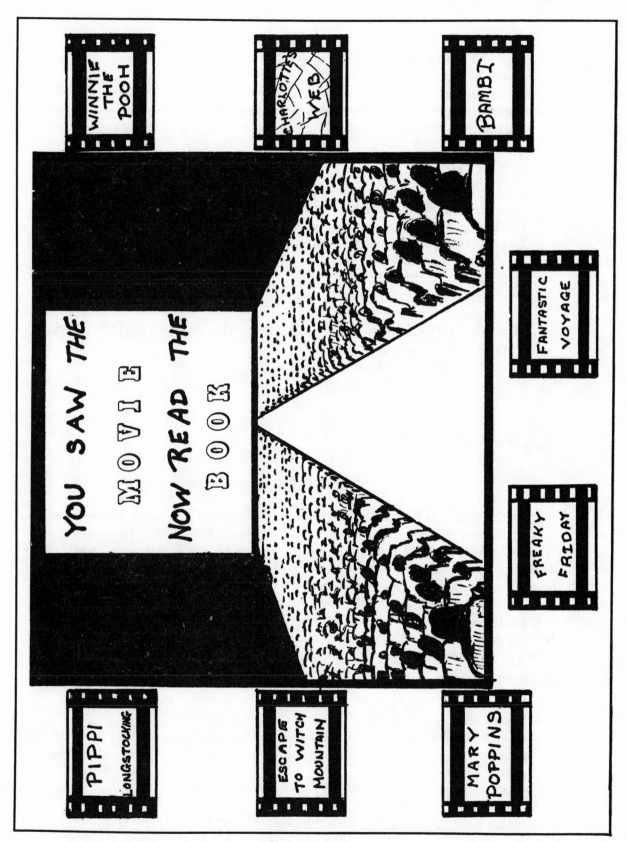

—several 8½″ × 11″ sheets of white construction paper
—black and red felt markers
—red tissue paper (optional)
—rubber cement
—scissors
—overhead projector

PREPARATION:

1. Copy the interior of the theater on gray construction paper with a black felt marker. Use the overhead projector enlargement technique described in the October chapter. The finished theater should measure 18″ × 17″.
2. Cut a 9″ × 7½″ rectangle out of white construction paper to make the screen.
3. Use black and red felt markers to print "You Saw the Movie, Now Read the Book" in 1″ high letters.
4. Use rubber cement to paste the screen onto the theater.
5. Use a red felt marker to color the walls of the theater. Or use red tissue paper that is gathered to suggest curtains.
6. Draw 4″ × 3″ title frames on white construction paper with a black felt marker. Print the book titles in the frames.
7. Paste the theater and the title frames onto the posterboard.

Library Art Activity

"READ" BUTTONS

Publicize National Library Week by having everyone in your school—the children, teachers, principal, and even custodians and cafeteria workers—make and wear "READ" buttons during the entire month of April. Everyone will enjoy designing and wearing the buttons, and there will be a greater awareness of reading and of the significance of National Library Week. Encourage everyone to participate by designing a poster similar to the one shown.

If possible, this activity should be done in conjunction with the art teacher. The buttons can be designed during art class, and the art teacher will be available to help you put them together.

MATERIALS:

—kit for making badges
—circle cutter
—enough top and bottom metal discs and clear plastic discs to make a button for everyone in your school (These items can be purchased from some library supply houses.)
—white vellum, enough to make a disc for everyone in your school
—felt markers in assorted colors
—brown paper bags, enough for each class in your school

PREPARATION:

1. Cut 2½″ discs out of white vellum using the circle cutter. You should have more than enough for everyone in the school.
2. Have every child print "READ" on a disc with a pencil. The students can decorate the discs in any way they wish. They should go over the word "READ" with felt markers.
3. Upper grade children can print "READ" on the kindergartners' discs, but they should let the kindergartners decorate the rest of the discs themselves.
4. Cover each white disc with a clear plastic disc.
5. Follow the kit instructions for putting the buttons together.
6. Make sure that the children's names and homerooms are on the backs of their buttons.
7. Place all of the buttons for each class in a brown paper bag and give the bags to the teachers. The front of each bag should indicate the date when the buttons should first be worn. (If you are concerned that the children will forget to wear the buttons to school, the teachers might collect them at the end of the day and redistribute them the next morning.)

8. Have faculty members design their own discs and offer to put the buttons together for them. You might want to have some children design extra discs for the principal, the office staff, and others who might not have the time or inclination to make their own buttons but still want to wear one.

You will be amazed at the versatility and creativity of the "READ" buttons. Seeing four or five hundred during a school day makes quite an impact on everyone.

Note: If you would prefer to do this activity at a different time of year, it is an excellent way to publicize the book fair discussed in the November chapter.

Library Enrichment Activity

TYING INTO TELEVISION*

Turn television watching into a plus for your media center program by arranging for children in your school to see a show that encourages them to read good books— public television's "Cover to Cover."

"Cover to Cover" is a fifteen-minute weekly program for fourth and fifth grade students. There are two series: "Cover to Cover I" is directed toward fourth grade students, "Cover to Cover II" has selections that are more suitable for fifth graders. The program is narrated by John Robbins, who talks about one or two children's books each time. Episodes from the spotlighted book are dramatized to pique the viewer's interest. The narrator's summaries of the action alternate with the dramatizations, all of which use the actual words of the author. Enough is told to get the children genuinely interested, but their curiosity about the story is not satisfied.

If you have television sets available, try to have classes watch the program on a regular basis during school hours. If the time of the program is not convenient and you have videotape equipment, you can tape the shows and have the children view them at a different hour. If there are no television sets in your school and the program is scheduled for after-school hours, publicize the time it will be on and encourage children to watch it at home.

It is very important to have the spotlighted books available for circulation at the end of the program. The children will be clamoring for them and will read them eagerly. If you have only one copy of a book, consider purchasing paperbacks if they are available. Generally, as soon as one child finishes, the book is passed along to someone else in the class. Often, more than half of the class will end up reading a particular book.

A teacher's manual designed to accompany "Cover to Cover" summarizes each featured book and mentions other titles on the same subject for further reading. These books will also be read and passed around, but they will not be as eagerly requested as those that are featured on the show.

In addition to "Cover to Cover," there are occasional television specials that are derived from popular children's books. Be on the lookout for the occasional good program that might spark a child's interest in reading. You should be aware that sometimes the title of the program is different from that of the book. It is a good

---

* Based on an article by Ruth Toor that appeared in *The Reading Teacher*, November 1977, p. 204.

idea to get on the mailing lists of television network publicity departments so that you will be advised of upcoming specials. When one comes along, publicize it and afterward display the featured book or books in a prominent place in your media center. Some children who do not enjoy reading and are addicted to television might be surprised to find that a show they saw was adapted from a book that is invitingly featured in the media center. This might be just the motivation they need to begin reading.

Storytelling Suggestions

SPRING WEATHER

Respond to the uncertainties of April weather with stories of wind, rain, and the coming of spring.

Barrett, Judi

The Wind Thief
illus. by Diane Dawson
Atheneum, 1977

On a cold and blustery day, the wind decides he needs a hat to keep warm and picks a stocking cap with rainbow stripes. Making a huge gust, he lifts the hats from the heads of all of the people on the street. When he stops blowing, the hats land on the wrong heads. Everyone goes home with a new hat, including the wind. (kindergarten to second grade)

Clifton, Lucille

The Boy Who Didn't Believe in Spring
illus. by Brinton Turkle
Dutton, 1973

King Shabazz, a city boy, doesn't believe in spring. He and his friend, Tony Polito, search for spring with the cityscape always present in the background. On an apartment roof they find a nest with four light blue eggs. "Man, it's Spring." With contemporary illustrations and a fully integrated neighborhood, you couldn't ask for a better book for early April. (kindergarten to second grade)

Craig, M. Jean

Spring Is Like the Morning
illus. by Don Almquist
Putnam's, 1965

A nonfiction account of the coming of spring as seen by a young boy. Each of his senses perceives the differences around him, alerting him to the changes that take place as the world wakes up in spring. Two sessions are required to read this, and much discussion will follow on how to "smell" or "taste" spring. (first to third grade)

Garrison, Christian

Little Pieces of the West Wind
illus. by Diane Goode
Bradbury, 1975

A tale about an old man who sends the mighty West Wind to find his lost socks, holding as hostage a piece of the Wind to insure its return. The search grows complicated, and the Wind loses additional pieces until it is reduced to a tiny breeze. The process is reversed when, befriended by a little girl, the Wind fulfills all requests and regains its full strength. (kindergarten to second grade)

Ginsburg, Mirra   *Mushroom in the Rain*
                                   adapted from the Russian tale by V. Suteyev
                                   illus. by Jose Aruego and Ariane Dewey
                                   Macmillan, 1974

A mushroom is just large enough for an ant to fit underneath. As increasingly larger animals come seeking shelter from the rain, the group squeezes together to make room. When the rain stops, the ant is amazed to realize how many animals were under the mushroom. But you know what happens to mushrooms in the rain—they grow! (kindergarten to second grade)

Hutchins, Pat   *The Wind Blew*
                                   Macmillan, 1974

As the wind blew, it scooped up umbrellas, scarves, newspapers, and much more in this rhyming story with an English setting. Before it blew out to sea, all of the flying articles were dropped back to earth—but not where they belonged. Children delight in discovering what happened to the items. (kindergarten and first grade)

Raskin, Ellen   *And It Rained*
                                   Atheneum, 1971

A pig, a parrot, and a potto always sit down to tea in the jungle at four o'clock, just five minutes before it rains. When they grow tired of weak tea and soggy biscuits, they try various solutions before finding one that is quite satisfactory to all of them—very strong tea, very hard biscuits, and a little rain to soften things a bit. (first and second grade)

Scheer, Julian   *Rain Makes Applesauce*
                                   illus. by Marvin Bileck
                                   Holiday House, 1964

This is a tricky book to read aloud, so do it only if you really love the humor. Silly phrases with great sounds such as "Monkeys mumble in a jelly bean jungle" occupy center stage. Meanwhile, two children plant an apple seed, and with care and the help of the rain, they grow a tree, pick apples, and make applesauce. Delicate illustrations contribute to the special mood. (kindergarten and first grade)

Silverstein, Shel   *The Giving Tree*
                                   Harper and Row, 1964

"Once there was a tree . . . and she loved a little boy." He picked her leaves, ate her apples, and rested in her shade, and the tree was happy. As the boy grew older, she gave him her apples to sell, her branches to build a house, and her trunk to make a boat. Finally, she had nothing left but an old stump on which the boy, now an old man, could sit and rest. (All ages)

Here is another suggestion if you are telling stories on the right day:

Krahn, Fernando   *April Fools*
                                   Dutton, 1974

This story without words follows the action of two boys as they construct a sea monster to fool people. When they become lost in the woods, their April Fools' Day gag saves them by alerting rescuers to their location. (kindergarten to second grade)

Teaching Unit

SUBJECT INDEX TO CHILDREN'S MAGAZINES

Sixth graders, and fifth graders who have mastered the elements of the card catalog and basic reference tools such as encyclopedias and dictionaries, can be introduced to periodical indexes. The *Readers' Guide to Periodical Literature* and its abridged version index adult magazines. Most elementary schools do not subscribe to enough of these magazines to warrant the purchase of either index, but the *Subject Index to Children's Magazines* is an excellent resource for your media center. It indexes many of the periodicals commonly found in elementary media centers such as *Cricket, Ranger Rick, Highlights,* and *Young Miss,* and it uses the format that students will later encounter in the *Readers' Guide.* Issues appear ten times a year on a monthly basis, with two double issues and semi-annual cumulative indexes.

This teaching unit is designed as a classroom learning center to be developed with the classroom teacher. However, the unit can be taught in the media center if necessary. Students must pass the library skills proficiency test before using the task cards.

MATERIALS:

—ditto master of library skills proficiency test
—materials for sample entry display:
  • sheet of 11″ × 14″ oaktag
  • black felt marker
  • small sheets of construction paper in assorted colors
  • string (optional)
  • rubber cement
—several 9″ × 14″ sheets of posterboard
—10 strips of 6″ × 2″ posterboard
—clear self-stick vinyl
—5 sheets of 6″ × 9″ posterboard
—2 large manila envelopes and 1 smaller manila envelope
—6″ × 9″ sheet of light-colored construction paper

PREPARATION:

1. Prepare a proficiency test on library skills previously learned by the students. (See sample test on page 214.)
2. Make a large sample entry, copying from any issue of *Subject Index to Children's Magazines.* Label all parts of the entry as shown in the illustration (page 215).

  • Print entry on 11″ × 14″ oaktag.
  • Use assorted colors of construction paper to prepare labels. Use one color for author, another for name of magazine, and another for subject heading, and so on.
  • Paste the labels on both sides of the entry.

Library Skills Proficiency Test

Choose the correct word to complete each sentence from the list below.
WORDS FROM THE LIST MAY BE USED MORE THAN ONCE.

not true
Dewey Decimal Classification
System
author
illustrated
alphabetical
biography

subject
index
title
numerical
true
call number

1. Nonfiction means _____.
2. Fiction means _____.
3. Fiction is arranged in _____ order.
4. Nonfiction is arranged in _____ order.
5. The method used for arranging nonfiction is called _____. (Not the same answer as # 4.)
6. The card catalog is arranged in _____ order.
7. The card catalog contains _____ cards, _____ cards, and _____ cards. (3 different answers)
8. The numbers and letters appearing in the upper left-hand corner of a catalog card are called the book's _____.
9. When the top line of a catalog card is printed entirely in capital letters, it indicates a(n) _____ card. (example: MYSTERY AND DETECTIVE STORIES)
10. When the top line of a catalog card has the first letter of the first word capitalized and all other letters, except the first letter of a proper noun, in lower case, it indicates a(n) _____ card. (example: This is New York)
11. The card catalog is sometimes called a(n) _____ to the media center.
12. When "illus." appears on a catalog card, it means the book is _____.
13. When the top line of a catalog card has a last name that is followed by a comma and then by a first name, and only the first letter of each name is capitalized, it indicates a(n) _____ card. (example: Cameron, Eleanor)
14. On the spine label of every book in the media center, you will find the book's _____.
15. When a "B" appears above a call number, it indicates that the book is a(n) _____. (example: B NAMATH)

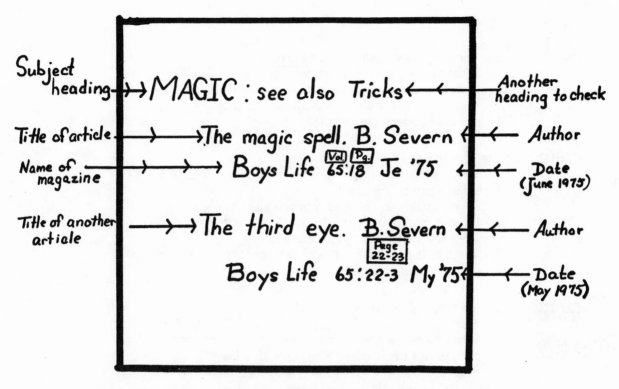

- Draw lines or use string to connect the labels to the appropriate sections of the entry.
- For tight spots such as volume and page, paste the labels directly over the information.

3. Make several photocopies of a page in the *Subject Index*. (See the sample on page 217.)
4. Paste each photocopy on a sheet of 9″ × 14″ posterboard.
5. Select ten subject headings from the *Subject Index* that are of interest to the students and are represented in most issues. Print the headings on the posterboard strips and cover with clear self-stick vinyl.

Note: If you use posterboard strips to play the catalog card game described in the January Teaching Unit, be sure that the strips for this unit are of a different size and color. This will help prevent the materials from getting mixed up when students take them from the classroom and return them to the media center.

Sample subject headings:

ARCHERY	POWER CONSERVATION
BICYCLES	PUPPETS AND PUPPET PLAYS
FIRST AID	SNAKES
GLIDERS	SWAMPS
HAIR	STORMS

6. Prepare five task cards on the 6″ × 9″ sheets of posterboard. Note that the questions on the first four cards apply to the sample page. This gives students practice with entries that can be checked easily. The fifth card requires them to actually use the *Subject Index*.

Sample Task Cards:

Card 1   Use sample pages from Subject Index.
1.   What is the title of the article listed under CACTI?
2.   In what magazine did the article appear?
3.   In what month and year did the article appear?
4.   On what page is the article?

Card 2   Use sample page from Subject Index.
1.   What is the title of the article listed under BUSINESS?
2.   Who wrote the article?
3.   In what magazine did the article appear?
4.   In what month and year did the article appear?
5.   On what page does the article begin?
6.   What tells you that the article is continued on another page in the magazine?

Card 3   Use sample page from Subject Index.
1.   How many articles are listed about BUTTERFLIES?
2.   What magazine has an article on Eleanor Cameron?
3.   Who wrote the article "Alaska on $5 a Day"?
4.   Where should you look to find articles on BURROS?
Answer these questions in complete sentences.

Card 4   Use sample page from Subject Index.
1.   How many subjects are listed on this page?
2.   Which article on CALCULATING MACHINES was published in Popular Mechanics?
3.   What magazine had an article on BURGLAR ALARMS? Who wrote it?
4.   If you wanted information on monarch butterflies, which two magazines would you choose? Give the complete date of each article.
5.   You are going camping and you are worried about fire safety. Which two articles should you look at? Give title of the article, magazine name, date, and page.

Card 5   1.   Take one of the strips.
2.   Look up the heading in the Subject Index to Children's Magazines.
3.   Which issue did you use?
4.   How many entries are listed under the subject heading you chose?
5.   Give the names of the magazines that have information on this subject.
6.   Put a star next to any magazines that we have in the media center.
7.   Choose two articles and write them in proper bibliographic form.
8.   Repeat for each strip.

7. Print the directions and requirements that students must follow to complete the teaching unit on the 6″ × 9″ sheet of construction paper.
8. Display the unit on a classroom bulletin board. Include the sample entry, the student directions, a manila envelope containing the five task cards, a manila envelope for the photocopies of the sample page, and a small manila envelope for the posterboard strips.

Sample Page from *Subject Index to Children's Magazines**

BUDGETS - U. S.
    The 1976 federal budget dollar.
    Search 6:9 Ap 10 '75
BUFFALOES
    Our playful bison. C.Hellyer.
    Pacific S 9:28 My '75
BULL, OLE BORNEMAN, 1810 - 1880
    Ole Bull - musician, adventurer.
    A.Sorenson. Badger Hist
    28:50-61 Ja '75
BURGLAR ALARMS
    Add an emergency alarm to your
    wireless garage opener.
    R.V.Putterbaugh. Pop Mech
    143:210 My '75
BURROS: see Donkeys
BUSINESS
    How to succeed in business while
    really trying. G.Hiller.
    Am Girl 58:26-7+ Ap '75
BUTTERFLIES: see also Moths
    Be a butterfly tamer.
    M.K.Hultsch. Wee Wisdom
    81:38-9 Ap '75
    Butterflies and moths in winter.
    E.Munroe. Nat Canada
    4:26-9 Ja-Mr '75
    Junior, the monarch. Parade
    56:4-5 Ap 23 '75
    List for life. Explorer
    36:2-3 My 8 '75
    Monarch butterfly. (Picture
    only) Ranger Rick
    9:1 Ag-S '75
    ...Spicebush Swallowtail butter-
    fly. C.H.Sloan. Geog Sch B
    53:464 Ap 28 '75
CABINETMAKERS
    Nelson Way, second career man.
    C.Stapleton. Md Mag
    7:54 Summer '75
CACTI
    Saguaros. Ariz Highw
    51:28 Ap '75
CALCULATING MACHINES
    Electronic checkbook... J.R.Free.
    Pop Sci 207:11 Ag '75
    PS readers share their calculator
    shortcuts. D.Huff.
    Pop Sci 206:102-3+ Je '75
    Super math from simple kits.
    I.Berger. Pop Mech
    143:104 My '75
CALDECOTT MEDAL AWARDS
    Caldecott Award acceptance.
    G.McDermott. Horn Bk
    51:349-54 Ag '75
    Newbery and Caldecott awards.
    Horn Bk 51:98+ Ap '75

CALENDARS
    May 1975.   Wee Wisdom
    81:49-50 My '75
    Wee Wisdom presents March!
    Wee Wisdom 81:centerfold
    Mr '75
CAMBODIA
    Cambodian refugees crowd into
    capital. Sr Wkly R
    29:3 Ap 2 '75
    Southeast Asia... At war again!
    [or still?] Jr Schol
    76:9-10 Ap 10 '75
    Transpacific update.   Sr Wkly R
    29:3 Ap 23 '75
CAMERON, ELEANOR
    Meet your author. Cricket
    2:42-4 Je '75
CAMP COOKERY
    The wok for walkers.
    Pacific S 9:44 My '75
CAMPING
    Alaska on $5 a day. A.Satter-
    field. Pacific S 9:40 Je '75
    Camping goes compact...
    B.McKeown. Pop Mech
    143:116-7 Mr '75
    Camping safely with fires and
    heaters. Pacific S 9:46
    My '75
    Dear Ranger Rick.   Ranger Rick
    9:18-23 Mr '75
    Electric RV fridge makes camping
    a cool experience. W.S.Anda-
    riese. Pop Sci 207:91 Ag '75
    A fire ethic. Pacific S 9:41
    Je '75
    For backpackers: a lightweight
    stove that behaves itself.
    C.Maurer. Pop Sci
    206:57 Ap '75
    Make-it-yourself camping lantern.
    E.Adams. Young World
    12:53 Ag-S '75
    Pop-up tent camper you can build.
    Pop Mech 144:50 Jl '75
    Rancho poncho: a quick-change
    bivouac bag. E.P.Haddon.
    Pop Mech 143:122 Mr '75
    Recreation roundup. H.Shuldiner.
    Pop Sci 206:30 My '75
    A safe outdoor fire.   Boys' Life
    65:46 Je '75
    '75 pace-setting RV's.
    H.Shuldiner. Pop Sci
    206:100-1+ Mr '75
    Steens Mountain: lava flows and
    five life zones. J.Spurr.
    Pacific S 9:43 Jl-Ag '75

* Reprinted from the March-August 1975 issue of *Subject Index to Children's Magazines* with permission from the editor.

Professional Responsibilities

HARDWARE MANAGEMENT

Although distributing hardware (see the September Professional Responsibilities) is one of the first things you do at the beginning of the school year, the circulation of equipment is actually the last step in a series of procedures that begins when the equipment is purchased. To circulate hardware with maximum efficiency, you should process each piece through the steps described below.

Organizing all of the files suggested here may sound too time-consuming; however, you will find that in the long run it saves time. A volunteer with clerical talents can be of great help in creating and maintaining your hardware management system.

CHECKING OPERATION: Do not assume that any equipment is operational just because it is new. Each piece must be thoroughly checked out according to the directions booklet. Become familiar with how the equipment works because you will have to instruct faculty, students, and volunteers in its operation.

OPERATIONS MANUAL: Once you know how to operate the machine, it is a good idea to write a step-by-step description of the procedures. Indicate the type of equipment and the model number at the top of the page. Keep all of the directions for one type of equipment together in one section of a loose-leaf operations manual.

Whether or not you rewrite the manufacturer's explanation of how to operate the equipment, keep the booklet of directions that accompanied the equipment in a file. When the equipment malfunctions—and it will—the booklet will come in handy. By checking the directions, you can get an idea of whether outside repair is required. In addition, the booklet gives directions for cleaning and maintaining the machine and changing the lamp if it has one. Each brand, each model, each type of hardware has its own peculiar method for changing the lamp. If you are fortunate and lamp changes are few and far between, it is easy to forget the procedure.

INVENTORY CHECKLIST AND SUPPLIES FILE: To use equipment efficiently, you must maintain an adequate inventory of supplies. Otherwise, your stock of supplies may be suddenly depleted just as the demand rises. A simple method is to have a checklist of all materials needed. (See sample at top of facing page.)

In this abbreviated example, lamps and film are listed by type. Film mailers, transparency supplies, and other miscellaneous items are also listed. Every three to six months an inventory of supplies is taken and checks are entered in the appropriate column.

This checklist keeps you aware of the state of your supply closet and alerts you to impending problems. For example, if the supply of one type of lamp is drastically cut from one inventory to the next, it indicates a piece of equipment is being used more frequently or one of the machines or outlets is causing lamps to burn out.

In addition to the checklist, a file of 3" × 5" cards listing the supplies needed by type of equipment is helpful. On each card, write the name of the equipment, the

SUPPLIES CHECKLIST		SEPT.	JAN.
LAMPS:	CAL		
	DAY		
	EKE		
FILM:	Type 108 Verichrome		
	Pan 126		
	Mailers		
TRANSPARENCY SUPPLIES:	Acetate (boxes)		
	Pens		
	Pencils		
MISCELLANEOUS:	Lens Cleaner		
	Tape head cleaner		

model number, the number of pieces, and the supplies needed. This is a handy file to have when a lamp burns out. You can check it to find out which lamp is needed, and you have ready access to the vendor's name in case of repeated breakdowns.

PROJECTOR, Filmstrip, Silent

SINGER GRAFLEX 400 Code—FS
  10 Projectors
        VENDOR: YEAR PURCHASED:

LAMPS: CAL
      Estimate 3 per Projector per year

SERIAL NUMBERS AND CODING: The next step is to record the serial number of each piece of equipment in a file or book. Organize your list by model and type. Frequently serial numbers are difficult to locate, are not easily read, and are too cumbersome to use when charging out equipment. Therefore, it is helpful to assign a simple letter-number code to all equipment. The code should include a designation of equipment type, such as OP for overhead projector. The number is similar to an accession number; if you have 15 overhead projectors, they are numbered OP-1 through OP-15. Enter the code name next to each serial number in your file. Label the equipment with this code name in a conspicuous location. An engraving tool, permanent felt marker, or label covered with white paste is suitable for marking equipment. If a label falls off or the marker fades, check the serial number on the machine against the one in your file and relabel.

Note: If you ever lend equipment outside the building, perhaps to another school, choose two or three letters to designate your media center and put these letters before the equipment code. This insures that the user will know where to return the equipment.

REPAIR RECORD: All equipment is subject to breakdown and may have to be sent out for repair. Some machines need repair more often than others. To know which machines malfunction regularly and to obtain an accurate picture of the breakdown time for various types and models of equipment, set up a repair file. Use 5″ × 8″ index cards and divide each into three columns labeled Date Out, Date In, and Reason for Repair. Put the equipment code at the top of each card. Arrange this file by type of equipment and numerical sequence.

Code FS- 201		
Date Out	Date In	Reason for Repair

CHECKING COMMERCIAL BIBLIOGRAPHIES AGAINST THE CARD CATALOG

Your collection probably contains a number of commercial bibliographies such as *Index to Poetry for Children and Young People, 1970-1975,* compiled by John Brewton and others (Wilson, 1978), *Index to Fairy Tales 1949–1972* by Norma Olin Ireland (Faxon, 1973), and *Index to Young Readers' Collective Biographies,* 2nd ed., by Judith Silverman (Bowker, 1975). In order for these bibliographies to be of maximum assistance to you and your students, the books that they list should be checked against your card catalog so that anyone can tell at a glance which titles are in your media center.

Ask a volunteer to sit at the card catalog with the bibliography and a pencil and to complete the following procedures:

1. Begin checking the selections listed in the bibliography against the card catalog. The selections are arranged alphabetically by the author's last name.

2. After finding the author's name, check to make sure that the title is the same.

3. If the title is the same, make a check with the pencil next to the listing in the bibliography and write the call number of the book. This will save the user the time needed to recheck the catalog for the call number.

4. Continue this procedure until the whole list has been checked against the card catalog.

5. Write the date at the top of the list. When several years have passed and materials in this category have been added to the collection, the bibliography can be rechecked and updated.

Note: If you do not have many of the listed titles, you might consider basing future orders on the bibliography.

TYPING CATALOG CARDS

Explain to your volunteers that there are four basic kinds of catalog cards: author card (or main entry), title card, subject card, and shelf list card. The samples shown here indicate that each card should be typed in a different format. Be sure to emphasize the need for accuracy and for adherence to the proper form. To help keep the spacing uniform, you may want to purchase catalog cards with red guidelines for typing from a library supply house. Otherwise, your volunteers can use regular blank catalog cards.

Catalog cards for audio-visual materials have a similar format. However, the main entry card will often be the title card, and there will be no author card. The type of media described by the card can be indicated by the call number. For example, FS might stand for filmstrip, CAS for cassette.

AUTHOR CARD

    FIC   Fleischman, Sid
    FLE   McBroom tells the truth
                Norton, c1966.
                47 p. ill.

            A farm where beans can be planted
            and harvested in one hour can start
            a lot of rumors, and McBroom sets
            down the "facts."

            1. Gardening—Fiction   I. Title

TITLE CARD

            McBroom tells the truth
    FIC   Fleischman, Sid
    FLE   McBroom tells the truth
                Norton, c1966.
                47 p. ill.

            A farm where beans can be planted
            and harvested in one hour can start
            a lot of rumors, and McBroom sets
            down the "facts."

            1. Gardening—Fiction   I. Title

SUBJECT CARD

GARDENING—FICTION

FIC
FLE

Fleischman, Sid
    McBroom tells the truth
        Norton, c1966.
        47 p. ill.

A farm where beans can be planted
and harvested in one hour can start
a lot of rumors, and McBroom sets
down the "facts."

1. Gardening—Fiction   I. Title

SHELF LIST CARD

FIC
FLE

Fleischman, Sid
    McBroom tells the truth
        Norton, c1966.
        47 p. ill.

S-12,407

1. Gardening—Fiction   I. Title

Open End

SHOULD FILING OF MEDIA BE INTEGRATED?

In an ideal media center, all materials—whether books, filmstrips, cassettes, study prints, or transparencies—would be filed together so that anyone needing information on a subject would find it all in one place. Multimedia units would almost leap off the shelves into the user's arms, and every type of material would get optimum usage. However, most library media specialists either cannot or do not want to integrate different types of media and arrange them by subject.

The physical layout of your media center and the dimensions of your bookshelves often make it impossible to file all media together. Although a few producers of sound filmstrips are now turning out packages that are shaped like books, many are still using huge boxes that could never fit on a regular shelf. Records and cassettes are hard to shelve normally; so are transparencies, slides, film loops, and 13″ × 18″ study prints.

Different types of media may be filed separately because the library media specialist does not use the Dewey Decimal System for cataloging audio-visual materials. In addition, some library media specialists feel that audio-visual materials should not be easily accessible to children because they cost too much to replace. In this case, the materials are filed in a closed cabinet, in a separate room, or on a high shelf. When audio-visual material is requested, it must be found and brought to the person who has made the request. Of course, this contradicts a policy of "open access," which means that anyone is able to lay hands on anything in the media center. Children can be taught to handle most types of media without causing any problems. In fact, first grade children can operate an 8mm. film loop projector with very little training.

Consideration should also be given to the distance between your audio-visual equipment (hardware) and the materials that are used with that equipment (software). If your software is stored at a great distance from the related hardware, optimum usage will not be made of it. Instead, you might store your 8mm. film loops in a carrel that contains an 8 mm. loop projector and keep your records in a bin next to a record player.

If you are fortunate enough to be involved in planning a new media center or redesigning an old one, you should seriously consider including the integrated filing of all media in your plans. Otherwise, keep in mind some of the points mentioned, and come up with a media filing system that is best suited to your school and to your own philosophy.

May

Happy Birthday To...

5   **Leo Lionni** (1910)—author and illustrator
       Mostly large picture books using bold colors and collage techniques, including *Swimmy* and *Frederick*

6   **Giulio Maestro** (1942)—author and illustrator
       Illustrates his own humorous picture books, such as *The Remarkable Plant in Apartment 4*, as well as both fiction and nonfiction works by other authors

7   **Nonny Hogrogian** (1932)—author and illustrator
       Picture books and easy folk tales such as *One Fine Day* (Caldecott winner) and *Rooster Brother*

9   **Sir James Barrie** (1860)—author
       Creator of *Peter Pan*

      William Pene Du Bois (1916)—author and illustrator
       Author of picture books and stories for intermediate grades, including *Bear Party, Lazy Tommy Pumpkinhead*, and *21 Balloons*

      Eleanor Estes (1906)—author
       Fiction for intermediate grades, including *The Moffats* and *Ginger Pye*

      Keith Robertson (1914)—author
       Intermediate and upper grade fiction, including *Henry Reed, Inc.* and *Three Stuffed Owls*

11   **Zilpha Keatley Snyder** (1927)—author
       Fiction with an other-worldly aura for upper grades, including *The Egypt Game* and *The Changeling*

12   **Edward Lear** (1812)—poet
       Renowned for his limericks such as the famous "There was an old man with a beard . . ."

Farley Mowat (1921)—author
Stories about animals for upper grades, including *The Dog Who Wouldn't Be* and *Owls in the Family*

18   **Lillian Hoban** (1925)—author and illustrator
Pictures for Russell Hoban's Frances books as well as easy-to-read stories of her own such as *Arthur's Honey Bear*

Irene Hunt (1907)—author
Fiction for upper grades, including *Up a Road Slowly*

21   **Virginia Haviland** (1911)—compiler and specialist in children's literature
Compiler of the multi-volume Favorite Fairy Tales series

22   **Sir Arthur Conan Doyle** (1859)—author
Creator of Sherlock Holmes

Arnold Lobel (1933)—author and illustrator
Easy-to-read books and picture books such as the Frog and Toad series and *Lucille*

23   **Scott O'Dell** (1902)—author
Fiction on survival themes for upper grades, notably *Island of the Blue Dolphins*

27   **Rachel Carson** (1907)—author
Leading conservationist who may be said to have begun it all with *The Sea Around Us* and *Silent Spring*

30   **Millicent Selsam** (1912)—author
Science books on an easy-to-read level such as *Egg to Chick* and *Tony's Birds*

31   **Jay Williams** (1914)—author
Picture books and intermediate fiction including the Danny Dunn series and *Forgetful Fred*

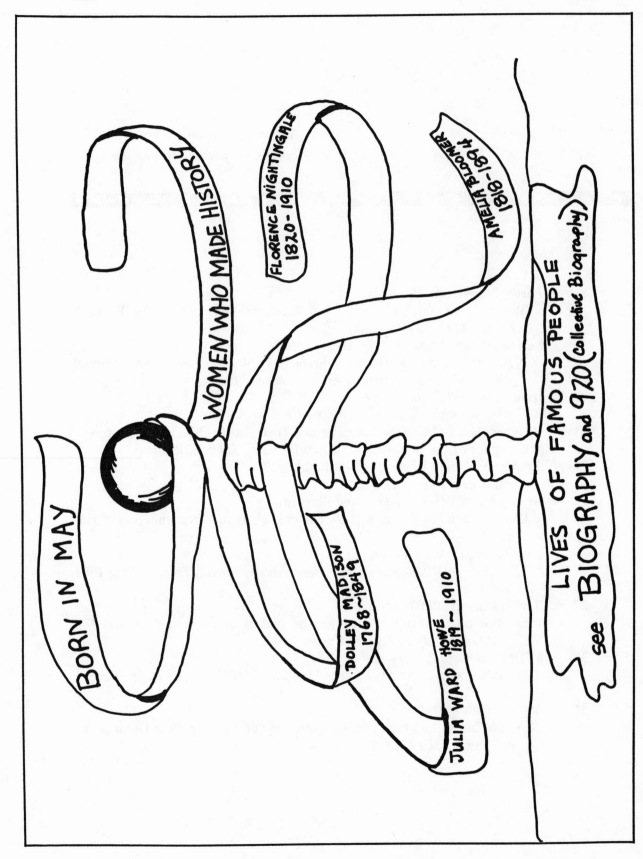

BORN IN MAY

WOMEN WHO MADE HISTORY

FLORENCE NIGHTINGALE 1820-1910

AMELIA BLOOMER 1818-1894

DOLLEY MADISON 1768-1849

JULIA WARD HOWE 1819-1910

LIVES OF FAMOUS PEOPLE see BIOGRAPHY and 920 (Collective Biography)

Bulletin Boards

MAYPOLE

Four determined women were born in May. Use them as the subject of a quick, attactive bulletin board and promote the reading of biography and collective biography at the same time. (See illustration.) If there is space available, display biographies about these four women and others.

When you make this bulletin board, be aware that all sizes given are approximate and are to be used only as a guide. Do not worry about exact measurements. As you draw the outline for the ribbons around the Maypole, allow the pencil to swirl freely to obtain the effect of ribbons curling in the breeze.

Slightly diluted poster paints will look best and should be your first choice if you are experienced with this medium. Good quality crayons are an attractive alternative.

MATERIALS:

—1 sheet of 22″ × 28″ yellow or light green posterboard
—paints or crayons in 6 pastel shades (blue, pink, orange, violet, yellow, green)

Note: If you are using crayons, you will not need to use the color that is the same as the color of the posterboard. Outlining the yellow or green ribbon in black will be sufficient. However, yellow paint on yellow posterboard or green paint on green posterboard will show up well.

—black felt markers, wide tip and narrow tip
—pencil

PREPARATION:

1. Draw the Maypole and swirling ribbons in pencil.

    • The ball on top of the Maypole is approximately 2½″ in diameter and 18½″ from the bottom of the posterboard.
    • The pole is 1½″ wide.
    • The ribbons are 1½″ to 2″ at the widest part.

2. Use the wide-tip marker to print "Born in May" and "Women Who Made History" in 1″ letters on two of the ribbons.

3. With the narrow-tip marker, print the four names and dates on the four remaining ribbons.

4. Use the wide-tip marker to draw a flowing line 2½″ to 3″ from the bottom of the posterboard. This line will simulate the ground.

5. Use the wide-tip marker to outline the banner at the bottom that directs students to biography and collective biography.

    • The banner is 18″ wide and 1½″ high.
    • Use the narrow-tip marker to print information on the banner.

6. Use the wide-tip marker to go over your pencil outline of the Maypole and ribbons.

7. Color the ribbons, the Maypole, the interior of the banner, and the ground with paint or crayon. The Maypole ball is orange or gold.

   Note: If you use paint, the letters may fade slightly. Should this occur, go over the letters with the felt marker when the paint is dry.

NONSENSE BY LEAR

Salute Edward Lear, the noted Victorian author of limericks and other kinds of humorous verse. If you accompany this bulletin board with this month's Library Art Activity, students will be guided to the poetry section. Those who find Lear dated might enjoy his literary descendants such as Ogden Nash.

The bulletin board shown here looks striking, and the only difficult part is the portrait of Lear. Use an overhead projector to enlarge the drawing shown here, find one in an encyclopedia, or choose one of Lear's self-caricatures. All of his works and illustrations are included in *The Complete Nonsense Book* by Edward Lear (Dodd, Mead, 1912).

MATERIALS:

—1 sheet of 22″ × 28″ posterboard in a light color
—1 sheet of white construction paper
—4 sheets of construction paper in a color that complements the posterboard
—black felt markers, fine tip and wide tip
—scissors
—rubber cement
—overhead projector
—pencil

PREPARATION:

1. Use the overhead projector to make a 5½″ × 6½″ drawing of Edward Lear on white construction paper with the fine-tip marker. It is easier if you use a pencil to trace the drawing and then go over your work with the marker.
2. Frame the drawing with the wide-tip marker. Cut it out and paste it onto the posterboard 5″ from the bottom.
3. Letter "A Sample of" in 1¾″ high letters and "Nonsense" in 2½″ high letters. The words "by Edward Lear" are about 1″ high.
4. The birth and death dates are ¾″ to 1″ high.
5. Select four of Lear's works that you think will appeal to the students. Print each of them on a sheet of construction paper. Draw a wavy line around each poem for an interesting effect. Cut out the poems and paste them onto the bulletin board.

Library Art Activity

ILLUSTRATE A LIMERICK

Students will discover humorous verse for themselves if the Lear bulletin board is expanded into an art activity. They can select a limerick or another type of

A Sample of NONSENSE

by

Edward Lear

Born:
May 27, 1812
Died:
January 29, 1888

Laughable Lines

How pleasant to know
Mr. Lear!
Who has written such
volumes of stuff!
Some think him ill-
tempered and queer,
But a few think him
pleasant enough.

LIMERICK

There was an Old Man of
the Coast
Who placidly sat on a post;
But when it was cold, he
relinquished his hold
And called for some hot
buttered toast.

LIMERICK

There was an old person
of Ware,
Who rode on the back
of a bear;
When they said "Does it trot?"—
he said, "Certainly not!
He's a Moppsikon Floppsikon bear!"

from a
Nonsense Alphabet

R

R was a rabbit
Who had a bad habit
Of eating the flowers
In gardens and bowers

r
Naughty fat rabbit!

nonsense verse—including tongue twisters—and illustrate their selections. Decorate the media center with the results. Students with literary talents can be encouraged to write and illustrate their own limericks. Keep drawing paper and crayons at the desk for anyone who wishes to work in the media center. Announce the activity with a poster similar to the one shown here.

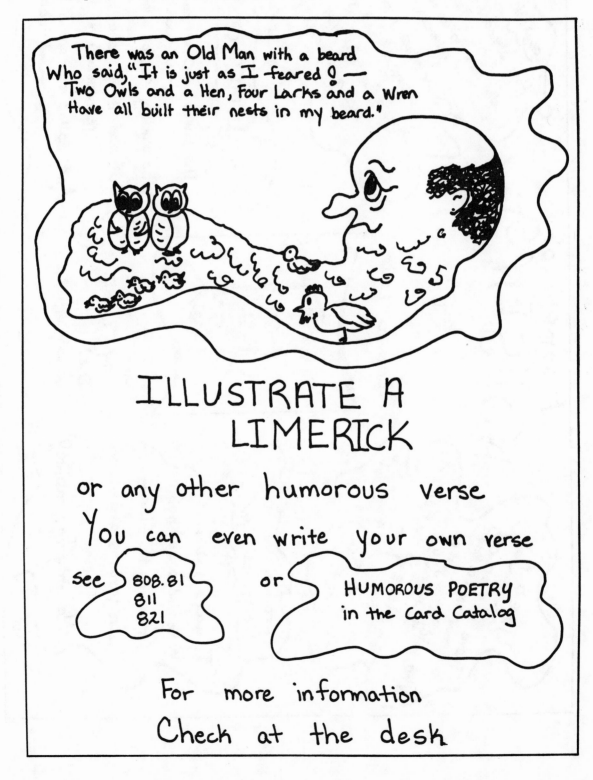

MATERIALS:

—1 sheet of 11″ × 14″ posterboard in a light color
—construction paper in a contrasting shade
—felt markers, wide tip and narrow tip
—rubber cement
—easel back
—scissors
—pencil
—overhead projector

PREPARATION:

1. Block out the area of the poster where the drawing will go and use a pencil to lightly print the letters for "Illustrate a Limerick" below it. Leave space for the two balloons showing Dewey decimal numbers and card catalog information. Lightly print the other directions with a pencil.
2. Choose a limerick and illustrate it on the construction paper. You can use the overhead projector to copy the picture shown here or trace one of Lear's own illustrations from *The Complete Nonsense Book* (Dodd, Mead, 1912). Use the narrow-tip marker to make the drawing and to print the limerick.
3. Use the wide-tip marker to make a wavy outline around the illustration and then cut it out.
4. Print the appropriate Dewey decimal numbers and the subject heading HUMOROUS POETRY on construction paper using a fine-tip marker.
5. Use the wide-tip marker to make wavy outlines around the Dewey decimal numbers and the subject heading and then cut them out.
6. Use the wide-tip marker to go over the letters you have printed in pencil.
7. Paste the three construction paper cutouts on the posterboard.
8. Attach the easel back.

Library Enrichment Activity

TURN IN RIDDLES

Begin preparing for the June "Riddles" bulletin board in May. Because June is such a busy month, anything you can do ahead of time is a great help. If you use this activity, you will have your June bulletin board ready to go by the end of May. The students will do most of the work by turning in their favorite riddles. The display for the activity requires very little time. All that is necessary is a simple poster and a box for collecting the riddles.

MATERIALS:

—box (use an empty book card box, catalog card box, or shoebox)
—aluminum foil
—scraps of colored construction paper
—tape
—1 sheet of 11″ × 14″ colored posterboard

—felt marker
—easel back
—30 pieces of 5″ × 2″ unlined paper
—scissors

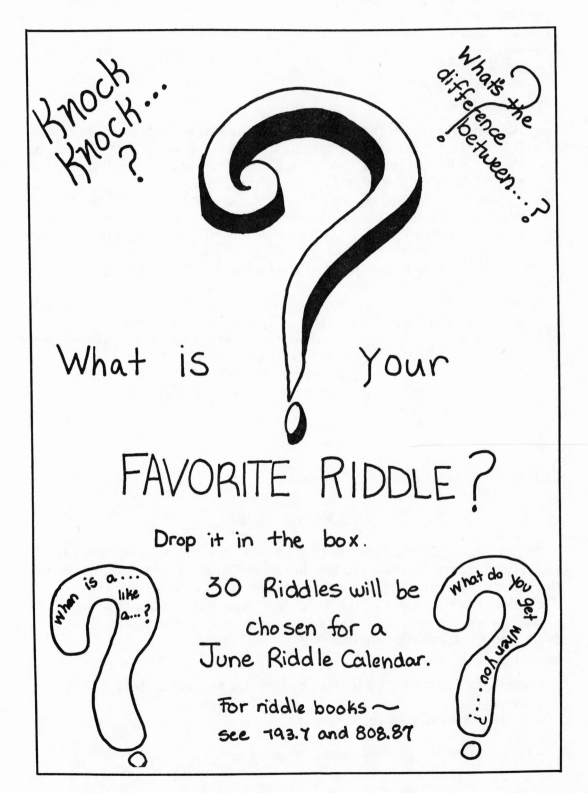

PREPARATION:

1. Cover box with foil.
2. Make a slit in the top of the box.
3. Cut out question marks of different heights and shapes from the construction paper.
4. Roll pieces of tape so that they are sticky on both sides. Use the tape to attach the question marks around the box.
5. Prepare the poster. Draw a very large question mark and print the directions to the students. (See the illustration.)
6. Attach the easel back and display the poster.
7. Empty the box full of riddles several times during the month.
8. Select 30 of the best riddles. (A volunteer can do this task.)
9. Fold the pieces of unlined paper to form 2½″ × 2″ rectangles.
10. Keeping the fold line along the top, write a number (1 to 30) about ½″ high on each of the slips. Be sure to leave room for the riddle.
11. Print the riddle on the outside of the folded paper. Print the answer on the inside.

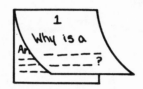

12. Put the slips aside in a safe place until you are ready to assemble the June bulletin board.

GOOD BOOKS TO READ

Encourage children to suggest books that other children might want to read by posting a "Good Books to Read" list in your media center. As students finish books they especially enjoyed, ask them to add the titles, followed by their own names, to the list. When other students just don't know what to read, have them consult the "Good Books to Read" list made by their peers for ideas. Sometimes students are more likely to pick up a title from the list than to follow through on recommendations made by the library media specialist. Generally, a variety of books is listed because students from all grades participate in this activity. It is interesting to see which titles are added. Occasionally, you may be surprised at a title that someone considered good enough to add to the list.

The following directions are for preparing a booklet containing the "Good Books to Read" list. You should also prepare a simple poster that encourages students to contribute to the list and to consult it for reading ideas. (See the illustration on the next page.)

MATERIALS:

—2 pieces of 9″ × 12″ construction paper in a light color
—10 sheets of 8½″ × 11″ lined paper
—pencil
—string

—2 paper fasteners
—masking tape
—felt markers
—hole puncher

PREPARATION:

1. Use a felt marker to draw a book entitled "Good Books to Read" on a sheet of construction paper.
2. Place the sheets of lined paper between the two sheets of construction paper. Punch two holes through the left side of the layer of paper, one near the top and one near the bottom.
3. Insert paper fasteners into the punched holes, making a booklet with your drawing of a book on the front cover.
4. Attach a piece of string to a pencil with masking tape.
5. Anchor the loose end of the string to a wall with masking tape.
6. Use tape to attach the back cover of the booklet to the wall just under the place where the string is attached.

Storytelling Suggestions

STORIES IN RHYME

Continue May's poetic theme with a flock of stories all in rhyme. Rhyme helps words flow easily, making reading a pleasure and listening a delight.

Gelman, Rita Golden
Hey Kid
illus. by Carol Nicklaus
Watts, 1977

An unexpected gift in a padlocked crate is revealed to be a big white thing named Sam who won't stop singing and won't stop talking. The girl who now owns him is driven to distraction; she finds another strong crate, locks up Sam, and takes him far away. In turn, she presents him to another child, calling, "Hey kid. Today's your lucky day." (first and second grade)

Hall, Katy
Nothing but Soup
illus. by Doug Taylor
Follett, 1976

In this unusual book, an unusual boy, Q. Leonard Faroop, eats nothing but soup. The illustrations are bold, glossy, and cartoon-like. (second and third grade)

Hutchins, Pat
Don't Forget the Bacon
Greenwillow, 1976

A boy gets sent to the store for "six farm eggs, a cake for tea, a pound of pears, and don't forget the bacon." As he passes various people and stores, the first three items in his head keep changing. He finally remembers them but forgets the bacon. (kindergarten and first grade)

Lobel, Arnold
The Man Who Took the Indoors Out
Harper & Row, 1974

One beautiful day, Bellwood Bouse invites his furniture to come out of his house. When all of the pieces run off, he is left with just a rocking chair. A year passes, and one winter day the furniture returns, tattered and torn. Although he is glad it is back, Bellwood is wiser now and locks it safely inside. (first and second grade)

Lord, John Vernon   *The Giant Jam Sandwich*
                                     verses by Janet Burroway
                                     Houghton Mifflin, 1972

The town of Itching Down, inundated with four million wasps, makes a giant sandwich in which to trap them. Using trucks, helicopters and human resources, the townspeople finally get rid of the wasps—to their delight and that of the birds who feast on the Giant Jam Sandwich. (first and second grade)

O'Neill, Mary   *Hailstones and Halibut Bones*
                                     illus. by Leonard Weisgard
                                     Doubleday, 1961

A serious collection of poems with words that capture the mood of colors. Things associated with each shade are explored, as well as the colors of emotions. A springboard for creative discussion. (second to fourth grade)

O'Neill, Mary   *Winds*
                                     illus. by James Barkley
                                     Doubleday, 1970

Every type of wind is described with scientific precision in O'Neill's lyric poetry. The illustrations are black, gray, and the palest of pinks. Reminiscent of William Blake, they keep the listener "celestially attuned." A very special book for very special groups. (second to fourth grade)

Schweitzer, Byrd Baylor   *The Man Who Talked to a Tree*
                                     illus. by Symeon Shimin
                                     Dutton, 1968

This book is not in rhyme, but it is poetry nonetheless. An old man, who says he speaks the language of trees, tells some boys the story of how a tree was planted by a young couple who settled out West and how it was nurtured through a drought. The book is illustrated in sandy pink and blue; no green is used. The lack of water and the loneliness of the West come through powerfully. The book may take two sessions to read, but it is well worth it, for its impact on the students is incredible. (first to fourth grade)

Wells, Rosemary   *Noisy Nora*
                                     Dial Press, 1973

Nora gets annoyed whenever her parents are busy with her brother and sister, and she hangs around trying to get attention. But no one notices her until she goes away and silence reigns. (kindergarten and first grade)

Zemach, Harve   *The Judge: An Untrue Tale*
                                     illus. by Margot Zemach
                                     Farrar, Straus & Giroux, 1969

A judge refuses to believe the accounts of five prisoners as each of them tell him that "a horrible thing is coming this way." He gets his just desserts at the end of the story, when a monster enters the court and eats the judge to the gasps and applause of the group. (first to third grade)

Teaching Unit

ONE-VOLUME REFERENCE BOOKS

Students in the high-intermediate and upper grades who are able to accomplish simple research (using the card catalog, general and subject encyclopedias, and perhaps a periodical index) should be encouraged to broaden their knowledge of reference books. This Teaching Unit takes the form of a classroom learning center and encompasses the use of an almanac and two other one-volume reference books: *Famous First Facts* edited by Joseph N. Kane (Wilson, 1964) and *Facts about the Presidents* edited by Joseph N. Kane (Wilson, 1974). The inclusion of an almanac with the other volumes may seem unusual, but there are two good reasons for this juxtaposition.

First, any learning center must include enough books to allow several children to work at the same time. Even if the groups are not large, two books are certainly not enough. Adding an almanac is helpful, for several back issues can be used. Although only the *Information Please Almanac* edited by Ann Golenpaul (Simon & Schuster, annually) is used in this unit, you can easily expand the learning center to include other almanacs.

Second, an almanac, like the other reference books, presents a large amount of information in one volume. To find information in all three books, the user must learn to use the index intelligently and then must frequently skim several pages to find the appropriate section.

To give students practice in using one-volume reference books, you should select information for them to find on subjects that interest them. If the students in your school have not yet become highly skilled at using the *Guinness Book of World Records* edited by Norris McWhirter (Sterling, annually), you can also use this book as part of the unit.

As with all classroom learning centers, much of the work involved in setting up the display and monitoring the students' progress is done by the teacher. The job of the library media specialist is to present the learning center and to develop the questions. The questions in this unit are designed for the above-average sixth grader.

No introductory lesson is necessary for this unit. The students learn as they search, asking questions when they have a problem. This effectively avoids teaching them what they already know and thus boring the academically talented student.

MATERIALS:

—15 pieces of 6″ × 9″ colored posterboard

Note: You might use a different color posterboard for each of the three volumes and make five cards in each color.

—3 manila envelopes, large enough to hold the cards
—piece of oaktag, about 18″ wide
—felt markers
—masking tape

PREPARATION:

1. Prepare five task cards for each book so that you have a total of fifteen cards. (See the sample task cards.)
2. Print the name of one of the reference books on each of the three manila envelopes. Place the appropriate set of task cards in each envelope.
3. Print ''Find the Fact—Using One-Volume Reference Books'' on the 18″ wide piece of oaktag. Attach the manila envelopes with the task cards inside them to the oaktag.
4. Mount the oaktag on a bulletin board or wall.

SAMPLE TASK CARDS:

Card 1A	Use <u>Famous First Facts</u> to find the dates of these "firsts": 1. The first ice cream cone 2. The first chop suey 3. The first popcorn 4. The first lollipop machine 5. The first bicycle factory in the United States 6. The first crossword puzzle book 7. The first toothbrush 8. The first electric toaster 9. The first book matches 10. The first safety pin
Card 2A	Use the Year Index in <u>Famous First Facts</u>. Go back 100 years. 1. Find one "first" related to a modern invention and give its date and location. Example: first interstate telephone call. 2. Find one sports "first." 3. Find one transportation "first." 4. Find one strange or humorous "first."
Card 3A	Use the Day Index in <u>Famous First Facts</u>. Check under your birthday. (Give the day in your answer.) 1. What is the oldest event listed? What happened? 2. What is the most recent event listed? What happened? 3. What funny or very special event happened? What year?
Card 4A	Use the Geographical Index in <u>Famous First Facts</u>. Look up our state. 　Find five "firsts" that occurred in our state that you think are funny or important.
Card 5A	<u>Famous First Facts</u>—Special Task Card Make a Calendar 1. Choose a month and make a calendar for that month. 2. Find an interesting fact for each day of the month. 3. Print the fact and date on the calendar. 4. Choose one fact and illustrate it to accompany your calendar.

Card 1B	Use <u>Facts about the Presidents</u> to answer these questions:

1. What was the date of John Adams' death? What was the date of Thomas Jefferson's death? Who was older?
2. Look under Zachary Taylor. What was his political party? What happened in his administration on April 10, 1849? Where was his horse pastured?

Card 2B	Use <u>Facts about the Presidents</u> to answer these questions:

1. Who was the vice-president under Harry S Truman?
2. In the 1948 election, who were the Republican candidates for president and vice-president?
3. What was the name of Truman's wife? Give her maiden name (before marriage).
4. How many brothers and sisters did Truman have?

Card 3B	Use <u>Facts about the Presidents</u> to answer these questions:

1. Where was William McKinley born?
2. Who was McKinley's vice-president during his second term?
3. How many political parties had presidential candidates in the election of 1900? Name them.
4. Who assassinated McKinley? When? Where?

Card 4B	Use the Comparative Data in <u>Facts about the Presidents</u> to answer the following questions on presidential wives:

1. How many wives lived to be over 80 years old? Who?
2. Who was the first presidential wife to regularly attend school?
3. Who was the first wife of a president to graduate from college?
4. How many presidential wives had fathers who were planters or farmers? Who were they?

Card 5B	Use the Comparative Data in <u>Facts about the Presidents</u> to answer these questions:

1. How many presidents did not attend college? Name them.
2. How many presidents were under 5'7" tall? Name them.
3. How many were 6'0" tall or taller? Name them.
4. Name the presidents who died in office.
5. What were the last words of James Madison?
6. Which president had 15 children?

Card 1C	Use the <u>Information Please Almanac</u> to answer these questions:

1. What is the address of the American Motorcycle Association? The National Basketball Association?
2. Who was the Cy Young Award winner in 1963?
3. Where were the Winter Olympics held in 1972?
4. Which team won the Stanley Cup in 1970?
5. Which teams played in the Rose Bowl in 1971? What was the score?

Card 2C   Use the <u>Information Please Almanac</u> to answer these questions:
1. What was the date of the first manned orbital flight? Who was the astronaut? Name his ship.
2. Who was the first American in orbit? What was the date?
3. Who were the crew members on the first manned lunar landing? What was the date?
4. Who were the American astronauts and Russian cosmonauts involved in the first international manned rendezvous and docking? How many hours was the American flight? How many hours was the Russian flight?

Card 3C   Use the <u>Information Please Almanac</u> to answer these questions:
1. What is the world's longest river? How many miles long is it?
2. How large is the Gobi Desert?
3. What is the world's highest mountain? How high is it?
4. Where is the second highest waterfall in the world?
5. How deep is the deepest lake in the world? Where is it located?

Card 4C   Use the <u>Information Please Almanac</u> to answer these questions:
1. Earthquakes: What was the date of the San Francisco Earthquake? On March 27, 1964, an earthquake hit Alaska. How high was the seismic wave? (Use a dictionary to find out what a seismic wave is.)
2. Floods: What is the earliest date given for a major flood? Where was it?
3. Shipwrecks: When did the Titanic sink? How many lives were lost?
4. Aircraft disasters: When did the zeppelin <u>Hindenberg</u> explode? How many lives were lost?

Card 5C   Use the <u>Information Please Almanac</u> to answer these questions:
1. Who invented the helicopter?
2. Who is credited with inventing the first automobile?
3. Who gave the first successful television demonstration? When?
4. Who invented the first passenger elevator?
5. Who invented the first friction match?

Check your answers for 4 and 5 with <u>Famous First Facts</u>. Do they agree?

Professional Responsibilities

TIPS OF THE TRADE

Keep your book shelves in good order by teaching children to use book paddles when they are selecting a book. Get some paint stirrers from a local hardware or paint store and paint them in a color that complements your media center. You can use any type of paint, including spray paint, for this job. Get some large coffee cans, cover them with self-stick vinyl, and store the book paddles in them.

Whenever the children come in to look for a book, they take a paddle with them to the shelves. When they pull a book from a shelf, the paddle goes in its place. If they decide not to take that book, it is easy to see where it belongs on the shelf. They remove the book paddle, replace the book, and look elsewhere.

Be sure that the children get in the habit of removing the paddles and replacing them in the nearest storage can; otherwise, you will have paddles sticking out all over your book shelves. It is not hard to get children to use the paddles and to replace them when they find a book. They will enjoy using them, and your shelves will stay much neater.

If you have the inclination and the space, you might consider setting up special collections of books for holidays such as Christmas, Halloween, and Easter. If all of these books are shelved together in one place, they will be easier to find, and the children will know where to find a holiday book whenever they want one.

It is also helpful to color-code holiday books by placing a piece of colored tape above each spine label. If you buy rolls of green tape (for Christmas books), orange tape (for Halloween books), and pink tape (for Easter books), it is very easy to color-code the books as soon as you place the spine labels on them. You might consider purchasing colored dots from a library supply house and using them instead of the tape. Any type of colored sticker will remind your volunteers that the holiday books are shelved in a special place. The children will also get used to this system quickly.

If you decide to use this tip, you should be cautious about color-coding too many kinds of books. Otherwise, you will defeat your purpose by confusing the users of your media center.

Children are always asking where special books such as mysteries are kept. If you have an integrated fiction collection, the answer is that they are filed on regular fiction shelves by the author's last name and that they can be found by looking under the "MYSTERY AND DETECTIVE STORIES" subject heading in the card catalog. However, you can make it easier for children to find different genres of fiction such as mysteries, science fiction, and sports fiction by using subject labels that can be purchased inexpensively from most library supply houses. These labels are affixed to the book's spine either above or below the regular spine label. They make it easier for popular kinds of books to be spotted on the shelves. Children enjoy searching the shelves for these special books, and you or a volunteer can also spot them more easily if you are pulling a group of books for a special display.

Subject labels are equally effective for biographies and for reference books. Even though the books in each of these categories are filed together, the stickers denote that the books are special.

Consider purchasing color-banded plastic covers also known as "flags" for your circulation file. They have many uses and save you a lot of explanations.

A red flag over a book card signals that the book is on reserve. (See the November Volunteers section.) A yellow flag can be used when new book cards are needed. If the new card is typed after a child has signed the old card, the yellow flag holds both cards together until the book has been returned. The old card is then destroyed, the new card is placed in the book pocket, and the flag is removed. If the old card is filled and a child wants to sign out the book, a blank card is used for the child's signature and the two cards are held together with a yellow flag. When the information has been typed on the new card, the old card is destroyed and the flag is removed.

A black flag is used to indicate any type of mistake or problem; it signals "stop" to whoever is slipping books. The volunteer must check to see what is the problem, and the flag is not removed until the problem has been satisfactorily resolved.

You may find other uses for the color-banded covers, but, again, caution is necessary. Don't get carried away. Use as few colors as possible or you will confuse things instead of simplifying them.

If your filmstrip projectors are kept in carrying cases, you may find it difficult to get the top of the case latched into place. When this happens, you probably assume that you have the lid on backward and proceed to turn it around.

Avoid the problem of which way the top goes on by marking the case once it is properly closed. Draw a triangle with a permanent felt marker on the top and bottom halves. From now on, when the triangles match up, you will know that the lid is on the right way.

Help yourself and the students to return drawers quickly to their correct locations in the card catalog by numbering the drawers. It is even more helpful if the vertical rows are color-coded. Use colored tape to cover about 1½" of each drawer label. Write the numbers with a black felt marker on the tape.

You can achieve the same results without tape by using different color felt markers. Four or five different shades are sufficient. Use the markers to write the number and guide letters on the drawer labels. All of the drawers in one vertical row should be marked with the same color.

Make use of the professional magazines purchased for the faculty that are never quite used as often as the expense would warrant. When these periodicals are over a year old, cut them up and start a teacher resource file.

Subject headings for the file should include basic curriculum areas such as language arts, math, and science; these headings can be further divided into primary and intermediate levels. Other headings are bulletin boards, seasonal crafts, and anything else that your faculty would find useful.

As you clip the articles, do not exclude the clever but short ideas. Just paste the information onto an index card. Label each clipping with the appropriate subject heading. If possible, a separate drawer in a file cabinet could be used for this professional vertical file. Follow the procedures recommended for circulating vertical file material. (See the March Volunteers section.) In case of lack of space, a large folio envelope is extremely helpful.

Be prepared for the fact that some of the materials will not be returned, since adults are often more careless than children when dealing with vertical file materials. However, you do have a constant source of new materials. You also have the satisfaction of knowing that the money set aside for professional periodicals has been well spent since the materials are being put to good use.

Volunteers

PROCESSING MEDIA

When new audio-visual material arrives, here are some steps to follow in processing it:

1. All media should be viewed or listened to promptly in order to make sure that there are no defects. Sometimes a sound filmstrip is not synchronized, a cassette does not play, or a wrong title is inside a correctly marked box. Occasionally, a part may be missing. The time to catch any of these problems is as soon as the material arrives, before you have marked any of it or signed the purchase order for payment. Either you or a volunteer can check for problems, but if you have the time, previewing will help become familiar you with the contents of your media collection.

2. If catalog cards come with the material, check them over to see if you agree with the classification number or want to make any change in it. Problems in this area seem to occur more often with nonprint media than with books. (See the October Professional Responsibilities for a discussion about the reclassification of commercial catalog cards.) Frequently, items are placed in 372 (elementary education) when they would probably be more suited to and easier to find in a number of other designations.

3. If there are no catalog cards, you must classify the material yourself and make up a main entry card as a sample from which one of your volunteers can type the other cards. (See the April Volunteers section on typing catalog cards.)

4. Be sure to designate the type of audio-visual material as part of the call number. You might use CAS for cassette, SP for study print, and FS for filmstrip. If you color-band your audio-visual cards, do so now or immediately after the cards have been typed. (See this month's Open End.)

5. Fill out a scrap catalog card and place it in your file of new media so you can use it when preparing media bibliographies for teachers. (See the February Professional Responsibilities.)

6. If you keep a running inventory of materials, add the new items to your count.

Volunteers can now take over and perform the following tasks:

1. Write or stamp the school name on each piece of audio-visual material, including the teacher's guide.

2. Put the call number on each piece of material.

3. Type a pocket, catalog cards, and charge out card for the material.

4. Place a spine label on the box or container that indicates the name of the material and its call number.

5. For multi-media kits, it is helpful to place a list of contents inside the container.

MENDING

Often books need to be mended or repaired. Before you tackle this job, give it some thought. Fixing a simple rip on a page or a loose binding is not a problem. You can make these repairs with tape and glue in just a few minutes.

More complicated jobs should be considered carefully. Often, it is easier and cheaper in the long run to discard the book and purchase a replacement copy. Ask yourself some questions: Is the book worth the time and effort that must be expended to patch it? What will it look like when you are finished? If the book is no longer in print, has it outlived its usefulness? If it is a nonfiction work, is it dated? As you come across books that need mending, consider them as candidates for weeding (removal) from your collection. Of course, as your budget gets tighter and the cost of books keeps rising, the decision becomes harder to make.

If you've taken all of these factors into account and the answer is "mend it," arm yourself with a guide to mending. (You can request one free from any library supply house.) These guides give clear, step-by-step instructions on subjects such as mending torn pages, repairing worn spines, and tipping in loose pages. Try to find a volunteer who enjoys mending and turn over all repairs to that person. Work with your "mender" to develop a collection of basic mending supplies. Some of the mending—not bookbinding—kits offered by library supply houses are good starters. Other items such as book wings and perforated tapes can be added as needed. Encourage your volunteer to consult catalogs to find out what is available. Keep a supply of various kinds of tapes and glues on hand. If you have the money, there is a new Scotch book repair tape applicator, sold by library supply houses, that is a big help in mending.

One last point: Whenever the opportunity arises, stress to children, teachers, and parents that they should never mend pages that have been torn in books. Regular cellophane tape yellows with age; the tape that is needed for this job is a special Mylar tape that stays clear. Ask them to show you any pages that need repair rather than using the wrong tape to make the repairs themselves.

Open End

COLOR-BANDING OF CATALOG CARDS

No matter what system (open, integrated, or limited access) you use for shelving media, all cards are filed in the card catalog.

In some instances, a separate file is maintained for audio-visual materials. The materials are organized by type. The advantage of this system lies in not having to wade through the entire catalog for nonprint materials, and the question of color-banding does not arise. However, a divided catalog of this nature frequently contains just main entries, and it can be replaced by the shelf list. Even if subject cards are included, there are definite drawbacks to this system. Someone searching for all of the materials contained in the media center on a given subject must remember to check both catalogs. Unless there are compelling reasons related to your methods of operation or the kinds of services you offer, it is probably better not to increase the number of alphabets the patron must use.

If the card catalog is integrated, you must decide whether to color-band the cards. The approach recommended by the profession in library schools, workshops, and conferences is not to color-band. The primary advantage of not color-banding is saving time and money. If you do not color-band, you save the time it takes to mark each commercially processed card and you save money by not having to order cards in an array of colors for in-house cataloging. The extra storage space needed for banded cards is also saved.

The philosophy expressed by choosing not to color-band—that no distinctions are to be made between print and nonprint media and that within the catalog the integration of all media is complete—reflects the position of the professional establishment. Another reason not to color-band is that there is no standard color code. Even when color codes were at the peak of their acceptance and there were only a few types of software, there was no consistency among media centers as to what each color signified. Several books, notably *Developing Multi-Media Libraries* by Warren B. Hicks and Alma M. Tillin (Bowker, 1970), tried to offer one system for classifying code letters and colors. But with technology forever spawning new forms of media requiring new codes and new colors, any detailed system of differentiation would become mind-boggling. The current establishment philosophy arose in reaction to the "rainbow-banded" catalog.

One alternative that many library media specialists and media center users prefer is to mark all software catalog cards with a single color, such as red. To save time and money, you can use a colored felt marker to mark the tops of the cards. This is a rapid process that avoids extra costs, extra space, and extra cards. Anyone looking for nonprint media in a unified catalog can easily spot the banded cards, and even children in the primary grades can distinguish between books and audio-visual materials as soon as they are able to use the card catalog.

Whatever method you choose, be sure to weigh your decision carefully. It is too easy to create a situation that is filled with problems for patrons and extra work for you.

June

Happy Birthday To . . .

1   **James Daugherty** (1889)—author and illustrator
        Picture books such as *Andy and the Lion* and U.S. history such as *Daniel Boone*
        John Masefield (1878)—poet
        Poet laureate of England famous for sea poems such as "Sea Fever"

2   **Norton Juster** (1929)—author
        Writer of *The Phantom Tollbooth*, a humorous tale for middle grades
        Paul Galdone (1914)—illustrator and adapter of folk tales
        A longtime favorite with a variety of artistic styles to suit his many titles, such as *The Little Red Hen* and *Henny Penny*

5   **Franklyn M. Branley** (1915)—author
        Nonfiction for elementary and middle grades that emphasizes astronomy and space science, notably *The Nine Planets*
        Richard Scarry (1919)—author and illustrator
        Busy picture books on broad topics and preprimer subjects, such as *Richard Scarry's Best Counting Book Ever*

6   **Peter Spier** (1927)—illustrator and adapter
        Noted for extremely detailed and historically accurate full-color illustrations, especially his representations of songs such as *The Erie Canal* and *The Star-Spangled Banner*

10   **Nat Hentoff** (1925)—author
        Fiction for upper grades and nonfiction such as *Journey into Jazz*
        Maurice Sendak (1928)—author and illustrator
        Leading illustrator of picture books with a special awareness of children's

Tie it up and track it down.
It's inventory time!

fears and the way they view the world; noted for *Where the Wild Things Are*

24 **Betty Cavanna** (1909)—author
Fiction for upper grades, usually with a romantic twist, such as *Ruffles and Drums*

John Ciardi (1916)—poet
Although well known for his adult poetry, Ciardi is equally at home with humorous verse for children such as *I Met a Man*.

Leonard Everett Fisher (1924)—author and illustrator
Black-and-white scratchboard illustrations illuminate his American history series, such as *The Cabinetmakers* and *The Doctors*

25 **Jane Sarnoff** (1937)—author
Illustrated nonfiction books such as *The Great Bicycle Book* and *The Monster Riddle Book*

26 **Pearl S. Buck** (1892)—author
Fiction with an Oriental flavor, including *The Big Wave*

Charlotte Zolotow (1915)—author
Picture books dealing with basic emotions, such as *My Grandson Lew* and *The Quarreling Book*

27 **Helen Keller** (1880)—author
Her autobiography, *The Story of My Life*, is solid reading for upper grades.

30 **Mollie Hunter** (1922)—author
Historical fiction for upper grades, such as *Stronghold*

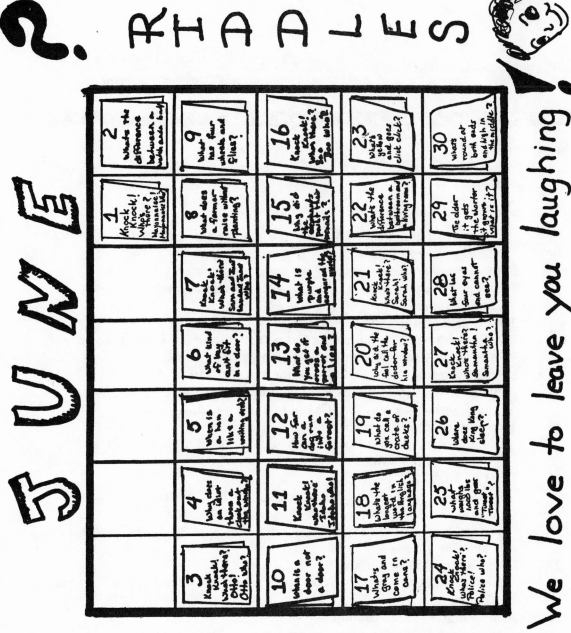

Bulletin Boards

RIDDLES

All of your May preparations come to fruition as you quickly set up your Riddles bulletin board. Be prepared for heavy traffic around the bulletin board as students check to see if their riddles were chosen and read those that were selected.

MATERIALS:

—1 sheet of 22" × 28" colored posterboard
—30 riddle slips (see the May Library Enrichment Activity)
—felt markers in assorted colors
—rubber cement

PREPARATION:

1. Use a felt marker to draw a 17½" × 15" calendar. (See illustration.) The top of the calendar is 4" from the top of the posterboard. Divide the calendar into the usual 5 weeks and 7 days; each box is 2½" × 3¼".
2. Use a felt marker in any color to print "June" in letters 3" high. Also print "Favorite Riddles" and the slogan "We love to leave you laughing" along the bottom of the posterboard.
3. Draw free flowing question marks in the two top corners.
4. Draw cartoon faces or more question marks in the bottom corners.
5. Paste the 30 riddles in the boxes. Be sure to put the first riddle in the correct box for the first day of June.

DIVE INTO READING

Remind everyone that reading is a form of recreation by using a summer swim as a theme for the final bulletin board of the school year. Accompany this bulletin board with dittoed summer reading lists if you wish. See the suggestions in this month's "Summer Reading Lists" section. The bulletin board can be prepared rapidly using felt markers. Use an overhead projector if you wish to copy the illustration shown on the following page.

MATERIALS:

—1 sheet of 22" × 28" yellow posterboard
—wide-tip felt markers in brown, blue, black, green, and red
—black fine-tip felt marker
—overhead projector (optional)

PREPARATION:

1. Draw or trace a 15" high tree. The overhanging branch extends 16" from the side of the posterboard. The tree is drawn with the brown marker, and black lines are added for effect.
2. Outline the grass and embankment in green. Add brown and green lines to the bank.

3. Draw the diver with the fine-tip marker. Color his suit red.
4. Use the blue marker to make the horizon line on the water.

   Note: Test the blue felt marker before using it. Some blue markers turn bright green on yellow posterboard. You will never get a real blue on the yellow, but a blue-green that does not look like grass is fine.

5. Use the blue marker to print "DIVE INTO" in 1¾" high letters.
6. Use the blue marker to write "Reading" with a flowing hand and to make some water lines.

Library Art Activity

BOOKMARKS FROM BARTLETT'S

Assume that students will be reading heavily through the summer and organize an art activity for creating bookmarks similar to the one shown. This project not only results in a useful item but also expands students' ability to use reference tools.

Bartlett's Familiar Quotations, 14th edition by John Bartlett (Little, Brown, 1968) is not used very much by elementary or even junior high-school students. The index

is more difficult to use than one in a multivolume subject encyclopedia. To rapidly locate a quotation, the user needs to skim the page. In short, using *Bartlett's* requires advanced ability in many of the library skills, which makes the bookmarks an excellent choice for an end-of-year activity.

This art activity can be presented in several ways. First, you can make a poster announcing the art activity, as you have done with previous art activities. Supplies for making the bookmarks would be available at the desk. Because the poster could not include a detailed explanation of how to use the reference tool, the students would be on their own. As has been noted, *Bartlett's* is difficult for the novice, and you and the volunteers would be called on frequently to assist students with problems. A second method is to use the activity as part of a mini-teaching unit and to have the students do all of the work in the classroom. *Bartlett's* would be placed on temporary loan to that class. However, this would restrict the activity to one group of students. A third approach involves another mini-teaching unit; this one synthesizes the other two approaches and is explained in detail here.

Make arrangements with the classroom teacher to give a half-hour presentation to the class. The material is best suited to grades six and up. During the explanation, you can suggest or require that the students make bookmarks. Students will go to the media center to select their quotations, but all art work will be done in the classroom. Because many culminating activities are taking place this month, it is simpler to keep projects in the classroom when they do not truly require the resources of the media center.

Because most reference collections have only one copy of *Bartlett's*, only one student at a time can select a quotation. Since each student needs only one quotation, the situation is difficult but not impossible. You can alleviate the problem by purchasing some paperback copies. The paperback version is not organized in the same way as the hard-bound volume, but sufficient similarities exist to make it a reasonable alternative.

Preparation for this activity is relatively simple and quick. All of the necessary materials can be made in under two hours.

> *Note:* If there is sufficient interest, encourage students to make extra bookmarks so that you can distribute them in September during primary grade orientation. (See the September chapter.)

MATERIALS:

—*Bartlett's Familiar Quotations*
—acetate to make two permanent transparencies
—1 piece of 7″ × 2½″ oaktag
—fine-tip felt marker

PREPARATION:

1. Select a quotation from *Bartlett's* that you find appropriate for a bookmark.
2. If you have a good photocopier, make a copy of the page in the index that lists the quotation you have chosen and a copy of the page where the quotation is located.
3. If you don't have a good photocopier, print in pencil an excerpt from the index that includes the reference to the chosen quotation. Also print an excerpt from the page where the quotation is located. (See the sample excerpts, pages 253 and 254.)

   • To keep your lines straight, place a sheet of lined paper underneath a sheet of unlined paper and put both sheets on the overhead projector. The lines will show through and you will not need to erase later.
   • To make the page of quotations, turn a sheet of standard-size paper so that the height is 8½″. Although you will not be able to copy the entire page, you should duplicate its format. Rule a top line and a line dividing the page in two columns; label the columns *a* and *b*, print the name or names that appear on the top line, and put the page number on the bottom.
   • Place the quotation you have chosen in the proper column. Print several quotations that appear on the page above and below the chosen quotation. Be sure to include several quotations that are followed by ''Ib.'' as well as quotations that list the works to which the ''Ib's'' refer.
4. Prepare two permanent transparencies of the two pages from *Bartlett's*.
5. Use a fine-tip marker to illustrate on the oaktag the quotation you have chosen.

PROCEDURE:

1. Begin the mini-unit by congratulating the students on the library skills that they have mastered over the years.
2. Explain that you have something special for them to discover and produce *Bartlett's Familiar Quotations*.

Readiness is all, 266b
Reading, affect you agreeably in r., 469b

after r. your work, 417b
contemplation more than r., 364b-365a
cursed hard r., 482a
digressions sunshine of r., 437b
English dictionary best r., 916a
I prefer r., 878a
maketh a full man, 209b
overset mind with r., 816b
peace makes poor r., 783b
to mind as exercise is to body, 395b
write things worth r., 421b

Readings, our r. secret, 951b
Read, all he r. assails, 404a
nothing but detective stories, 999b

3. Open the volume and show the students a sample page. Acknowledge that the format does not seem especially unusual. Then flip to the index. Let the students see how small the type is and then hold together all of the pages that comprise the index so that they can appreciate what a large proportion of the book is devoted to the index. The reason for this long index (the key word entry of the book) is what makes *Bartlett's* unusual.

4. Tell the class that there are several ways to use *Bartlett's*. The simplest way is to open to any page and browse through the quotations. A more difficult way is to find quotations by famous people such as Benjamin Franklin.

• Explain that *Bartlett's* is not arranged in alphabetical order but in chronological order. (A brief digression is necessary to remind the group that they know what alphabetical order and numerical order mean. Ask if anyone knows what chronological order is. If no one can explain this term, define it yourself.)

• Show the class that there is an alphabetical index of authors just before the quotation index. Look up Franklin in the author index; then turn to the proper page and read some quotations.

ADDISON - STEELE

a

We are always doing something for Posterity, but I would fain see Posterity do something for us.

Ib. 587 (August 20, 1714)

See in what peace, a Christian can die.

Dying words (1719)
From Young, Conjectures on Original Composition (1759)

SIR RICHARD STEELE
(1672 – 1729)

I am come to a tavern alone to eat a steak, after which I shall return to the office.

Letters to His Wife
(October 28, 1707)

b

A little in drink, but at all times yr faithful husband.

Ib. (September 27, 1708)

Though her mien carries much more invitation than command, to behold her is an immediate check to loose behavior.

Tatler No. 49 (1709-1711)

Reading is to the mind what exercise is to the body.

Ib., No. 147

When you fall into a man's conversation, the first thing you should consider is, whether he has a greater inclination to hear you or that you should hear him.

The Spectator No. 49 (April 26, 1711)

5. Inform the students that although these two ways of using *Bartlett's* are enjoyable, they are too easy for such accomplished users of the media center. What you have in store for them is the third and most difficult way of using this reference book. They will be using the main index to look up specific quotations.

6. Put the transparency of the excerpt from the index on the overhead projector. Explain the following points:

   • The index is alphabetical.
   • The first quotation for a word is given alongside the word; subsequent listings are indented and follow in alphabetical order.
   • The page references are followed by *a* or *b*.
   • When the entry word is within the body of the quotation, just an initial is used to identify it. If the initial does not appear, the entry word comes first in the quotation.
   • Plurals and other forms of a word have separate listings.

7. Read the quotation you have chosen and have a student find the page reference.

8. Put the transparency of the page on which the quotation appears on the overhead projector.

   • Have the students explain what *a* and *b* mean. (They can figure this out easily.)
   • Show how to skim the page to find the quotation you want; run your finger across the words until you come to a word beginning with the right letter.
   • Ask the class who is being quoted. Someone will figure out how to discover this.
   • Now remind them that who said it is not enough; they must discover where it was said. There will be dead silence, or someone will suggest it was "Ib."
   • Explain the meaning of "Ib." Then point to another quotation that is followed by "Ib." and ask the students to locate its source.

9. Tell the class that instead of completing ditto sheets or task cards that require them to look up certain words, they will participate in an art activity.

10. Produce your sample bookmark and explain that the children will be using *Bartlett's* to produce their own bookmarks.

    • They will come to the media center and use the index in *Bartlett's* to find a quotation.
    • They will write down the complete quotation, the person who said it, and where it was said.
    • When they return to class, they will print the information on precut oaktag (supplied by the teacher) and draw an appropriate illustration.
    • Although you may suggest entry words such as books, reading, library, and learning, allow them to choose quotations about anything that interests them.

11. As a general precaution, all quotations should be shown to the classroom teacher before the art work begins.

Library Enrichment Activity

SALUTE TO SUMMER AUTHORS AND ILLUSTRATORS

In addition to your June "Happy Birthday to . . ." display, you might want to give the students with summer birthdays some recognition by briefly saluting authors and illustrators born in July and August. Fewer names than usual are included here because the June birthdays are already on display and the two additional months might prove cumbersome, particularly while you are trying to wind down the year.

July

1   **Liesel Skorpen** (1935)—author
    Picture books including *Mandy's Grandmother* and *We Were Tired of Living in a House*

2   **Jean Craighead George** (1919)—author
    Fiction and nonfiction with ecological themes including *Julie of the Wolves* and *Who Really Killed Cock Robin*

10 **Julian May** (1931)—author
    Nonfiction on all subjects such as *They Turned to Stone* and *Arctic: Top of the World*

11 **E. B. White** (1899)—author
    Writer of the all-time children's best seller, *Charlotte's Web*

12 **Herbert Zim** (1909)—author
    Nonfiction for the beginning and middle reader on all subjects such as *Machine Tools, Elephants,* and *Cargo Ships*

14 **Isaac Bashevis Singer** (1904)—author
    Teller of Jewish folk tales such as *Zlateh the Goat,* and a Nobel laureate

17 **Karla Kuskin** (1932)—author and illustrator
    Simple rhymes that amuse such as *A Boy Had a Mother Who Bought Him a Hat*

23 **Patricia Coombs** (1926)—author and illustrator
    Easy fiction such as the Dorrie the Little Witch series

27 **Scott Corbett** (1913)—author
    Mysteries for middle and upper grades such as *The Hockey Trick*

August

2   **Holling C. Holling** (1900)—author and illustrator
    Stories with scientifically accurate illustrations recounting fictional versions of complex ecosystems such as *Paddle to the Sea*

7   **Betsy Byars** (1928)—author
    Fiction for middle grades on contemporary themes such as *The Eighteenth Emergency*

11 **Don Freeman** (1908)—author and illustrator
Picture books for the younger set with animal heroes including *Corduroy*, *Pet of the Met*, and *Beady Bear*

15 **Brinton Turkle** (1915)—author and illustrator
Picture books about a Quaker boy named Obadiah and illustrations for books by other authors

16 **Matt Christopher** (1917)—author
Sports fiction for middle grades such as *Catch that Pass* and *Shortstop from Tokyo*

Beatrice Schenk de Regniers (1914)—author
Picture books including *May I Bring a Friend?*

30 **Virginia Lee Burton** (1909)—author and illustrator
Picture books about anthropomorphic subjects such as *The Little House* and *Mike Mulligan and His Steam Shovel*. Perhaps the books are a little dated, but at the right moment they are a valuable part of your collection.

Sesyle Joslin (1921)—author
Picture books such as the Baby Elephant series and two excellent books on etiquette: *What Do You Say, Dear?* and *What Do You Do, Dear?*

CLASS CONTEST TO RETURN END-OF-YEAR MATERIAL

One way to quickly get back all library materials at the end of the school year is to set up a contest to see which class in each grade returns its materials first. Each child in the winning class who has brought back all books and other media receives a little prize. This activity requires no effort on your part that exceeds what you would normally be doing to get all of the materials back, and it gives the students an extra incentive to return things speedily.

MATERIALS:

—ditto master for notice to classrooms
—prizes, enough for all of the children in one class in each grade

PREPARATION:

1. Prepare and send a notice to each class that gives the final date when books and other materials are due and announces the contest. (See the sample notice.)
2. Purchase prizes. They should be very inexpensive because you will need to buy a large number and costs can mount. Consider some type of ice cream; it is generally very hot this time of year, and almost everyone loves ice cream. If this does not work out because of storage or distribution problems, go to a store that sells novelties and purchase a large quantity of items for under ten cents apiece. If you do buy ice cream, get the same kind for every class in the school; your selection of novelties, however, will vary according to the children's ages and interests. Do get only one kind for all of the children in one grade. Don't tell anyone what the prizes are before they are awarded. Keeping this a secret adds to the fun of the activity. Most children will be very anxious for their class to win and will persistently remind forgetful students to return their books.

NOTICE: TO ALL STUDENTS

ALL books, magazines, a/v materials, and anything else you have taken out of the library will be due on WEDNESDAY, JUNE 8.

No materials may be charged out after that date, although you may use them in the library.

Please check all of the places where missing books may be hiding, such as your desk in school, under your bed or behind the bureau in your room at home, and anywhere else you keep books. Return everything promptly so that we can get things back on the shelves before the inventory begins. All money for lost books should be paid now.

We are having a contest for speedy end-of-the-year returns. Each member of the homeroom in each grade that returns all outstanding materials first will win a prize for promptness.

Pitch in and help YOUR class be the winner in this contest!

Mrs. Toor

---

3. After the date when everything is supposed to be returned, have your volunteers make a list of all outstanding materials owed by each class. Distribute copies to each classroom and keep a master list at the circulation desk so that materials can be checked off as they are returned. This way, you can tell at a glance which class in each grade has returned everything first.
4. As one class in each grade wins the competition, check with the teachers to see when the prizes should be awarded. If possible, keep fairly quiet about which class has won so that the others will keep returning their materials.
5. Award the prizes to each grade.

SUMMER LOANS TO TEACHERS

The arrival of June brings up the question of lending materials from the media center to teachers over the summer. Often, busy teachers will set aside some time during their vacation to catch up with professional reading or to plan a new curriculum unit for the next year. They will come to you requesting the loan of books, periodicals, and possibly software and the accompanying hardware. Try to find out exactly what they hope to accomplish so that you can make suggestions for additional materials that can help them.

If you show that you are delighted to loan materials from your collection to the faculty during the summer, the teachers will be appreciative. If you have qualms about doing this, remember that materials sitting unused on the shelves all summer do no one any good.

Occasionally, you will have requests from teachers who plan to travel and want to borrow a camera or tape recorder to take with them. These requests should also be handled in a friendly manner. You should check with your principal about district policy on lending equipment, but once this matter is resolved, there should be no reason not to lend it.

Summer loans are one way that your policy of good service to your users carries on right through the summer.

SUMMER READING LISTS

Very often, right when you are in the middle of the many tasks involved in closing the media center, you will be asked by parents, faculty, or administration for a summer reading list to give out to students. Since compiling a professionally recommended reading list for various age groups takes a good deal of time, several alternatives are provided here.

1. Put together a student-selected book list by using suggestions from your "Good Books to Read" booklet. (See the May chapter)

2. Make a list of the favorite books chosen by the children in the Favorite Book Contest. (See the January chapter.) Like the contest, the list will be divided into three age groups: first and second grades, third and fourth grades, and fifth and sixth grades.

3. Check with the children's department of your local public library to see if the librarian has a list you can distribute. At the same time, offer to publicize the summer reading program at the local library.

4. Do none of these things, citing end-of-year pressures, but resolve that you will prepare a professionally recommended reading list for next summer beginning in February or March. If you put a note on your calendar to that effect, you will have plenty of time to make up a good list to distribute the following June.

5. Throughout the year, be on the lookout for commercially prepared reading lists and bibliographies that are listed in professional journals and compiled by large public libraries. These can be used as resources when you compile your list.

Storytelling Suggestions

STUDENT FAVORITES

You will probably be able to hold storytelling sessions during only the first part of June since you will not meet regularly with classes during inventory. Instead of selecting stories yourself, ask students to suggest some of their favorites and enjoy retelling them. The following books have been student favorites in our schools.

Charlip, Remy and   *Thirteen*
  Jerry Joyner   Parents, 1975

> An unusual picture book featuring 13 stories on each page. Some are wordless; some have a few words of explanation. Begin with "The Sinking Ship" (top right-hand side of page) and follow it through to the end. Then read another story or, if it is wordless, have the children tell what is happening in each picture. Allow the children to choose the next few stories. By now they will be familiar with the format. (first and second grade)

Hardendorff, Jeanne B.   *The Bed Just So*
                              illus. by Lisl Weil
                              Four Winds, 1975

> A tiny hudgin, looking for a comfortable bed, disturbs a tailor's sleep every night by pulling off his covers. The tailor tries to make a bed for the hudgin, but it still grumbles and complains every night until it finds comfort in a walnut shell that's made "just so." (kindergarten and first grade)

Hoban, Russell   *Bread and Jam for Frances*
                                   illus. by Lillian Hoban
                                   Harper & Row, 1964

Mother gives Frances just what she wants—bread and jam for all three meals.
After one day of this fare, Frances decides that variety is more interesting.
The lunch that the reformed Frances brings to school, complete with a paper
doily and flowers, will have the children's mouths watering. (kindergarten to
second grade)

Lionni, Leo   *Alexander and the Wind-up Mouse*
                                   Pantheon, 1969

Alexander, a despised mouse, seeks a purple pebble to give the magic lizard
in return for being transformed into a toy mouse like his friend Willie. He finds
the pebble, only to discover that Willie is being discarded. Changing his wish,
he rescues Willie. A beautiful tale of true friendship. (first to third grade)

Maestro, Betsy and Giulio   *A Wise Monkey Tale*
                                   Crown, 1975

Monkey falls into a very deep hole and cleverly figures out how to get out of
it. She manufactures a message from Gorilla that says, "If very wise you wish
to be; Come down here, wait and see," and she tricks Lion, Snake, Zebra,
and Elephant into climbing down to join her. When the hole becomes very
crowded, a second message from Gorilla ("When fitting in another is in doubt;
The first one in must climb out") allows Monkey to leave the others stuck in
the hole. (first and second grade)

Marshall, James   *George and Martha*
                                   Houghton Mifflin, 1972

Five short stories about two hippopotamuses who are great friends. The ridiculous situations appeal to everyone's funny bone and gently point out problems
and solutions in dealing with people we like very much. (kindergarten to
second grade)

Slobodkina, Esphyr   *Caps for Sale*
                                   Addison-Wesley, 1947

A peddler who sells caps that he wears in a stack on top of his head takes a
nap under a large tree and wakes up to find all but his own cap missing. He
discovers that a group of monkeys took the caps from his head while he slept
and tries to get the caps back from the monkeys. Children love to repeat the
peddler's phrases and carry out his gestures in dealing with the monkeys.
(kindergarten and first grade)

Thaler, Mike   *How Far Will a Rubber Band Stretch?*
                                   illus. by Jerry Joyner
                                   Parents, 1974

A boy hooks one end of a rubber band to his bed post and pulls to see how far
it can go. To the amazement of the students, he rides a bike, a bus, a train,
and even a rocket to the moon before "B-O-I-N-G," he is snapped back to
Earth and out of his dream. (kindergarten and first grade)

Waber, Bernard   *Lyle and the Birthday Party*
                                  Houghton Mifflin, 1966

The famous crocodile is green with jealousy as he watches Jonathan celebrate his birthday. A mix-up puts Lyle in the hospital where his usual helpfulness surfaces and rids him of his envy. A surprise party completes the cure. (kindergarten to second grade)

Teaching Unit

CLASSROOM ACTIVITIES USING THE CARD CATALOG

At best, a Teaching Unit in June is inconvenient. It is obvious from the rest of this chapter that end-of-year activities place enormous demands on your time. June and September require intensive clerical and administrative work. Most of your attention is focused on the operation of the media center, and you work more closely with volunteers and other support staff than with students and faculty. But care must be taken not to forget that patrons cannot be neglected no matter how pressing the demands of paperwork. This Teaching Unit, designed primarily for third and fourth grade students, can also be used as an enrichment activity in grade two and as a remedial activity for the fifth and sixth grades. The unit's chief virtue is that it is organized so that all work is done in the classroom.

If you have time, prepare the mock-up of the card catalog in April or May and select the sample cards or make the strips at that time. Then store the materials until June, when you will route them to the classroom teacher.

As is noted in the directions, you can use 11″ × 2″ posterboard strips (see the January Teaching Unit) or extra catalog cards (see the November Teaching Unit). The strips, which are labeled with authors, titles, and subject headings, are best suited to large group work. The more strips or cards you have, the better the unit will be. If you make the bingo game that is included at the end of this unit, you need a lot of strips or cards.

> *Note:* It is not necessary to prepare new strips or extra catalog cards for this Teaching Unit. The strips made for the January Teaching Unit or the cards made for the November Teaching Unit can be used.

MATERIALS:

—two sheets of 14″ × 11″ oaktag (one sheet if card catalog has only one side)
—two sheets of posterboard in two contrasting colors
—felt markers (black wide-tip marker, black and red fine-tip markers, yellow highlight marker)
—rubber cement
—30 to 60 strips of 11″ × 2″ posterboard (optional if cards are used)
—30 to 60 extra catalog cards (optional if strips are used)

PREPARATION:

1. Draw a replica of your card catalog on the oaktag. (See the illustrations on pages 262 and 263.) Be sure that the letters and numbers on the drawers match exactly with your catalog.

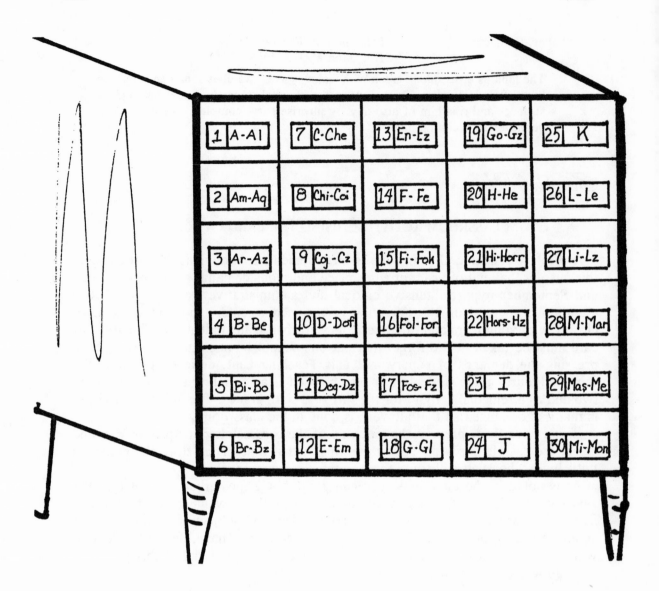

- Draw the outline with the red marker.
- Use the fine-tip black marker to outline the labels on the drawers.
- Use the fine-tip black marker to write in numbers and guide letters.
- Use the yellow highlighter to color the number portion of the drawer labels.

2. Cut the lighter shade of posterboard in an interesting pattern.
3. Paste the mock-up of the card catalog onto the light-colored posterboard.
4. Paste the catalog and posterboard onto the darker sheet of posterboard.
5. Use the wide-tip black marker to letter "Card Catalog" on the posterboard.

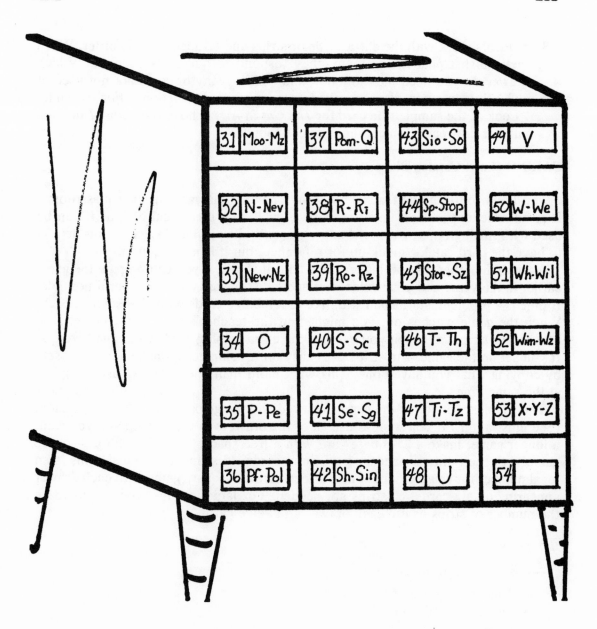

PROCEDURE:

Three different ways of using the strips or cards are given here. The one you choose will depend on the grade level and the teacher's preference.

1. The teacher shows the strips to the entire class. The students respond by giving the number of the drawer in which the author, title, or subject can be found. The teacher can also have a "spelling bee" with the strips; each student who gives a wrong answer is eliminated from the bee.
2. The teacher shows the students the extra catalog cards. They are directed to copy the top line on each card and to print the number of the drawer in which the card would be found.

3. Students work with the extra cards or strips and arrange them in order. When they finish alphabetizing them, they respond to questions such as "Which drawer do you need most often?" and "How many drawers are not used at all?" Students can also be asked more advanced questions. For example: "Look at the sample title card for *The Cat in Art*. Who is the author? In what number drawer will the author card be found?"

CARD-O (Card Catalog Bingo)

Third and fourth grade teachers will love having this game in their classrooms. It is an excellent reinforcement activity as well as a great deal of fun. It can be used with small groups or with the entire class. While playing this game, it is helpful to have the card catalog mock-up for reference, but it is not required.

As with the other part of this teaching unit, it is best if you can prepare the game earlier in the year. Use your volunteers and enlist the aid of the teacher if possible. If time is a problem, start small with five to ten bingo cards with nine squares each. When the game catches on, you might find the teacher's help forthcoming. It is best to use strips, although you can use the extra catalog cards with small groups. If you set up the game with strips, it is easy for a volunteer to make additional sets by copying what you have done. This way, more than one class can use the game at the same time.

The simplest version of the game is played with bingo cards with 9 squares each. (See illustration.) If you wish to use all of the drawers in the catalog and you want a longer game, make a 25-square card with a free space. For a five-card, 9-square game with each drawer appearing on three cards, 15 strips are needed. This is an ideal number for small groups. For a fifteen-card, 25-square game with each drawer appearing on six cards, 60 strips are needed. For larger groups, you can increase the number of strips or use each drawer on twelve cards.

MATERIALS:

—posterboard for bingo cards
  • 9-square cards are 6" × 7"
  • 25-square cards are 7½" × 8"
—11" × 2" strips of posterboard
—black felt markers, wide-tip and fine-tip
—counters or markers for covering squares on cards
—box large enough to hold the strips
—pressure-sensitive labels, ⅝" × 1¼"
—clear self-stick vinyl

PREPARATION:

1. Label the strips with authors, titles, and subject headings or use the strips from the January Teaching Unit. If the group is small, it is not necessary to have a strip from every drawer in the catalog, but a variety of strips is imperative. If more than one strip is from the same drawer, a player might have to cover the same square twice, so each strip should be from a different drawer.

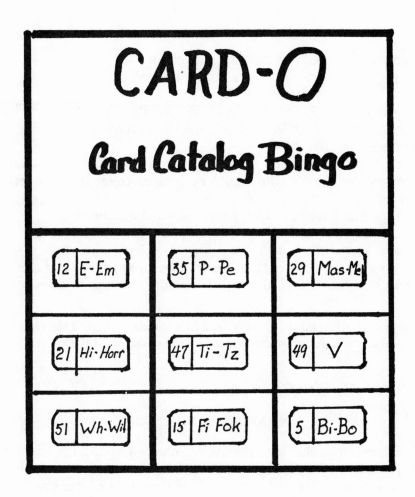

Note: You can prepare several sets of cards and strips for the small-group version of the game. By carefully selecting drawers with single guide letters or several guide letters or by choosing easy or difficult headings for the strips, you can regulate the difficulty of the game. If you do make several games on different levels, use a different color for each level. Be sure that the strips and bingo cards for each level are the same color.

2. Write the answer (the correct drawer number) in very small letters in the right-hand corner on the back of each strip.
3. Rule the bingo cards with the wide-tip black marker. Use pressure-sensitive labels to make the drawer fronts. Since the preparation for this game is so time-consuming, you might have a volunteer prepare the cards and then fill in the drawer numbers and letters yourself.
4. Use the fine-tip marker to make lines dividing the drawer numbers from the guide letters.
5. Refer to the posterboard strips before filling in the letters and numbers of the drawer fronts. For example, if a strip reads HORSES, write "22 Hors-Hz" on several cards. If you are making the fifteen-card, 25-square game using 40 strips, the same drawer front appears on nine cards.
6. Cover the bingo cards with clear self-stick vinyl.

PROCEDURE:

1. The strips are placed in a box and shaken up.
2. Each player gets one card and a stack of counters.
3. If there is a free square, it is covered with a counter.
4. The game leader takes a strip out of the box. Being careful not to let the other players see the answer on the back, the leader reads the strip and shows it to all of the players.
5. Players whose cards show the drawer front in which the author, title, or subject on the chosen strip would be located cover the appropriate square with a counter.
6. The strips that have been called are discarded face up.
7. The first player to arrange the counters in a vertical, horizontal, or diagonal row calls out "cardo" or "bingo."
8. Counters are removed from the winning card one at a time and checked against the backs of the discarded strips to be sure that the squares were covered correctly.

Variations: To win at bingo, players need to make an X, L, T, I, or H. The speed at which the strips are called can also affect the difficulty of the game.

Professional Responsibilities

PLANNING AN INVENTORY

Since you are responsible for the state of your collection, it is important to take an annual inventory. Theoretically, this can be done at any time, but practical considerations point to the end of the school year as the least disruptive time. If you have never taken an inventory, here are some helpful steps and suggestions for planning one.

First, be sure that you know the scope of your job and how you are going to accomplish it. The only print materials that will concern you are books; magazines, pamphlets, and similar materials are not inventoried. If audio-visual hardware and software are under your responsibility, they should also be inventoried.

Next, talk over your plans with your principal and reach an agreement about the amount of time you will need. Be sure to outline the procedures involved in the operation and to explain some of the expected difficulties. Clarify any school or district policy concerning how to handle books lost by students. One to two weeks is the usual amount of time for an inventory; two weeks allows time for a large print collection and a media inventory, as well as for unraveling errors in cataloging and slipping that will surface during this operation. If one week is all that you can manage, you may have to modify your plans and concentrate entirely on an inventory of books.

Now you must decide whether to close the media center completely or to undertake a modified closing. (See this month's Open End.) You should then inform your faculty of the dates of the inventory period and suggest that they charge out as many books and other materials as they will need for class use. (See the sample notice, facing page.) After all, school is still in session, and service to your users is your prime consideration.

NOTICE TO THE FACULTY

Southern Boulevard Media Center

May 27, 19__

We would like to have all books and a/v materials returned by <u>students only</u> before our inventory begins. The date when all of these materials should be in the library is <u>Wednesday, June 8th.</u>

You are welcome to choose any materials you need for your classroom collection and to keep them as long as necessary. Since materials are signed out to you and are kept in the classroom, we can physically check them at any time if necessary. We would, however, appreciate your looking through the books and a/v materials you now have and returning anything you no longer need.

The library may be used by students for research during our inventory period, June 13-17. Students should have work to do; they should not come in just to browse on their free time.

We are again having a contest for the homeroom in each grade that is the first to return all of the materials charged out by the students. The attached notice tells about this contest. Please discuss it with your class and then post it in your room.

Ruth Toor

Set a date on which all books must be returned by the students and after which no books can be charged out. This date should be several days before the inventory is to begin. However, you must accept the fact that you will never get back all of the outstanding books on time. This is always a frustrating problem, but you might as well plan to begin inventory with a large amount of materials still out. One way of making this task a little easier is to run a contest to see which class in each grade turns in all of its materials first. (See this month's Library Enrichment Activity.)

The more people you have helping with your inventory, the faster and more efficient it will be. You can ask your regular volunteers to contribute extra time if possible, but you should also send out a notice several weeks in advance requesting all parents in the school to volunteer their assistance for this one-time-only task. (See the sample notice, next page.) As responses come in, tabulate the dates when people have agreed to come. Try to have teams of two people working together, but don't worry if you have an extra person. A week before inventory begins, send out reminder notices to the parents who offered their services telling them the date and time for which you have them scheduled. (See the sample notice, page 269.) Your library chairperson should be very helpful in organizing the schedule.

The actual mechanics of taking an inventory are discussed in this month's Volunteers section.

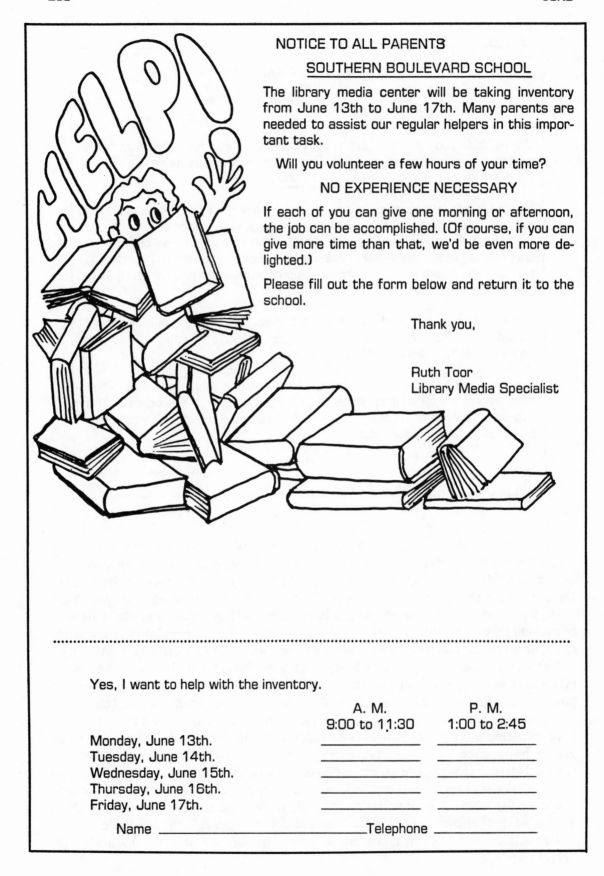

NOTICE TO ALL PARENTS

SOUTHERN BOULEVARD SCHOOL

The library media center will be taking inventory from June 13th to June 17th. Many parents are needed to assist our regular helpers in this important task.

Will you volunteer a few hours of your time?

NO EXPERIENCE NECESSARY

If each of you can give one morning or afternoon, the job can be accomplished. (Of course, if you can give more time than that, we'd be even more delighted.)

Please fill out the form below and return it to the school.

Thank you,

Ruth Toor
Library Media Specialist

Yes, I want to help with the inventory.

	A. M. 9:00 to 11:30	P. M. 1:00 to 2:45
Monday, June 13th.	_____	_____
Tuesday, June 14th.	_____	_____
Wednesday, June 15th.	_____	_____
Thursday, June 16th.	_____	_____
Friday, June 17th.	_____	_____

Name _____ Telephone _____

```
┌─────────────────────────────────────────────┐
│  REMINDER TO PARENTS                          │
│                                               │
│  SOUTHERN BOULEVARD MEDIA CENTER              │
│                                               │
│                            June 6, 19___      │
│                                               │
│  Thank you for offering to help us take inven-│
│  tory.                                        │
│                                               │
│  We will be looking forward to seeing you on  │
│  _____ from _____ to _____.    │
│                                               │
│                            Ruth Toor          │
│                            Library Media Specialist │
└─────────────────────────────────────────────┘
```

INVENTORYING HARDWARE

Basic maintenance of equipment requires a program of regular cleaning. Some school systems have a special audio-visual coordinator whose department is responsible for all cleaning and repair; other school systems contract for these services. If neither program is in operation in your district, the responsibility is probably yours. Without a trained staff, it is very difficult to schedule equipment for regular cleaning. However, unless you make time to clean hardware, you will have to send out an increasing number of items for major repairs. If you cannot seem to find time for basic maintenance during the year, it is imperative that all equipment is checked annually. The end of the school year is a convenient time for this check.

Rather than calling in all equipment during the inventory period, schedule the hardware roundup and cleaning for the two weeks before inventory begins. You can then recirculate the equipment to the teachers according to their needs and permit them to use hardware until the last day of school.

Send a notice to the teachers giving the schedule for turning in equipment. (See the sample notice, page 270.) Most of the equipment is scheduled in size order. Smaller pieces requiring multistep checking are called in first because the summer storage begins at this time and the smaller items do not take up needed floor space.

Be prepared for teachers who forget to follow the schedule. Sometimes the problem arises because a teacher needs to use the equipment on the day that it is scheduled to be returned. Wait to follow up missing equipment until the volunteers have cleaned most of the pieces that were returned. (See this month's Volunteers section for cleaning procedures.) Then see the teacher and exchange the equipment that is in the classroom with equipment that has already been checked.

Special procedures for circulating cleaned hardware are discussed in the Volunteers section. Keep in mind two main goals. First, all hardware must be cleaned and checked. It would be nice if it could then be stored for the summer, but do not be concerned if this is not possible. Second, service to faculty should be maintained with as little disruption as possible. The teachers have to deal with their own pressures at this time, and it would be contrary to all that the media center stands for to add to these pressures. As always, your object is to be helpful and make things simpler for those who depend on your services.

HARRY S TRUMAN SCHOOL

NOTICE TO TEACHERS

HARDWARE INVENTORY AND RETURN OF EQUIPMENT

The library will begin inventory on June 6. All books are due by that date.

Please follow the schedule for returning equipment. Once equipment has been cleaned and inventoried, it may be used in the classroom until the last day of school.

Date	Return
May 23	Cassette Players (Sharps)
May 24	Cassette Recorders (Avids)
May 25	Cassette Recorders (Panasonics)
May 26	Filmstrip Viewers (individual size)
May 27	Filmstrip Projectors
May 31	Overhead Projectors/Opaque Projectors
June 1	Record Players
June 2	Listening Stations
June 3	Cameras, Slide Projectors, 16mm and 8mm Projectors

Thank you,
Hilda

YEAR-END REPORT

As the inventory moves into its final stages, it is a good idea to prepare a year-end report, whether or not it is required. By writing down an account of the year, you can see what you accomplished and where your attention should be focused during the coming year.

Begin the report by recording the total circulation statistics. These may be broken down by Dewey Decimal Classification numbers. The first section of the report can explain and enlarge upon these statistics. The report should also describe any services you introduced and discuss the types of library skills you taught and the grade levels at which you taught them. Include explanations of projects that were launched and problems that were encountered, but do not dwell on the latter. Discuss your goals for the next year. If you have previously written a year-end report, show to what extent last year's anticipated objectives were met.

Copies of the report are sent to your supervisor (if you have one), to the principal, and to the superintendent of schools. Although year-end reports tend to be self-congratulatory, they are good to have on file. Looking back at them after a few years, you can see that, despite occasional problems, much has been accomplished.

Volunteers

TAKING INVENTORY

Your goal in taking inventory is to see if all of your books are actually on the shelves of the media center. Have your volunteers begin by placing all of the shelves in exact order. Each person can work on one section.

1. Fiction—Books are placed alphabetically by the author's last name and then by title. All copies of the same title are placed together.

2. Nonfiction—Books are placed in numerical order by the call number on the spine label (914, then 914.1, then 914.23, then 914.3). Within a specific call number, books are placed alphabetically by the author's last name (914A, 914 CAR, 914 COL, 914 D).

3. Biography—Books are placed alphabetically by the last name of the person they are written about $\boxed{\begin{array}{c}\text{B}\\\text{CAREY}\end{array}}$ $\boxed{\begin{array}{c}\text{B}\\\text{CUSTER}\end{array}}$. Biographies of the same person are arranged alphabetically by the author's last name.

After all of the shelves are in exact order, deploy the volunteers in teams of two whenever possible. If you are fortunate enough to have many teams at one time, be sure to space them so that they will not get in each other's way. It doesn't matter in which order the sections are inventoried, as long as all of the shelves are read.

Try to pair each of your regular volunteers with a first-time helper. (See suggestions for getting extra help in this month's Professional Responsibilities.) If there are several persons who have not been in the media center before, consider assigning them to fiction and saving the nonfiction shelves for your regular, more experienced helpers.

Have plenty of pencils and paper clips ready. Hand each team a pencil, some paper clips, and a section of shelf list cards. Explain that the shelf list is arranged in the same order as the books on the shelves.

Have one volunteer read out the information on the card—author, title, and number of copies—while the other person locates the book and pulls it off the shelf. The book should be checked to make sure that the pocket and book card inside match exactly. Mix-ups such as the wrong card being in the wrong book pocket can occur in any book, but they are especially prevalent when there are duplicate copies. This is a convenient time to correct any mistakes. You might also find mistakes such as the call number on the inside pocket and on the outside spine of the book being different.

If you are in a new position in an established media center, you may find a lot of "skeletons" at this time. Don't worry about it. This is one of the reasons that you are taking inventory. Keep your cool, deal with the most pressing problems immediately, and make a list of projects that need to be carried out next September.

The next step in taking inventory depends on the following circumstances:

1. If the book mentioned on the shelf list card is on the shelf and correct, it is returned to its position on the shelf but placed sideways so that its spine is parallel

to the top of the shelf. (See illustration.) The shelf list card is turned over, and the team goes on to the next card and book. The reason for turning the completed books sideways is so that you and your volunteers can tell at a glance how much of the media center has been inventoried. Everyone will gain a feeling of satisfaction from looking back to see how much has been finished already. Putting the books back in the correct position takes very little time, and it should not be done until a day or so before the final closing of the media center.

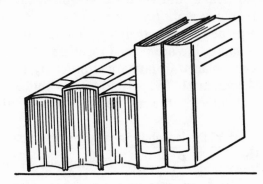

2. If a book is missing, a paper clip should be placed on the shelf list card to denote this fact. If the card lists several copies of the book, use a pencil to make a notation (such as M '78) next to the one that is missing in addition to placing the paper clip on the card. Explain to the volunteers that making notations in pencil and using paper clips on the card makes it very simple to correct the shelf list card if and when the missing book turns up.

3. If there is a book on the shelf that does not have a corresponding shelf list card, leave that book standing on the shelf. However, if the book is oversized, pull it off and set it aside. Assign a single volunteer to spot these books on the shelves after they have been inventoried and to list on separate scrap catalog cards the following information for each title: author, title, publisher, copyright date, pages, accession or copy number, and call number. The book can then be turned sideways to indicate that it has been inventoried, and the scrap cards can be checked and typed at leisure.

If you have one person left over after organizing your helpers into pairs, there are several ways you could utilize this person:

1. The person could work alone, looking at the shelf list card and then at the book. This may take a little longer, but it can work out very effectively, especially if one member of a team has to leave early.

2. You could work with the person, making up another team. However, you should avoid this if possible because you should be free to trouble-shoot and answer questions whenever they arise.

3. You might recruit a few interested sixth graders (with their teachers' permission) to work with your adult volunteers. Students at this age can be very conscientious and helpful.

4. The extra person can work at the circulation desk updating overdues, doing current desk work such as slipping and filing, or preparing a list of the materials that each teacher still has out.

5. If you plan to inventory your paperbacks, the extra volunteer can easily do this alone. All of the paperbacks must be arranged in alphabetical order by the

author's last name and then checked off your paperback card file. (See the December Volunteers section for tips on processing paperbacks.) The card and pocket in each paperback should also be checked at this time.

After all of the books have been inventoried, the same procedures are followed for audio-visual software. If you do not have enough volunteers to do a complete nonbook inventory, consider doing a partial inventory of audio-visual materials a few weeks before the book inventory is to begin. You might also consider inventorying just one type of software each year or letting your regular volunteers inventory the audio-visual materials as an ongoing task throughout the year. Since you probably have considerably less media than you do books, this type of inventory is much simpler to accomplish.

Here are just a few more general tips. Since there always seems to be a heat wave during inventory time, consider supplying your helpers with iced tea or some other cold drink. If your media center is not air-conditioned, round up some fans to make everyone feel more comfortable. Be gracious and grateful; often, one-time helpers discover that they enjoy working with you in the media center and come back to volunteer on a regular basis the following year. If you explain exactly what you are trying to do to all of your helpers, they will understand their task much better and work more efficiently. Remember to thank everyone for a job well done.

When your inventory is completed, your shelf list will show that you have a great many "missing" books. However, if you have allowed the teachers to charge out books for their classrooms, many of these titles are not really missing. You can handle this situation in two ways. You can either go through the book cards under the teachers' names and remove paper clips from the appropriate shelf list cards immediately, or you can wait until the books are returned to the media center before acknowledging them as "found."

If this is your first inventory, be aware that straightening out problems and snags takes up more time than does taking the entire inventory. Don't become overconfident if you finish early; you will need quite a bit of time for your follow-up work.

How you handle the balance of your missing books depends on your situation and inclination. Here are some steps you might follow:

1. If you are pressed for time, consider waiting until next fall and then having a very reliable volunteer go through all of the cards with paper clips on them and recheck the shelves for the books. It's amazing how often many of the books will turn up, right where they are supposed to be.

2. If you prefer to look for the books right away, you can check the shelves at the end of school to see if any of the books are there.

3. Leave the paper clips on the shelf list cards for at least one year. Often, missing books turn up months later.

4. After books have been noted as "missing" for two inventories, you can consider removing the cards from your catalog, subtracting the number from your book count, or placing the shelf list cards in your "consideration for purchase" file.

As you become accustomed to taking regular year-end inventories, the task will seem less overwhelming. Your collection will be in reasonably good shape, and the inventory itself will be less demanding. Try to think of it as just wrapping up a successful year in the media center.

HARDWARE INVENTORY AND CLEANING

The key to handling the annual inventory and cleaning of hardware is advance planning. Try to have extra volunteers on hand. If the media center is still open and offering full service, the regular volunteers will have enough work without the added task of taking an inventory of hardware. Prepare hardware checklists similar to the ones shown. If you are not sure what needs to be done, check your file of

HARDWARE CHECKLISTS

Cassette Recorder

Code #	Checked In	DeMag & Clean	Play Back	Record	Description of problem
CR/1	x	x	x	x	Works fine
CR/2	x	x	x	x	Works fine
CR/3	x	—	—	—	Does not play or rewind
CR/4	x	x	x	—	Sound distorted; does not record properly

Listening Station

Code #	Checked In	Jack Box	Earphones	Description of problem
LS/1	x	x	—	One earphone dead
LS/2	x	—	x	Earphones work in other jack box; this one dead
LS/3	x	x	x	Everything fine

Overhead Projector

Code #	Checked In	Bulb Checked	Lens Cleaned	Acetate Roll Cleaned	Description of Problem
OP/1	x	x	x	x	Functioning
OP/2	x	—	—	—	On-Off switch needs repair—hazardous

Record Player

Code #	Checked In	Speeds Checked	Pause Checked	Operation	Description of Problem
R/1	x	x	x	x	O.K.
R/2	x	x	x	—	Turntable makes rubbing sound
R/3	x	x	—	x	Pause works slowly

manufacturers' manuals (see the April Professional Responsibilities) for instructions on maintenance. Be sure to have all of the necessary cleaning supplies on hand. In addition to solutions such as lens cleaner and head cleaner, a supply of rags for dusting is helpful.

The volunteers can do all of the cleaning and checking in, but first they must be shown what to do. To avoid repeating the same demonstration, teach each volunteer only a small part of one operation. The volunteer then performs that segment of the task on each machine of the same type. To keep track of what has been done, a check is placed in the appropriate column of the hardware checklist. At all times during the inventory process, the code number assigned to each machine (see the April Professional Responsibilities) is used to refer to the machine.

Equipment will begin arriving at the media center in advance of its due date. The teachers who are early birds can cause as much of a problem as those who are late if you are not prepared. Take advantage of the early returns by getting some of the equipment cleaned and ready to recirculate. This way, you can easily accommodate teachers who need equipment on the day that it is scheduled for cleaning.

A new procedure for circulating hardware should be put into effect during the closing weeks of school. Since equipment is allowed to recirculate only after it has been completely inventoried and cleaned, having a new system helps remind teachers of the need to return the equipment. Have the teachers use sign-out sheets similar to the one shown. Sign-out sheets also help you make quick equipment check-ins; these become very important as the last day approaches and some equipment is still outstanding. With the sign-out sheets in operation, any piece of equipment that has already been inventoried can be returned at the last minute and quickly checked off the list.

YEAR-END HARDWARE SIGN-OUT SHEET			
Type of Equipment: Record Player			
Code #	Teacher Name	Date Out	Date In
R/17	Kaszuba	6/1	6/7
R/2	Beaubian	6/1	6/17
R/8	Segal	6/6	6/16
R/25	Rizzi	6/8	6/17

CLOSING TEA

Say "thank you" to your volunteers for their year-long help by having a closing tea in their honor some time during the last week of school after your inventory is finished.

Very early in the month, consult with your library chairperson to set a date and make up invitations. (See next page for a sample invitation.) If postage is a problem, distribute the invitations in person whenever possible. Be sure to invite your principal as well as the superintendent of schools. Invite everyone who has helped during the year, even those who are no longer volunteering. It is better to ask too

Please come . . .

Fold

Fold   Here

Southern Boulevard Library-Media Center

Wednesday
June 16
10:00 a.m.

to a tea honoring our library volunteers.

R.S.V.P.-Regrets only The Library

Here

many than to hurt the feelings of someone who volunteered during part of the year but can no longer do so. If possible, you might also invite anyone who offered his or her help during inventory. Not many of the one-time volunteers will come, but it is a good opportunity for those who do come to socialize with your regular volunteers and learn how pleasant it is to help in the media center. If you ask people to let you know if they are not coming, you will have a rough idea of how many to expect.

Ask a talented volunteer to make blank name tags from different colors of construction paper shaped as books. Leave the name tags, a felt marker, and some pins on the circulation desk the day of the tea so that your volunteers can fill in their names and put on the tags as they come in. This is important because many of them do not know each other. Next to the blank name tags, place a sheet of lined paper on which interested volunteers can sign up for the next year. They should list their names, telephone numbers, and days on which they would prefer to work. This will save your library chairperson some telephone calls and give you a good start toward setting up next September's schedule.

If you want to award certificates to your volunteers, you can design them yourself or order them from any library supply house. They should be filled in ahead of time. You can then award the certificates during the tea and mail them to anyone who does not attend. The certificates are optional, but volunteers seem to like them.

As for refreshments, keep them simple. Consider serving iced tea or coffee, but be prepared to have a hot beverage in case of a cool day. Bake or order some small pastries. Have a pretty tablecloth, some fresh flowers, and paper cups, plates, spoons, and napkins that blend with the decor. Your library chairperson should be able to help you with the details, but don't rely on the chairperson to organize the whole tea. Remember, you are the one who is saying "thank you" to your volunteers (including the parent who is library chairperson).

Schedule about one hour for the tea and be sure to post a sign indicating that the media center will be closed during that time. Otherwise, you will have lots of interested children wanting to know what is going on and offering to help sample the goodies! No formal program is necessary. When most of the volunteers have arrived, give out the certificates and thank everyone for his or her help throughout the year. After that, the volunteers will enjoy circulating and chatting with people they know and meeting those they don't know.

The tea comes at the busiest time of the year for you, but, with a little advance planning, it shouldn't be too much of a burden. It will show your appreciation of the volunteers, and you, in turn, will be greatly appreciated by them.

Open End

LIMITING ACCESS DURING INVENTORY

As the end of the school year approaches and you prepare to take inventory, you must set a date for closing the media center. With all that needs to be done, you might want to lock your doors and concentrate solely on the job at hand. However, if you have provided an effective program throughout the year, it is not only impossible but also undesirable and unprofessional to do so. Students and faculty depend on the services available, and they cannot function well without them.

The open-ended question is not whether or not to close the media center but rather how to determine the degree of access that will not disrupt either the classroom teaching or your inventory. Obviously, compromises are in order; regularly scheduled classes should be suspended as soon as inventory begins, but other services can continue with some restrictions.

The degree of student access to the media center is determined by the amount of room you have and the extent of the students' needs. Ideally, students should not be able to borrow materials but be allowed to use them within the media center. If the section being used has been inventoried or has been arranged for inventory, the books will have to be brought to the student and returned to the shelves by the staff. If time pressure builds or your facilities are limited, this personal service will be difficult if not impossible. In this case, try to keep the reference section open for use even if everything else is closed.

As for faculty access, you must make every effort to be as flexible as possible. See this month's Professional Responsibilities and Summer Loans to Teachers sections for some ways to help teachers while coping with your own end-of-year responsibilities.

As always, you will have to accommodate users who have learned to depend on media center services. You must adjust your own procedures accordingly while trying to operate as efficiently as possible. No single solution is perfect; no single answer is suited to all media centers. The challenge lies in seeing how close you can come to achieving your ideal program. Next year will be even better; after all, September is just two months away.

Index